Alone in Mexico

Alone in Mexico

The Astonishing Travels of Karl Heller, 1845–1848

by Karl Bartolomeus Heller

translated and edited by
Terry Rugeley

THE UNIVERSITY OF ALABAMA PRESS
Tuscaloosa

Manufactured in the United States of America

Typeface: ACaslon

∞
The paper on which this book is printed meets the minimum requirements of American National Standard for Information Sciences–Permanence of Paper for Printed Library Materials, ANSI Z39.48-1984.

Library of Congress Cataloging-in-Publication Data

Heller, Karl B. (Karl Bartholomäus), 1824–1880.
[Reisen in Mexiko in den jahren 1845–1848. English]
Alone in Mexico : the astonishing travels of Karl Heller, 1845–1848 / by Karl Bartolomeus Heller ; translated and edited by Terry Rugeley.
p. cm.
Includes bibliographical references and index.
ISBN-13: 978-0-8173-1588-7 (cloth : alk. paper)
ISBN-10: 0-8173-1588-8
ISBN-13: 978-0-8173-5456-5 (pbk. : alk. paper)
ISBN-10: 0-8173-5456-5
1. Mexico—Description and travel. 2. Mexico—History—1821–1861. 3. Heller, Karl B. (Karl Bartholomäus), 1824–1880—Travel—Mexico. I. Rugeley, Terry, 1956– II. Title.
F1213.H4813 2007
917.204′5—dc22

2007013796

Contents

Illustrations

Maps

Figures

Acknowledgments

The main thanks for this work go to my wife, Margarita, who heard it all a thousand times.

I am deeply indebted to Gerlinde Thompson and Robert Larson of the University of Oklahoma, who helped to improve my understanding of the German language dramatically.

My heartfelt recognition to the staff of The University of Alabama Press, who helped make this work a reality.

Jonathan Lawrence's careful copyediting helped bring both clarity and consistency to the text.

Finally, thanks to Karl Heller himself—out there somewhere in the Beyond, still traveling, still collecting, still jotting down his urgent observations.

Chronology

1824

November 20	Karl Bartolomeus Heller is born

1845

August 9	Heller departs from Vienna
August 10	Reaches England
October 11	Reaches Madeira
October 25	Reaches Barbados
October 30	Reaches Jacmel, Haiti
c. October 31	Reaches Jamaica
November 9	Reaches Cuba
c. November 14	Reaches Veracruz, Mexico
November 16	Reaches Mirador
November 30	Begins life in his hut
December 9	Trip to Tiger's Cave
December 15	Trip to San Bartolo
December 25	Christmas in Mirador

1846

January 5	Earthquake in Mirador
January 18	Departs for Huatusco
February 15	Trip to El Fortín
February 23	Trip to Los Baños
March 12	Returns to Huatusco
March 23	Departs Huatusco for Orizaba
March 25	Climbs Orizaba
March 28	Returns to Huatusco
April 27	Journey to Pueblo Viejo
mid-May	Returns to Huatusco
May 20	All Mexican ports blockaded by U.S. Navy

June 5	Maritime trade closed off
July 2	Heller departs for Orizaba, reaches Acatzingo
c. July 7	Reaches Puebla
July 11	Departs from Puebla, reaches Mexico City
July 30	Departs from Mexico City; passes evening in Lerma
July 31	Reaches Toluca
August 10	Departs for volcano Toluca
August 12	Reaches volcano
August 14	Returns, passes evening at hacienda Cocustepec
August 27	Departs for south of Toluca; passes evening in Tenancingo
September 5	Departs for Zacualpan; reaches Los Arcos mine
September 10	Departs Los Arcos to visit other mines
September 14	Visits La Golondrina mine
September 16	Departs Zacualpan for Toluca
September 18	Reaches Toluca
September 21	Departs for Mexico City
October 5	Returns to Toluca
October 15	Departs from Toluca
October 16	Reaches Mexico City
October 18	Departs from Mexico City; reaches Perote
October 23	Departs from Perote; reaches Zacuapan
October 29	Departs from Zacuapan; reaches Veracruz port
November 2	Departs from Veracruz port
November 3	Reaches Alvarado
c. November 8	Sets sail for Campeche
November 13	Reaches Campeche
November 14	Comes ashore in Campeche
December 25	Christmas in Campeche

1847

January 21	Departs for Champotón
January 26	Begins travel up Champotón River
January 28	Begins return journey
February 2	Sets sail from Champotón to Campeche
February 14	News of the wreck of the *Tweed*
April 2	Holy Week in Campeche
April 4	Departs for Uxmal
April 10	Returns to Campeche
May 22	Departs for Mérida; arrives the following day
June 14	Returns to Campeche

July 1	Departs for hacienda Chivic, visits dyewood forests
July 6	Returns to Campeche
September 5	Receives instructions from Europe, with half his stipend
September 14	Fiesta of San Román; Mexico City falls to U.S. forces
November 3	Sets sail for Tabasco
c. November 11	Sets sail upriver into Tabascan interior
November 20	Departs Villahermosa
c. November 22	Reaches Teapa
December 25	Christmas in Teapa

1848

January 16	Visits Cueva del Tigre
January 21	Departs for Chiapas
February 21	Travels in Pichucalco area
March 5	Reaches Pichucalco
April 19	Easter in Teapa
May 15	Departs Teapa for Tabascan coast
June 6	Boards *Arietes* in Frontera
June 19	Reaches Havana, Cuba
July 6	Boards *Lyre* for the United States
August 5	Leaves New York for Europe
September 4	Reaches Vienna

1857
Heller joins faculty of Theresianum Academy

1864
Heller's son Karl Maria is born

1880
Karl Bartolomeus Heller dies in Vienna

Alone in Mexico

Introduction

In the summer of 1845 a twenty-year-old Austrian botanist named Karl Bartolomeus Heller set out from Vienna for an extended scientific expedition in Mexico. His itinerary carried him to England, Cuba, the British West Indies, Haiti, and the Mexican port of Veracruz. Heller spent a year exploring central Mexico; in late 1846 he sailed from the Veracruz coast for the southeastern state of Yucatán, a region in those days accessible to Mexicans and the world only by boat. After a brief but observation-filled stay in the cities of Campeche and Mérida, he rambled westward through the virtually unknown states of Tabasco and Chiapas, and in 1848 he finally returned, via Havana and then the United States, to his homeland.

Heller's exploits were nothing short of remarkable, particularly given his youth and the anarchic conditions of midcentury Mexico. Among other adventures, the memoirist survived an earthquake, bandit attacks, and several near shipwrecks; ran naval blockades and repeatedly risked capture by U.S. forces; suffered recurrent attacks of tropical disease; flirted with attractive young women; rode on horseback through isolated virgin forests and treacherous mountainsides; passed sleepless nights in remote logging camps; attended Indian dances; traveled through brush fires; climbed trees in search of rare bromeliads; and even wrestled with a boa constrictor in his own hotel room. A gentleman-traveler in the classic nineteenth-century tradition, Heller composed a thoughtful account of his journeys and explorations. Published in Leipzig in 1853, his *Reisen in Mexiko in den Jahren 1845–1848* provided German-language readers with outstanding reportage on a nation whose history and culture few Europeans knew firsthand. Curiously, until now the book has never been translated into either English or Spanish, and indeed has remained virtually unknown to English-language scholars. Heller himself never won the fame of his hero and legendary predecessor Alexander von Humboldt or his U.S. counterpart John Lloyd Stephens, a fact that is all the more curious given the enormous vogue of Maya-area travelogues. After 150 years, Stephens's four volumes remain in print, while scholars continue to comb the pages of travelers and archaeologists such as B. M. Norman, Auguste Le Plongeon, and Theobald Mahler. Of academic scholars, only Howard Cline, in his classic unpublished dissertation on Yucatecan society and culture (1948), consulted Heller's work.[1] For modern readers and scholars, then, *Reisen in Mexiko* remains very much an astonishing and unfamiliar account.

Heller's Mexico

Karl Heller came to Mexico at a crucial moment. In 1821 this land, formerly the crown jewel of the Spanish empire, broke free and proclaimed its independence. Intractable problems soon racked the early republic. Despite important achievements in politics, art, and industry, Mexico remained a land of disunited provinces, with profound divisions of class and ethnic cultures. Experience at self-government—particularly of the democratic sort—was minimal. Nearly half of the nation's seven million inhabitants spoke indigenous languages rather than Spanish, while in many parts landowners ruled over their peons and neighboring peasants like feudal lords. The eleven-year independence war had inflicted terrible destruction; mines were flooded, much capital had fled during the previous three decades, while the country struggled with its centuries-old handicaps such as an extractive economy and the social and political marginalization of its impoverished majority. Church prohibitions on usury prevented the emergence of a modern, competitive banking system, while both the church and the army maintained privileges known as *fueros* (legal protection from civil courts).

To confront these challenges, Mexicans rallied behind the liberator Agustín Iturbide, who reigned as Agustín I until his preference for Spanish-style authoritarianism led to an overthrow in 1823. The following year Mexico's first constitution granted enormous powers to the states (more commonly known as provinces). Tensions between provincial and national government flared continually, and in 1835 Mexico City–based forces struck down the constitution and imposed a more conservative, centralist rule. But this failed to improve matters. In 1836 an ill-advised colonization scheme resulted in Texas independence, while several other provinces, frustrated by the betrayal of federalist principles, dreamed of following suit. Finally, Texas's annexation to the United States in late 1845, together with growing conflict over California, brought Mexico and the United States to the brink of war by the middle of the following year.

The Mexican-American War, fought almost entirely on what is today Mexican soil, engulfed the nation during Heller's residence. Indeed, Heller repeatedly had to confront the widespread breakdown in law and order that attended this conflict. Doubtless the problem was all the more evident to a young man raised in the security of the Austrian police state that Prince Clemens Metternich had erected in 1815 as a guard against future revolutions. Even taking exaggeration into account, though, it is clear that bandits, smugglers, and pickpockets plagued 1840s Mexico. Authorities exerted somewhat greater control over the cities, but once travelers set out on the open road they threw their lives open to chance. Even capable *arrieros* (mule drivers), who traveled armed and in numbers, feared highwaymen above all else. The problem only worsened until Mexico constructed its own police state after 1867.

Heller fled central Mexico only to enter a Yucatán peninsula that had just embarked on four decades of endemic violence. First came the federalist revolt of Santiago Imán (1836–40), culminating in Yucatán's independence from the larger republic. This was soon followed by the failed Mexican invasion (1842–43), a brief reunification, then an intertwining of civil wars and ethnic peasant uprising known as the Caste War (1847 onward). Yucatán was preparing yet another separation even as Heller's boat neared the Campeche port. In Tabasco Heller witnessed firsthand the U.S. occupation, and here and in Chiapas he was able to see the first glimmerings of the three decades of civil wars spun out of the occupation and ensuing Reform wars. We might say that Heller caught Mexico in that critical interstice between the hope and naïveté of the early national period and the bitter infighting of the Reform era.

In terms of his southeast observations, Heller's book offers an unrivaled glimpse of the Campeche area and of the seldom-seen people and folkways of Tabasco and Chiapas. His archaeological accounts of Uxmal, while doubtless astonishing to his German readers, are today somewhat less so, given the ruins' extensive treatment in contemporary English-language memoirs. Although Heller spent less time in the Yucatecan capital of Mérida, his observations here will nonetheless prove welcome to anyone interested in the mood of a society on the brink of a prolonged Maya peasant uprising known as the Caste War (1847–1901). Suffice it to say, then, that while many travelers wrote their accounts of Mexican society and folkways, few saw the nation at such a critical moment in its history.

Heller and His World

Such was midcentury Mexico. But what of the man who penned this unusual account? Karl Bartolomeus Heller was born on November 20, 1824, in the town of Misliboritz, district of Mähren, in what is today the Czech Republic but which then belonged to the Austro-Hungarian Empire's province of Bohemia. The Heller family relocated to Vienna shortly thereafter. Karl's father served as groundskeeper to the emperor's minister of horticulture, and consequently young Karl grew up with extensive exposure to the world of nature and the science of botany. He distinguished himself as a precocious scholar, and by the time he graduated basic studies at the age of eighteen he had assembled a scientific collection of insects that included more than six thousand specimens.[2]

Once he left the gymnasium Heller found himself torn over career choices, or lack thereof. His first inclination was to study medicine, but the family's limited means forced him to withdraw from medical school before taking a degree. (The dream was slow to die, and throughout his travels in Mexico he never passed up an opportunity to try his hand at healing.) The young man seemed condemned to arid government service, but at the last moment an opportunity arose. The Royal Botanical Society was then planning an expedition to collect specimens from the Americas, and Heller's old patron, society president Baron von Hügel, recruited young Karl for the job. Heller spent the next two years preparing himself for the challenge, reading whatever was available on Mexico, acquiring scientific instruments, and mastering Spanish, English, and French. The original text of *Reisen* even includes an appendix (here omitted) that provides a fairly accurate account of the basics of Yucatec Maya. Heller also readied himself for the expedition by reading available sources on Mexico, such as the letters of Hernán Cortés, the writings of the Franciscan friar Diego López Cogolludo, and the best-selling travelogues of John Lloyd Stephens.

Though challenging, Heller's expedition was nothing new. The eighteenth century had witnessed an explosion of interest in the subject of botany, fueled in part by the work of Swedish pastor and amateur naturalist Carl Linnaeus (1707–87), who created the system of plant classification still used today. A second impetus derived from the century's increased colonial competition, as European powers sought to wring what advantage they could from the natural kingdoms of Asia, Africa, and the Americas. London's Kew Gardens and Paris's Royal Garden amassed huge collections of specimens gathered from the remote corners of global empires, sometimes with an eye to profit, partly from mere scientific curiosity. Botanical studies also made inroads into Mexico at this time, mainly under the instigation of Spain's Bourbon monarchy, although conflicts between peninsular and creole (American-born) Spaniards complicated the process. A number of scientific expeditions probed the Spanish Americas between 1750 and 1808, culminating in the watershed travels (1799–1804) of Alexander von Humboldt. The political instability that followed Mexican independence necessarily limited national scientific advances, but the onset of nationhood did open up the society to a wide variety of visitors previously excluded under the old imperial system. They came on errands of archaeology, business, diplomacy, or mere sightseeing. Heller's expedition in many ways resumed the great botanical explorations of the late Bourbon era, but without winning the fame of such precursors as Humboldt or Joseph Banks.[3]

While we may question the degree of imperial clout that his cuttings of sweet potato and Mexican sage actually provided for Austro-Hungary, no one can fault Heller for inactivity. Indeed, once in Mexico he carried out his assignment far more thoroughly than the tight-fisted society had any reason to expect. In the course of his travels he collected and sent back to Vienna some fifty crates of materials. These included approximately hundreds of insects and small vertebrates; two thousand seashells; and his real forte, six thousand live and ten thousand dried plant specimens. Heller's writings also provided what were then virtually the only available accounts of Tabasco and Chiapas. Oddly enough, the modern reader's sole contact with Heller's exploration legacy probably comes through the local pet store: the tropical swordtail, beloved inhabitant of so many household aquariums and indigenous to the waters of southern Mexico and Belize, was in fact a Heller discovery, and today bears his name: *Xiphophorus helleri* (see chapter 5).

Money problems recurred throughout the expedition. Funding supposedly came from the Royal Botanical Society, which provided for its agent by setting up credit accounts with various commercial houses in port cities, principally Veracruz. But as sometimes happens with research grants, the allotted money failed to match the objective difficulties of the project. Heller's frequent and unexpected changes of plans elevated the costs, while political upheavals in both Mexico and Europe often delayed both funds and instructions. Burglaries, extortionate pricings, and armed highway robberies compounded the problem. Fortunately, the young man's gregarious personality served him well, because at various points (and particularly in Campeche) he was forced to rely on loans from friendly locals. But the matter of shortfalls persisted until the end, and one of the book's more moving passages comes in the final chapter with the hard-up Heller standing alongside the boulevards of Havana as the well-bred señoritas of high society ride by waving, while their carriages cover him with dust.

Karl Heller's later life built profitably on his Mesoamerican rambles, but success did not come immediately. Upon returning to Austria he encountered only more hardships, for with Vienna still convulsed in the aftershocks of the

1848 revolutions, the young man found that no work was available. Reduced to poverty, he began to publish sketches of his travels in the Viennese newspapers, and it was from these miscellaneous sketches that *Reisen in Mexiko* eventually took shape. Heller received other offers to undertake exploratory travel, but his parents were now sick and elderly and he considered it impossible to abandon them, choosing instead to eke out an existence in Austria. Only in 1851 did he take the first of a variety of teaching posts. From that point on, his fortunes moved steadily upward. He published at a furious pace, and in late 1853 *Reisen* earned him the emperor's gold medal "pro literis et artibus." In 1858 he joined the faculty of the gymnasium of Theresianum in Vienna, a school that trained sons of nobility for imperial civil service.[4] Here he served until his death in 1880. In the course of his twenty-two-year career, Heller became the king of instructors and the instructor of kings, providing scientific and mathematical training not only to numerous Hapsburg archdukes but also to the young Prince Alfonso of Spain (1857–85, crowned in 1875), who, before assuming the throne in Madrid, studied for two years in Theresianum. Alfonso XII's grateful memories of this time later earned Heller membership in the highly exclusive Order of Isabel.

Heller's life, though brimming with hard-won triumphs, was destined to be brief. During his final years he suffered an unidentified but recurrent gastrointestinal illness, possibly some form of chronic inflammation related to his near-fatal ordeals in Veracruz. In 1877 his condition began to deteriorate, and he traveled to spas seeking to recover. Even in sickness Heller's creative spirit persevered, and he managed to eke out one more essay, the curiously titled "Arthropods as Enemies of Mankind." In 1879 Heller was forced to give up teaching for good. The following summer a trip to his beachfront home in Ebensee turned to disaster when high waters inundated the house and forced the wheelchair-bound Heller and his family to make the difficult journey back to Vienna. Matters eventually reached the point where the patient could not so much as stir in his bed; a scholar to the end, he requested that his family read to him. On the night of December 14, 1880, a mere eleven days before the holiday he loved so well, the tenacious Karl Heller at last slipped away at the age of fifty-six.

Though virtually unknown today, Heller left a palpable imprint on the scientific community of his time. During his professional years he published extensively in scientific venues. In addition to a number of articles in the *Austrian Botanical Weekly,* he authored several science texts, including a manual on microscopes and a history of natural science.[5] He also became an early German-speaking authority on and ardent champion of Charles Darwin's theories, and self-published his own defense of evolution in 1869, a mere ten years after *The Origin of Species.* Even in later and strictly professional writings Heller occasionally revealed a literary yearning that set him apart from the often dry technical prose of his colleagues. Regardless of his place in the history of botany, the non-scientific memoir *Reisen in Mexiko* remains his most enduring work by far. Emperor Franz Joseph's highly educated brother Maximilian almost certainly read the book when he contemplated accepting the crown of Mexico; if so, perhaps *Reisen*'s account of a nation plunged into chaos convinced Maximilian that Mexicans would welcome the sort of ossified absolutism that the Hapsburg family had to offer. Whatever the truth on this point, the author's legacy survived in other ways. Heller's son Karl Maria (born March 21, 1864) inherited his father's love of natural science and longing for travel. Himself a zoologist of mention, Karl Maria carried out his own fieldwork in such far-flung locales as Syria and southern Bulgaria and won particular fame for a museum of exotic scarabs that he established in Dresden, a city that became his permanent home. Karl Maria Heller somehow survived the terrible Dresden fire-bombings, only to succumb to the ravages of old age seven months after the end of World War II, on December 26, 1945.[6]

Most of our knowledge of the elder Heller's personality derives from information within the text of *Reisen* itself. Single at the time of his epic journey, Heller later married, and in addition to Karl Maria he had at least one other son, of whom nothing is known. Heller appears to have been quiet and introspective, but almost always with a resilient sense of humor; he enjoyed the company of friends but was most at peace when wandering alone through the vegetation of rural Mexico. His eulogy refers to him as an individual of gentle demeanor, much loved by colleagues and students alike, and with a discretion that made him the confidant of an Austrian nobility long addicted to intrigue. It is clear, however, that beneath this calm exterior lay extraordinary intellectual gifts and a steely determination to carry out his mission.

Religion clearly formed a part of his life, although his piety was hardly conventional or dogmatic. Himself a Catholic, Karl Heller personally inclined more toward a meditative spirituality that—appropriate to a romantic age—drew inspiration from nature and shunned man-made pomp and ostentation. Above all, his temperament and profession drove him toward a religious worldview compatible with the recent advances of science. As he himself put it, the only reason for rejecting evolutionary doctrine was "the Almighty of prejudice and the unauthorized mixture of feelings which have nothing to do with natural research."[7] The young man finds himself dazzled and yet somewhat put off by the grandiose cathedrals of central Mexico. He evinces little love for the Mexican clergy, openly condemns the Catholic friars of colonial days, and has brickbats for the syncretic folk Catholicism that had taken root among Mexico's indigenous peasantry. Nevertheless, in his memoir Heller manages to convey useful descriptive information about the religious practices he witnessed, including nineteenth-century churches, rural religious ceremonies, popular deference toward the clergy, and a singularly vivid portrait of Holy Week in Campeche.

While it would have pained Heller to admit it, the Austro-Hungarian Empire of his lifetime in some ways resembled Mexico itself: less a nation than a chaotic patchwork of provinces and ethnicities quilted together by bureaucratic oversight and an enforced religious conformity. At the time he wrote, its peoples had just embarked on a series of failed revolutions to determine whether the emerging Germany would be large or small, authoritarian or democratic. The dreamed-of nation-states failed to materialize; republican forces were turned back, and power passed to the hands of Emperor Franz Joseph, the dynastic and seemingly immortal bureaucrat whom generations of European liberals loved to hate. Young intelligentsia like Karl Marx were permanently radicalized, and the aspirations of German nationalism had another quarter century to gather into an explosive force. The far-flung Austro-Hungarian Empire's problem of suppressed nationalisms continued to fester, and has plagued successor states to the present day. Despite political frustrations, however, the nineteenth-century German people enjoyed a florescence of learning and literacy. More citizens than ever were now reading. North German higher education in particular had already begun to surge ahead of its continental counterparts. Austrian strides remained somewhat less impressive, but Vienna, with its cafés, salons, and universities, proved an insatiable consumer of ideas and information. Heller's work thus fell upon a public hungry for news of the vast world beyond the Rhine.[8]

Bringing Heller Back Alive

Reisen in Mexiko presents all the difficulties we might expect of a nineteenth-century German text. Numerous spellings and usages have changed over the years. German grammatical constructions often require modification to prosper in English form. I have tried to render the prose as closely as possible to the diction of modern English, and at times I needed to subdivide both sentences and paragraphs to make them more comprehensible to the reader. The botanist's tireless deployments of *auch, doch, jedoch, noch,* and *schon* often fail to justify a word-for-word rendition (as Mark Twain put it, "Every time a German opens his mouth an *Also* falls out; and every time he shuts its he bites one in two that was trying to get out").[9] Redundant adjectives also abound, here distilled to a common essence. Heller relied heavily on passive and impersonal constructions, which drag when translated literally; whenever possible, I have wrestled these into active, transitive form.

One of the more curious features of the text is its odd mishmash of weights, measures, and currencies. Heller employed a welter of terms from different systems to render quantitative information. For example, to capture distances he used German, English, and Spanish measurements as well as nautical miles. Doubtless these inconsistencies reflect his international experience as well as a world where standard measurements were in flux (he uses the metric system occasionally, but only when he applies the term *meter* to relatively small objects). Here long distances appear in their equivalents as English miles, and smaller ones in feet. For Mexico's basic monetary unit Heller adopted the German term *thaler,* here replaced with *peso.* I have also rendered his temperature readings from the now-defunct Réaumur into Fahrenheit readings. Finally, whenever possible I have substituted the common names of plants for the latinate scientific terms that the Austrian scientist slung about with such abandon (a point we can forgive; he was, after all, a botanist).

Beyond matters of style and grammar, Heller's cultural preconceptions often intrude upon the narrative. The greatest baggage these explorers carried was not their suitcases, and the task of deconstructing the accounts of gentleman-travelers has today generated a growing literature.[10] Heller committed more than his share of mistakes and misinterpretations. Among the most irritating of his quirks was the insistence on mentioning every single European he met along the way. The memoirist tended to paint them in saintly adjectives—"worthy," "upright," "stout-hearted"—that contrasted visibly with the barbs he reserved for uncooperative Mexicans. Doubtless these encounters mattered deeply to a homesick lad of twenty, but today they appear nowhere as compelling as they must have been in their moment, and they often detract from the text's more enduring descriptive passages.

The reader will also notice a curious interiority conditioning the narrative; Heller seldom shares the stage with other characters, and even more rarely attempts to reproduce actual speech or conversation of the Mexicans or anyone else. In fact, the young Austrian appears to have been far more at home either in the world of objective and measurable data (doubtless a reflection of his scientific training) or in romantic exploration of his emotions. Scenic locales often take on an almost metric precision as Heller deals out numbers concerning elevation above sea level, average temperature fluctuations, and Greenwich-based latitudes and longitudes. At times this insistence on statistical verities reaches an almost comic extreme: upon arriving at the lovely Yucatecan city of Mérida, Heller immediately proceeds to measure the square feet of the town's central plaza!

Certain themes clearly drew his attention more than others. His interest in mineral springs borders on the obsessive. Not only does Heller summarize their chemical content, but he also tirelessly berates Mexicans for not commercializing and promoting them. The young author clearly had a fascination for boats of all variety, and often describes them in great detail (see, for example, his opening portrait of a transatlantic steamer). More comprehensible, surely, is his eye for the ladies. When in female company Heller can be counted on to pay attention, whether those women are the "enchanting water nymphs" of Chiapas and Tabasco or the señoritas of Campeche who sojourned to Sambulá in hopes that the santo would find them a sweetheart. This keen interest is not surprising for a single twenty-year-old who was desperately lonely and far from home.

On a more ominous note, his social preconceptions and prejudices barge into the text at numerous points. Heller shared the prevailing nineteenth-century belief that cultural traits passed through the blood, like DNA. The memoir's comments on slavery and African Caribbeans (chapter 2) are nothing short of offensive. His attitudes toward Indians are less hostile but nonetheless tend to present Mexico's indigenous peasantry as uncouth and benighted children even while envying them for a supposed simplicity that had vanished from the urban life of midcentury Europe. Heller took special note of their sullen demeanor, their primitive housing, their inclination to drink heavily, and their strangely syncretic religious practices, all of which he took as proof of inferiority. The question was where to assign blame for these perceived shortcomings. To the biological nature of the Indians themselves? To the exploitative nature of colonialism? To Spanish Catholicism? His answer tends to fluctuate. In all of this he faithfully echoes misconceptions of the times. In the era during which he lived, even the origins of America's native people remained very much in debate. Scholars (and a good many Latin American elites) disputed any direct link between the region's ancient cultures and its contemporary peasantries. Heller wrote without benefit of the immense body of scientific knowledge and cultural self-examination accumulated over the past 150 years. That being said, we must confess that he was frequently guilty of the colonial prejudices he decried among Spaniards and Mexicans.

Despite all his defects, though, yesteryear's explorer enjoys one signal advantage that entitles him to the respect of modern historians: he was there, and we were not. The Victorian voyagers and Teutonic travelers risked placing their names beside a hand-authored account of things personally witnessed and roads their own shoes had walked. For such reasons, the works of those memoiring souls—Heller included—have outlived the preconceptions of their day and age, and will continue to speak to those who take the time to listen. Moreover, this Austrian's shortcomings find some counterbalance in his own suffering. While Alexander von Humboldt lived on a sizable personal inheritance, enjoyed the company of Latin American dignitaries, and went on to become the toast of intellectual Europe, Karl Heller stumbled through Mexico as a penniless twenty-year old, endured disease and hardship, received little recognition for his labors, and had to claw his way into a middling academic post, only to see an early death.

For all its defects of style and preconception, Heller's account retains its powerful charm after languishing forgotten for more than a century and a half. Significant powers of observation and description were clearly at work here. The author's immense determination, curiosity, and unpretentious goodwill still communicate themselves in force, and anyone who has done prolonged research in a foreign country will sympathize with Heller's saga of loneliness, adventure, despair, and discovery. The introductions behind us, we now board a steamship with one Karl Bartolomeus Heller, Austrian botanical expert and aspiring author. Our destination is deepest Mexico, in search of a lost world that nineteenth-century Europeans knew only through hearsay, and which readers of the modern era all too often visit only in daydreams and web pages.

First Part

Travels in Veracruz, Puebla, and Mexico

If the traveler is to describe the highest pinnacles of our globe, the nature of the greatest river, or the winding paths of the Andes, then he risks the danger of tiring his reader through his unvaried expressions of wonder.

—Alexander von Humboldt

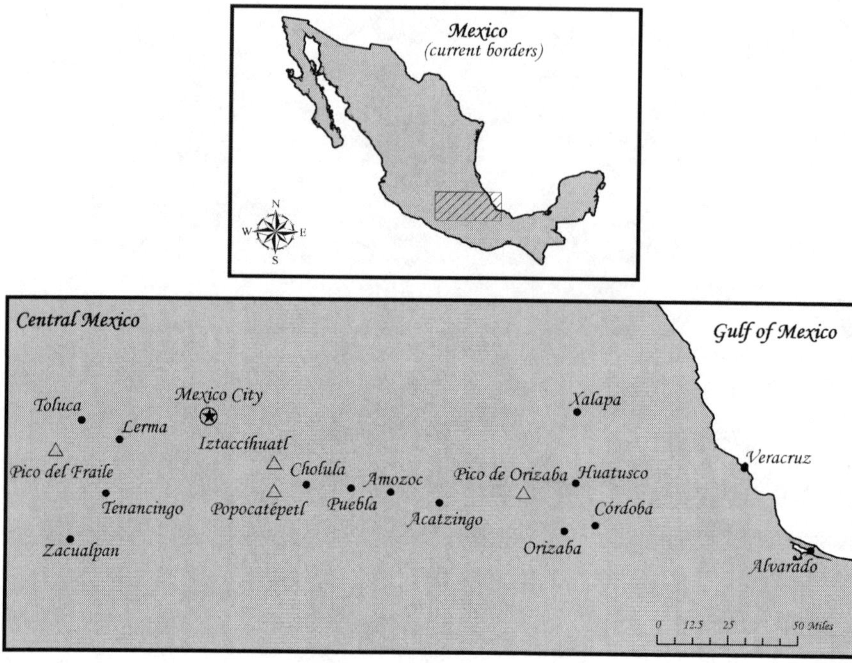

Central Mexico

Chapter 1

It was on August 9, 1845, from the deck of a handsome steamship that roared downstream on the Donau River, that I waved my last farewell to the beloved fields of my fatherland. I was enrapt by the youthful fantasies that necessarily occupy a twenty-year-old lad setting off on such a protracted and dangerous journey. But for the longest time my soul sank into those reveries that the traveler always experiences when leaving his home. Separation . . . and farewell! What an affecting moment it will be in the life of men, when after many years filled to the brim with troubles, sorrows, and struggle, we will have reunited!

It is a bitter feeling when for the first time a man must separate himself from everything he has known, loved, and held sacred since the moment when the child's initial glimmer of awareness awakened. That familiar scene, a mountain, a valley, a spire, become the very points on which one desperately ties the weak threads of hope of seeing home once again. They sink from view . . . some tears perhaps, and the struggle is over.

I watched the bank of the Donau in silence as it quickly passed. My gaze darted from one point to another, as though something inside me were calling, "Here! here! Tarry a second longer!" The steamship pushed on, until we crossed the borders of my fatherland, and my soul once more found calm and strength. From this moment my life belonged to my journey's path. One region now took the place of another, city followed city; in ten days I had put Germany and Belgium behind me, and in Ostend welcomed the high seas for the first time.

Just as a man stares thoughtlessly or rather unconscious of his thoughts at the devastating flames of a bonfire, recoiling in terror from the frightful element and yet mesmerized by the captivating spectacle of the flames, so too the wanderer stands as though bound on the ocean shore. He stares out into the angry, raging waters that thrust upon the coast, crashing with foam on the rocks. Waves rapidly roll in one upon the other and push onto the sand, then retreat for an instant, only to pound the adjoining shore with renewed power.

In this way, I might say, the wanderer stands like a dreamer, lost in contemplating the unimagined and captivating splendor of the waters. Then a passing sail or a roaring steamship startles him from his mute wonder and reminds him of reality.

A day later and the first sea journey, including a six-hour crossing to England, was complete. England, or rather London, stunned me for four weeks with its turmoil, curiosities, and sights of interest, when I stood once more on the seacoast at Southampton to embark upon the great sea to the West Indies and Mexico.

On October 2, 1845, we boarded the steamship *Tay,* anchored an English mile from the coast. The reader will permit me to describe this unforgettable moment. I was extremely fortunate to have the famous and experienced Herr Theodor Hartweg as travel companion; his work had brought him to England, and in him I found a friend to whom I am eternally indebted.[1] He was headed to California, and we thus enjoyed the prospect of a companion in our journey to Mexico. At two hours before midnight we stepped on the deck of our ship. Everything was fully alive here. The steamship *Tay* was one of those travel ships that sail every month from England to Middle America, and I will endeavor to describe its outfitting, since readers in our countries can only have an imperfect notion of such vessels.

The ship had eighteen hundred tons[2] carrying capacity; it measured one hundred paces in length and fifteen to twenty paces in breadth. The engine was of five hundred horsepower. On its spar deck rose two mighty seventy-foot-high masts, from which innumerable large and small cables ran and for the novice form an inextricable web. Benches stood here and there on the extraordinarily clean deck, not only for the convenience of passengers but also to keep those passengers from impeding the incessant work of the sailors. At the hind part of the ship stands the mighty helm; before it are two well-maintained compasses, which, with an extra in the middle, formed a pointed triangle.

Two boats hung backward on iron bars bent outward on both sides of the deck. They could be easily lowered from these into the sea and hoisted up again. On each wheel casing lay an iron sheet-metal lifeboat, each holding fifty men and always kept ready with provisions. In the middle of the deck between the two mastheads rises the colossal smokestack, and next to it the stables for sheep, pigs, and poultry. Here too we found assorted barrels of water. Some glass roofs (skylights, they are called), which are well sealed with iron clasps and which give light to the rooms beneath, and different stairs behind make up the otherwise remarkable features of the spardeck.

Such a steamer comfortably holds eighty-four passengers and a ninety-six-man crew, and at certain hours its deck is everyone's meeting place, or as we would say on land, the promenade. During good weather the lone traveler enjoys fresh sea breezes, feasting his eyes on the azure tide of the ocean. On a clear night he refreshes himself in the further shimmering lights of the moon, or perhaps admires the myriad sparks in the foam of the waves, sparks produced by a small organism with phosphorus light. Moreover, passengers seldom lack the news of the day, which is circulated and discussed within the bounds of the ship's world. The landsmen gather to shorten the time by smoking, singing, and sometimes by dancing as well; the good-natured German is seldom missing; the Frenchman casually joins in, while the Englishman, half mute and gloomy as the mists of his fatherland, wanders up and down, or comfortably sips a glass of whiskey punch.

We descended the stairs and found ourselves on the main deck. Behind those stairs were the first-class cabins, which were neatly arranged in rows opposite one another. These led to a small outermost elegant room abutting a very proper salon under the ship's wheel. This room is of course for the ladies. The middle of this deck was occupied by the galley, a cowshed, and the carpenter's workshop, including the storeroom. Toward the front were the cabins of the officers and engineers and the small rooms for the crew. One flight of stairs below lay the salon deck, which takes its name from the great dining hall. Four long tables, which are set four times a day, fill it up; at the back stands a small chimney, and over it a modest library, in which Bibles of all great and printed varieties play a major role. At the entries of both sides are the bars (tavern tables) for all sorts of spirited drinks, beer, and wine, which are not included in the passage cost, and there must be paid for weekly. During bad weather and in the evening, this comfortably lit hall is the principal sort of pleasure. Whist and other games are arranged, and unfortunately games of chance also find generally universal approval.

Cabins for second-class passengers occupy all other space of this deck. At last, on the fourth or engine deck stands the steam engine with its four huge boilers and coal chambers. The engine's levers rise into the third deck, like an untiring monster that threatens destruction and wants to wrench itself with a groan from its chain.

That was the ship on which we found ourselves, a colossus which—or so I believed at the moment—could defy all the seas of the world. Soon, however, I was to receive a more accurate idea of the matter.

When everyone had boarded, the sign was given to lift the anchor and to remove all persons who were not passengers. This moment was deeply moving; since while here the departing daughter fastened herself once more on the breast of the loving parent, over there a father blesses his departing son;

while here, the sobbing wife tears herself from her enterprising husband, friends embrace themselves for the last time, sunk in tearless, silent sorrow.[3] At that instant for the first time I felt how alone I was.

When the anchor was lifted, the last song of the sailors rang out monotonously, and the small steamboat that had brought us aboard encircled us until at last we were at sea. The sailors climbed up the rope ladders in a mob, cried out a three-times hip-hip-hurrah into the air as a farewell, and the answer from the small steamer faded away. We pushed on in a mass of foam, and the ship became our world.

A strong northwest wind had arisen and prevented us from reaching the open sea. For that reason we had to spend the night in a channel of Southampton, in order to be able to pass the dangerous Needles reef at the Isle of Wight the next morning. An intrepid pilot brought us out with the break of day, and presently we swam on the roaring waves of the ocean, which became higher and higher the further we went from the land toward an ever darker horizon.

I have earlier spoken of the impression that the first glimpse of the sea produces; but he who has only considered it from the land can form but an inadequate notion. Only that man who travels the ocean itself will truly know it. Waters in the vicinity of the coast are consistently gentler than those on the wide ocean. There the waves are small, short, and choppy, while here they often roll upon one another like mountains; their oscillations never entirely cease, perhaps because of the rotation of the earth on its axis. No pen will ever be capable of describing the spectacle of how this bottomless mass of water churns.

When we were on the open sea the situation filled everyone with horror and alarm. The northwest wind ranged over the agitated high water, while gigantic waves rolled by continuously with their spray-capped peaks like frenzied hydra. Seasickness claimed its victims, the deck was forsaken and the salon empty, and only a few lone individuals dared to glimpse out, too terrified to withdraw, for a storm was upon us. We soon found ourselves in the waters of Vizcaya. The elements' fury grew even stronger, and the sea seemed to want to devour us. It came raging over the deck, unleashing barrels, planks, and other objects, angrily slinging overboard whatever it found unsecured there; while in the ship's interior, tables and chairs, glasses, bottles, and dishes flew hither and thither and shattered against one another. Women wept, men stood despairing, clinging to anything firm. The disconsolate sailors shouted, while among them resounded the commands of the officers among them, the storm in all its fury howling through the ropes of the barren tackling. Only the two sailors bound to the helm stood mute like marble pillars, with that stoical calm which made them seemingly indifferent to everything that was happening all around. The engines churned in unison with the rattle of the ship in a dull moan as they struggled vainly against the elements. We progressed scarcely half an English sea mile in the space of an hour. This frightful situation persisted for three days and three nights.

The storm reached its worst during the evening of the sixth to the eighth of October. It dashed to pieces our forward jibmast and tore down a wheel casing. We did not know whether we would live to the coming morning, but the sun rose up with daybreak on the clear horizon, cheerful and with its blessing, proclaiming deliverance, filling everything with joy. To be sure, the sea continued to swell, yet always becoming softer and softer, until at last the immense surface had smoothed out. It resembled a mirror in which we could not tire of seeing our reflection. Meanwhile, we repaired what we could of the ship's damage, leaving it as it had been when we left the harbor with everything perfectly in order. On the eleventh at noon we neared the island of Madeira, opposite the coast of Morocco. Only ten days had passed since we left England—ten days, however, that seemed an eternity to a novice—and we rejoiced over our approach to that island.

The weather was splendid. A spotless and dark blue expanse stretched over the tranquil sea, another breeze warm and mild blew upon us, and the cold, unfriendly European sky disappeared. Finally, the rocky coasts of Porto Santo shot up over the waters: it was the barren and thinly populated island of Madeira, little more than a stopping point for a few fishermen. The sea foam stretched like a white band along the coast, and the rays of the setting sun brilliantly illuminated the rock masses on which the naked eye can discern neither trees nor bushes. A voyager's gaze rested immovably upon them, since one values the land ever so greatly after becoming acquainted with the fury of the ocean.

Gliding along Porto Santo and the Desiertos,[4] we came to Madeira proper, an island that rose up on the western horizon like a cloud. Meanwhile, night had fallen, but not a night such as we had ever seen. Out of the dark blue sky twinkled thousands upon thousands of stars. Among them, and reflected in the waves of the sea, lay the silvery gleam of the moon. Balmy winds blew to us from the land, breezes that can only be found in the climate of the Madeiras, perhaps the loveliest in the world. As soon as the contours of the land became clearer, we all strained our eyes to discover a house or a light at the first opportunity. As soon as we had rounded the eastern point we found the scenery delightful, since only the southern slope is much populated, while the remaining mountainous parts of the island scarcely seemed to offer a table-sized expanse for cultivation.

At midnight we noisily dropped anchor at Funchal, the main city of Madeira. The thunder of two cannons announced our arrival, and at once came the splashing of oars, bringing the port authority's boat as swift as an arrow to the side of our ship. The customary forms of greetings passed quickly, and the usual quiet in the cabins of our ship soon prevailed. We hastened to enjoy the few remaining hours of sleep, in order to be able to go ashore the next morning. At 5 A.M., when the sun rose on the horizon, the foredeck was already cheerfully animated. Countless canoes competed with Portuguese ardor, shouting and struggling, dragging themselves on board our ship, to bring the passengers ashore, and many times we had the entertainment of seeing the straining canoemen unintentionally refresh themselves in the cool water.[5]

While all this hubbub erupted around me, I lay engrossed in the spectacle of Funchal. To the left an isolated and bare rock jutted out of the sea; a mighty fortress stands at its tip and presides over the landing place. Behind this same the city's neat houses emerge, rising up the steep slopes distinctly and gracefully among the fresh greenery of the trees. The traveler is almost tempted to take it as a picture from some vivid fantasy rather than as a scene from nature.

A canoe swiftly brought us to the land, and an array of new scenes presented themselves. Funchal is a small city with narrow streets mostly going uphill; for that reason they use either a horse or the sedan in order to get from one place to another. The inhabitants themselves are Portuguese, since for a long time the island itself has been the property of Portugal. Although suitable, Madeiran clothing differs little from European, with the exception of a small cap made of cloth and furnished with a long point, something that lends a comic appearance to the men and women.

The stone-built houses are small and seldom seem particularly inviting. The flat-roof construction calls to mind southern Spain or Italy. Here and there, however, one finds very attractive buildings. Winsome gardens lend them a special flavor, all the more so since those gardens are decorated with a greenery that is foreign to the European. For example, the coffee tree, the banana, and the orange, the fig, and other trees of the tropical climate flourish in abundance.

After inspecting this fascinating vegetation, we hurried to one of those famous nuns' cloisters that normally cater to the visiting foreigners. Upon reaching the same, the nuns received us in the conversation parlor, offering us flowers assembled from bird feathers in the most artful form and entirely faithful to nature, and which procure respectable if small amounts of money for the saintly sisters when great ships touch port. More than the flowers, I enjoyed the magnificent view that the elevated position of the cloister furnished of the city and the wonderful ocean bay.

From there we descended the mountain along a small river. The steep banks of this stream abounded in dense rushes (wild cane, caladia, and ferns, with an avenue of plane trees and chestnuts) that shaded the charming path; over the walls of the garden protruded hibiscuses, oranges, and roses covered with flowers. All this in the month of October, when in Europe frosty winds already storm over the mountains and heaths, and force Nature into a months-long sleep!

Next came the fish and fruit market, memorable for its countless and novel products. From giant tuna fish to tiny anchovies, this market overflowed with the most splendid seafood. Next to that stood the fruit market, in which oranges, figs, bananas, wonderful grapes, and even stone fruit lay in huge piles. A lovely garland of heliotrope and oak-leafed geraniums sown with sweet-smelling blooms surrounded the whole, and no one from our ship could resist the temptation to take a rich supply of Madeira's fruit on board. A short promenade along the seacoast concluded our agreeable ramble, where we caught sight of two blue-gum eucalyptus standing in bloom among the most beautiful sycamores. The scene took us by surprise.

We were reveling in the magnificent view of this picturesque bay and its city when a cannon blast called us to return to the ship. Two hours later we were racing along the wide ocean that separated us from our destination by hundreds of miles. The wonderful weather (77 degrees Fahrenheit)[6] allowed us to reflect back with pleasure on the fatherland of malmsey, that asylum of so many consumptive Europeans.[7]

Doubtless as well, a visit to Madeira will remain unforgettable to the majority who cross the sea for the first time. After a dangerous if brief sea journey, could there be something more pleasant than to land on such a splendor-filled oasis of the ocean? If it were nothing more than a bare rock, the traveler would still appreciate it; but Madeira is a place where of splendid climate, where luxurious and fertile nature charms the European for the first time. The famous traveler Poepping[8] observes quite accurately that one retains a certain predilection for one's first landing place, because one sees an embodiment of the fantasies he has entertained for so long. We abandon such a place only with regret, all the more so if we believe—indeed, are convinced—that the visit was too short to observe all its beauty.

When the island had vanished from our sight, then began the prolonged monotony of sea life. To be certain, our approach to the tropics afforded more variety than did the northern latitudes, since in addition to the inhabitants of the sea we now saw flying fish and mollusks of extraordinary form.[9] Sea grasses and shellfish danced in the waves. Almost every day the sunrise and sunset allowed us the most phenomenal show, and the magnificent evenings made the deck an enjoyable place in all regards.

October 18 was one of the hottest and sultriest of days, and toward evening a frightful storm gathered in the heavens. Soon lightning crossed the ominous clouds in such quantity that the horizon glowed almost incessantly in fire. Indeed, we feared the evil consequences of such a storm. The captain gathered in the sails, stationed the sailors, and awaited the worst. However, how relieved were we all when the weather spent itself in a heavy rainfall, after which the sky soon cleared, and all danger passed.

On that day we crossed into the tropical latitudes and thereupon entered into the tropics proper, where we hoped that a favorable trade wind would soon push us along. Sadly, our hopes were deceived; for although we rarely encountered contrary winds, we had not even the most trifling wind behind us. The next day, October 19, we found ourselves completely calmed. The sea was like a glass mirror, and for the first time since our departure we were able to hold Sunday religious service. The crew stretched a canopy over the aft of the ship; in the center a *prie-dieu*[10] was set up, on which the English priest conducted the sea service. Two long rows of well-dressed sailors stood on the left and right, and near the helm the officers and remaining men and women gathered without regard to differences of religion. When worshiping the supreme being on the waves of the ocean, who would quibble over the different formulas of faith? I am convinced that the simply worded prayers of the priest moved everyone. The women glanced mutely among themselves, deeply affected by the sublime mood of the scene, and fully convinced of the great power that undiluted faith possesses. After a quarter of an hour the ceremony was completely over on the great English ship, and soon the onlookers lost themselves in different quarters, where they spent the remaining hours of Sunday quietly and tranquilly.

Five days of the most lovely weather had once again passed. In fact, the trade winds did not appear even once, and with this weather a sail ship would have found itself in a wretched position, since the calm lasted for many days. Finally, on October 25, at 9:00 in the morning we glimpsed the island of Barbados.

Chapter 2

At noon we reached the island, which we accurately recognized even at a distance because of its level east coast and because we could already see the stout coconut palms with their green tops swaying in the breeze. Barbados is the easternmost of the Caribbean islands. The Portuguese discovered but never occupied it, and for that reason Barbados passed to England when a British ship landed there in 1605, and has remained in their possession to the present day. It was the first English colony in the West Indies and was settled only a year earlier than St. Kitts (1623). Barbados lies between 59°50′ and 60°2′ west longitude (from Greenwich) and between 12°56′ and 13°16′ north latitude, and lies scarcely 238 miles from the South American mainland. Its surface area consists of 107,000 acres or 428,000 *Joch,*[1] all of which are superbly cultivated. The entire population, including the Negroes, comes to approximately 121,000 souls.

The capital and port city is Bridgetown, where a highly industrious life prevails, and not even the most trifling European article is wanting. The city is rather large for so small an island, and the houses are constructed in the European fashion. The mother tongue is English, but in the mouths of the Negroes this undergoes spectacular distortions. In Bridgetown there are six newspapers in the English language.

Since we had required thirteen days to cover the distance from Madeira to Barbados, the sight of this island came as a great pleasure. But the coast is not at all picturesque, for only the northeast part, called Schattland, rises to eleven hundred feet. How new and different from all others was the character of this island! How splendid the groves of coconut palms, how unique the beaches covered with cacti! One cannot say that this sight is eternally magnificent, for although the freshness beguiles, the monotony of this picture quite soon becomes evident; still, it is here that one sees tropical vegetation in its full dimensions for the first time.

We hurried to the shore and through the busy streets to a small plaza where the statue of Nelson stands, and from there to the so-called ice establishment,[2] a place that serves drinks with ice. To anyone who knows the heat of the West Indies from descriptions it will sound peculiar to hear mention of an icehouse on the island of Barbados, and yet it is so. Ice, an important article of commerce from the United States of North America, is sent from Boston, not only to all the West Indian islands but also to many points in South America and even China. He who has drunk nothing but stale ship water for more than twelve days will understand the inestimable value of a fresh drink under a heat of more than 95 degrees. Mixed with the suitable proportion of soda, this drink was so inviting that we did not merely enjoy it; rather, everyone fell upon it as if through some irresistible attraction. Never before had I known the value of a chip of ice as at that moment, and many times in the course of my journey I let myself pay extravagant and prodigious sums at the sight of this article so common in Germany.

Refreshed as we were, Herr Hartweg and I hurried to the outskirts of the city in order to more closely inspect the vegetation, even though the sun burned down on us with frightful intensity. A knot of fresh-looking trees and shrubbery presented itself to our sight. Here stood splendid tamarinds, there sea grapes, tecoma flowers, cordia, poinsettias, Jerusalem thorns, and cinnamon; begonias dotted with flowers; mimosas, shrimp plants, and deep blue sweet potato flowers, among which here and there we glimpsed the exuberant croton pictum. Captivated by the abundance of outstanding produce, we hastened to the fruit market, a visit that gave me once more the opportunity to learn much concerning new tropical products. There was an abundance of colossal pomelo (or as they say in England, shaddock), oranges, bananas, coconuts, soursop, alligator pears, mangoes, and even apples and pears that were brought from North America. Among the vegetables we saw the roots of the camote, the winged yam, and the cassava, the seed pods of different chiles, and the many squash. The extraordinarily delightful flavor of these different tropical fruits, of which I will speak more when the occasion permits, tempted most of our fellow travelers to return to the ship with good supplies. In particular they carried off half-ripe bunches of bananas.

The evening had arrived, and with it the hour for us to return to the ship. When the sun had sunk into the tranquil sea we found ourselves well under way to the island of Grenada, some 140 miles away; so it was that at dawn of the following day this group of islands already stood before us. The Grenadines are a cluster of approximately 120 islands, which because of their mass of reefs are highly dangerous to the seafarer in stormy weather. A product of volcanic activity, something to which their existence of almost pure porphyry testifies, these rocks often assume wonderful shapes. Among them, for example, I saw a colossal archway towering out of the sea and standing in solitary fashion over the waves. Others form perforated cones resembling petrified giants from a distance, and still others, worn away by the eternal breaking of the waves, scarcely rise above the water level.

Since the weather was better than ever, we passed quietly through these reefs to Grenada. One can scarcely imagine a sight more beautiful than this island. It rises among the aforementioned bare and uninhabited rocks like a garden. Although quite mountainous, it is nevertheless wholly covered by the most lovely greenery, and it seems as if in earlier times someone had paid a great deal of attention to its cultivation. Columbus discovered Grenada on his third voyage, in 1650 it passed to France, and in 1763 to England. It lies between 12°1′ and 11°15′ north latitude and 61°20′ and 61°35′ west longitude from Greenwich; for that reason it is only 104 miles from the South American mainland. Its surface area comes to eighty thousand acres. After a period of sixteen years England had to hand it over yet again to France, and it returned once more with the peace accords of 1783. The capital is Georgetown, which like Funchal is built on a slope and is protected by a strong fort. Although small, the harbor is good; as in Madeira, vessels of the greatest tonnage can anchor just short of the land. The bay of St. George is boundlessly picturesque and romantic, animated by the mass of Negroes, who make up the greatest number of inhabitants, loitering about.

Here for the first time I could marvel at the astonishing swimming ability of the Negroes, who with unbelievable swiftness retrieved whatever object was thrown into the sea, even the smallest coin. Not only did they search underwater, often for a long time, but when two of them simultaneously glimpse a sinking piece of money, a heated struggle would break out, not infrequently lasting for several minutes. Moreover, I must say that for my tastes the Negroes of this English island exhibit a greater shamelessness than even among the wild Indians.

In spite of its southern position, the island's temperature swings between 77 and 100 degrees, and the frequent rains make Grenada highly fertile. It exports such products as sugar, coffee, rum, cotton, and tropical fruit. For the most part the vegetation resembles that of Barbados, although here I again discovered more new plants, among which crape myrtle, leadwort, jasmine, and more begonias stand out for their handsome flowers; joining them as well are cacti, Spanish moss, bamboo, and daffodils, on whose flowers golden-feathered hummingbirds flit about with arrowlike swiftness.

Since landing here we had strolled for several hours, something that exhausted us not a little, with the tremendous heat and being unaccustomed to the walking. For a long time we rested in a small hotel lying on a knoll, from which point one enjoyed a wonderful view, until the reloading of our luggage from the steamship *Tay* to the steamship *Tweed;* that is to say, in Grenada the traveler changes ships. The latter vessel provides service between the islands until another steamship comes from England; it then takes on passengers and departs, touches down at still other points via Bermuda, and returns home. Here most travelers split up for different destinations. Many go to the Windward Islands,[3] others to South America, and only a few stay behind for the islands lying to the west. Of eighty-four passengers, only twenty-five remained on board the *Tweed,* and since it was considerably larger than the *Tay,* we could enjoy unrestricted all the comforts a ship can offer; in fact, even the charming ladies' salon now stood open to the gentlemen.

Around 11:00 at night we set out in this handsome vessel (which seventeen months later suffered a frightful shipwreck near the coast of Yucatán, wherein more than a hundred human lives were lost),[4] content and cheerful to be at sea, and struck a course for Haiti, which lies 720 English miles from Grenada. On October 30 we entered the bay of Jacmel after sailing along the coast since daybreak.

Since the steamship only traveled here to bring passengers and correspondence to the nation and to take the same out again, it was impossible for the other passengers to go ashore in the short space of time. This was no great loss, insofar as Jacmel is an entirely wretched place better seen from the ship than up close. The town is situated in the very lovely bay of the same name, which, because of its great depth and because of the many other bays of the island, is extremely difficult for inexperienced ships to find. Its streets are miserable and dirty, just like the inhabitants, and except for the accommodations of the president, who usually resides in the Haitian capital of Port-au-Prince, there is no respectable house to be seen.

Haiti, Santo Domingo—or as Columbus called it, Hispaniola—was discovered by that gentleman in 1492. It lies between 18° and 20° north latitude and 68° and 75° west longitude and is 360 miles long and 60 to 120 miles wide. Its circumference, the bays excluded, amounts to a thousand miles, thus making it is as large as Ireland.

This island, which the French call the Queen of the Antilles, may well be the most beautiful as far as vegetation and nature scenes are concerned. An unbroken chain of eternally green mountains, a few rising to a height of six thousand feet, cuts across the entire island and makes the southern coast a singularly picturesque place. Among other things, the overland journey from Jacmel to Port-au-Prince carries the wanderer past the most wonderful region the eyes can imagine, and for that reason it is all the more deplorable that this fertile and lovely land is of late so neglected and so little cultivated. Since the establishment of the black government many people have been settled on the land, and in spite of the fact that we sailed along near the coast, we could discover neither well-cultivated plots nor scarcely more than three houses, Jacmel excluded.[5]

The total population of Haiti amounts to no more than 850,000, that of Jacmel 6,000–7,000. The president of this republic is black; he receives a yearly salary of 40,000 Haitian gourde,[6] and on top of this, if he tours the island, enjoys an extra allowance of 30,000 gourde. He was elected for life and has the power to name his successor. The Haitian government appears to have made it its business to drive its beautiful land little by little back to its former condition of wilderness.

We had soon concluded our business in Jacmel and set out along the island for Jamaica. Since we left Grenada, the weather had remained quite lovely, and under the expansive sky the heat on the ship became almost unbearable. The thermometer continually read 95 degrees in the shade, and in the cabin fell to not under 84 degrees, even at night. The tremendous heat tormented us, as did the huge number of rats we had on board the ship, and which began to run about as soon as night fell. Indeed, not infrequently a small set of four paws ventured to scurry over someone who was trying to sleep peacefully. These irritations bothered us so terribly that on most evenings we wandered around the deck until midnight.

We had scarcely lost sight of the mountains of Haiti the next day when those of Jamaica rose up on the western horizon. The proximity of this island to Haiti and Cuba has given rise to the assertion that there is a point between these three islands where one can see all of them. However, the assertion falls rather into doubt, since this point, which is equidistant from the three, lies seventy-one miles away from each, and in fact the most colossal mountains would be needed in order to be able to glimpse them at such a distance over sea level.

Toward 6:00 in the evening we neared an island, and since the eastern coast was dangerous for the seafarer owing to sandbars and reefs, a lighthouse and repeated soundings provided for the safety of the ships. Moreover, we took someone on board who guided us to Port Royal without harm; here, however, he refused to bring us in, since the wind was against us. The next morning we therefore busied ourselves with a slow entry into the narrow channel, which is constructed from the mainland and a large sandbank. The waterway itself is marked out and winds its way hither and thither through floating blocks that are anchored to the bottom, for sailing vessels have the greatest difficulty entering. The high point of this sandbank, which is, strictly speaking, a spit of land, bears the name Port Royal. At the same time it forms the splendid natural harbor of Kingston, the principal city of Jamaica, before which we anchored an hour later. The Jamaican harbor is the main station of the English flotilla for the West Indies, and there lies the famous double-decker *Imaum* of ninety cannons.[7] Beyond this the harbor teems with many vessels of all nations, which give to the whole the appearance of lively commerce.

We landed as soon as we were able, and since we did not have to journey again until morning, a little time remained for us to see Kingston at somewhat closer hand. But first, a bit about the island itself. Jamaica, or as he called it, Xaymaca, which is to say, "Land of Eternal Spring," was discovered on May 3, 1494, by Columbus. This island has an oval form, is 160 miles long and 45 miles wide, and has a surface area of 400,000 acres. The Jamaican Blue Mountains run the length of the isle and in many places tower eight thousand feet above sea level. The sight of these mountains, whose slopes reveal a great deal of cultivation, together with the lovely harbor of Kingston and the crowd of ships, provides a wonderful scene. Fertile Jamaica passed from Spain to England in 1670 by treaty and was divided into three counties—namely Middlesex, Surrey, and Cornwall—and these in turn into twenty-three parishes, which include six cities, twenty-seven villages, and many dispersed settlements.[8] The yearly income amounts to 60,000 pounds sterling, of which 10,000 are revenue for the crown. The fertility of this island depends on heavy rains, which are more frequent in particular on the north side (where one occasionally counts 116 rainy days per year) than on the south side.

Kingston is a large but no less beautiful city. The streets are passably wide but dirty and in places filled with a mass of washed-up sand. The homes are constructed from bricks; most are only one story high and throughout the city display unpretentious verandas, which because of the rays of the sun offer a most opportune shade to the pedestrian. Attractive buildings are rare, and as such can scarcely be ranked alongside English or Scottish churches.

Kingston has three banks—the Colonial, the Jamaica, and the Planter's Bank—and two theaters. Beyond that, it has a society for the improvement of land and agricultural, which maintains a small and quite neglected zoological museum, where I found nothing interesting outside of a manuscript concerning plants of Jamaica and including hand drawings. Since 1841 a society dedicating itself to raising silkworms has been in operation; it has its headquarters in St. Anne and is making important progress. This land produces all the articles of the West Indies, and mangoes already spread wild on the nearby hills. In all of Jamaica nine English newspapers appear.

Since we lacked sufficient time to make a journey to the distant mountains, we therefore had to restrict ourselves to the city, which however remained far beneath my expectations. Even our attempt to catch up with Dr. MacFadyen, publisher of the flora of Jamaica, proved unsuccessful. Instead we visited with Dr. Macnab, an old acquaintance of Herr Hartweg, whose hospitable reception I believe must be mentioned here thankfully.

Since the time was passing so rapidly for us, in the evening we hastened to the Commercial Hotel, where we had intended to spend the night. But there the mosquitoes, whose acquaintance I made here for the first time and in an unhappy fashion, seemed unwilling to grant us much rest. We therefore hurried while it was still dark, stumbling through the streets, on board our ship in order to avoid these obtrusive guests. The next morning at daybreak we went ashore again to set forth on our small rambles. This acquainted us with nothing more than what we had seen on the previous islands, but at least they allowed us to breathe in once more the refreshing and fragrant land breezes. We finally departed from Jamaica, over which hundreds of vultures circled, in order to hasten to Havana some 740 miles away.

This journey was as pleasant as the previous ones. The wind and weather were favorable, once again the magnificent moonshine illuminated the refreshing nights, and I often stood on the deck wondering at the Southern Cross and the other stately constellations until late evening. The more that new matters appear to the traveler—whether they are islands, nations, peoples, or stars—the more he feels himself far from his homeland, however fascinating and agreeable these novelties may be. I have to confess that the first glimpse of the sea, a tropical island, or the Southern Cross made a deep and lasting impression on me.

Thirty-five days after leaving England we approached the favored island of Cuba, Pearl of the Antilles. Cape San Antonio was the first land we saw; it soon disappeared from view once more, because the safety of the sea voyager demands that he travel in a large curve around the western coast, which is lined with dangerous sandbars, in order to be able to approach the Havana harbor, lying on the north coast. Toward evening we spied the beautiful lighthouse that stands on a high rock, and arrived shortly thereafter.

Every traveler who sees Havana for the first time is certain to be greatly astonished. To the left, the citadel of El Morro, perhaps the greatest fortification in the world, defends the narrow entry of the harbor; to the right, the fort of El Puntal. The former cost 6,622,900 guilders, and one anecdote relates that King Philip, when an accountant submitted the bill to him, stepped over to the window with a telescope, saying, "If a fortress costs that much, I ought to be able to see it from here." The harbor, a work of nature, is also one of the most beautiful in the world. Its water is deep enough to be able to accommodate the greatest ships, of which it holds some thousand or so.

The city, which lies to the right,[9] distinguishes itself by its splendid buildings, which are all made of stone with flat roofs, painted blue and white, something that lends them a peculiar but also charming character. The wealth and luxury of Havana are almost proverbial, and it is certainly a city of the first rank in the Western Hemisphere. The island of Cuba lies between 74° and 85° west longitude and 19° and 23° north latitude. Its form is extraordinarily irregular, and the greater part of it faces northward toward Florida. It is the westernmost and the largest island, and since it opens into the Gulf of Mexico it is built along two channels. The north channel consists at most of thirty-two hours' travel, and the south thirty-eight hours'; from one point Cuba is merely fourteen hours away from San Domingo and fifteen from the southern Bahama Island. The maximum length from east to west is 572 miles, and its surface area covers 31,468 square miles. Since its discovery it has remained continually under the Spanish scepter, but all along has stirred up the jealousy of other nations. The last census for Havana and its suburbs showed 106,968 inhabitants, and for the entire island 946,819. The land is rich in precious metals, superbly cultivated, and owing to its tobacco and sugar commerce one of the most important points of the Americas. From the beginning the island was a gold mine for the Spanish, and who knows how Spain would have turned out if it did not have Cuba?

When we came ashore it was already evening, and to be certain one of those evenings that Havana counts among the most beautiful in the whole year. The smoldering heat of the summer months, which sadly make this city a dangerous residence as a result of yellow fever, had ended by the time of our arrival. Fresh sea breezes wafted over from the ocean, and the clean streets teemed with people of all classes strolling about in the cool air. Doubtless it would have been very difficult for us to find ourselves in the right place had not Herr B. May, a German who is established here and whose charming acquaintance we had made on ship, taken the trouble to serve as our guide.

We first reached a lovely space called the Plaza de Armas, which is marked by the most handsome buildings in the city. In the center of the same towers the statue of Ferdinand VII,[10] surrounded by lawn and shaded by many stupendous royal palms. A sidewalk lined with a handsome wrought-iron fence formed a square around the statue, and the entire world (for Havana is not poor) strolled about there every evening. From 8:00 to 9:00 in the evening the sounds of a military band add enticing incentive. In this one place the visitor can see the Spaniards, clad in white with their elegant dark cloaks and followed by slaves, smoking their Havana cigars in the streets. To many, however, this stroll is excessively crowded, and they come in their two-wheeled, wonderfully shaped carriages (*volantes*), which often display boundless luxury, driven in order to be able to hear the music without having to disembark. From there the crowd moves to the refreshment houses, of which there are many and sumptuous, in order to choose from among the numerous confections and iced drinks. In general, I must repeat that the luxury, and consequently the cost of living, is here higher than I have ever found in the greatest city in Europe! For us this evening had passed delightfully, and afterward we repaired to one of the better hotels to pass the night. It was this, the Fulton Hotel, a building with spacious interiors and lovely corridors, where we spent a pleasant night under protective mosquito netting in a cool room lined with marble, once more on land after a long time. On the following day Herr May, although himself quite busy, extended us the courtesy of being our guide. We were thus able to visit the most preeminent parts of Havana in the shortest possible time. He immediately led us along a first-rate promenade, the Paseo de Isabel II,[11] which extends beyond the city walls, decorated with flowers and handsome trees, to the shore of the sea. From there we passed to the Paseo Tacón, which consists of a beautiful boulevard of fig trees and ironwood, and in whose center stands an elegant fountain. These two promenades are for Havana what the Prater is for Vienna or the Corso for Milan. Here the residents of the city display their extravagance, Sunday in particular being the most popular moment.

From here we set out again on our walk until we came to an elevated point an hour away from the city, a point called El Cerro, where the archbishop has his villa and garden. In earlier times El Cerro was a highlight of Havana. It merged art with nature to make this the most interesting place. Stately grounds, aqueducts, menageries, splendid trees and shrubs, the impressive view of the city and the sea were on hand to attract locals and foreigners in multitudes. I would say that currently nothing remains other than the relics of that earlier splendor. For example, there stands even now the wonderful avenue of royal palms; the sight is still the same, but sadly the immediate surroundings suffer from marked deterioration, and without doubt will lose more as the years go by. Concerning the vegetation of the environs of Havana I can say but little. This much is certain, that it is quite poor when the magnificence of the island's interior is considered. The low hills are bare, planted with camote or corn, while the shore is covered with ordinary cacti. The few attractive palms and trees that one encounters there are for the most part planted; nor is there to be seen anything of the tobacco cultivation that is carried out exclusively on the western and southern coasts.

We returned toward evening and hastened to see the cathedral, a huge church built in the Spanish Byzantine style. Beyond its monument to Christopher Columbus, it held little attraction for me. The memorial to this extraordinary man stands to the left of the high altar and bears a portrait of the great discoverer fashioned from marble and a simple inscription:

A Castilla y León
Dio un nuevo mundo
Cristóbal Colón[12]

Beyond this church there is still a great deal more that I was not able to visit. Remaining buildings include the Governor's Palace as well as the Tacón Theater, one of the largest in the world, and the Tacón Prison, together with a few private residences. These homes struck me as something wonderful, as I stared at the prodigiously high windows with iron lattice and no glass pane, in which women sat on rocking chairs and smoked their cigars. Moreover, the breeziness of the houses—for they are so constructed that one can often look through all the rooms with a single glance—is something very odd for the German, accustomed to closed, confined quarters. I will later speak of Havana's cigar factories, which I first had the opportunity to see in the year 1848, on my second visit.

My brief stay in this city allows me to say nothing more of it, but as far as I could tell, the land and the city already enjoy a very high degree of culture. Only one thing strikes the European as disagreeable, and that is slavery. But he who knows the West Indies somewhat more intimately understands that for many long years the prosperity and culture of the region has depended exclusively on slavery. He will have to approve all the more when he sees the English islands where slavery was indeed abolished, but where prosperity and brilliance perished along with it.

Slavery has been an essential part of the West Indies for as long as the trade in white workers has existed, and since the latter support the climate only with difficulty, so will this other commerce continue for a long time.[13] In other regards, may it be said to the credit of mankind that the treatment of slaves is nowhere nearly as bad as many have depicted it, and it has been shown that the instant one gives freedom to the Negro he changes into a useless and insolent idler. It would not greatly surprise me if England had realized that, and had manumitted its Negroes for another reason: to definitively undermine the Spanish and French settlements, whereupon England's own East Indian colonies could be developed to the highest possible level.[14]

Chapter 3

On November 9, 1845, we departed from the Havana harbor in order to sail for Veracruz, which lay 810 miles away. A strong northwest wind churned up the sea, so that once again many of our fellow travelers fell seasick. The north winds, or *nortes,* are very frequent around this time on the American coasts, and endanger ships because of their intensity. No winter passes without at least one vessel falling victim to them, or at least their making for long and unpleasant journeys. They often last eight to fourteen days without interruption.

We neared the Campeche bank at evening the following day. It was rather favorably situated, and we were able to pass this bank without danger, something that required fifteen hours. The weather once more turned quite lovely, and since one could observe the outlying coast with precision, we sometimes passed so near that on the tenth at midnight with unaided eyes we glimpsed the much dreaded Alacranes,[1] on which our ship was to suffer the aforementioned shipwreck a year later. The sea at the upper half of this bank was sometimes only four feet deep and consequently calm, and has a dirty yellow color. Such banks are usually populated with innumerable fish, and one frequently sees whole schools of dolphins and vast swarms of flying fish, while voracious sharks follow the movements of the ship for hours. Sea grasses and mollusks are in any event extraordinarily common, and we often troubled to fish something out of the sea, a feat we managed only with difficulty owing to the very swift motion of the steamship.

Several days thus passed rather pleasantly for us, and our approach to the mainland of America became more and more evident owing to the mass of land and sea birds. Many of these feathered creatures, worn out by a long flight, rested on our ship's tackle, something that quite often gave us a few hours of entertainment, since the sailors tried to catch them in all possible ways. With this intention they silently climbed up the ropes, until they had come so close to a bird that they could grab it. It happened only after many fruitless attempts to seize the animal by a foot or by the tail; the exultation was then boundless and only ended when they set the poor captive free once more. These seemingly childish amusements are capable of drawing all the passengers onto the decks for a moment of pleasant entertainment, if for no other reason than that such antics momentarily interrupt the monotony of life at sea.

Mexico was now only a few more miles away from us, and everyone had assembled on the deck gazing toward the west in order to catch sight of our intended destination. For a long time, however, our efforts were in vain. Only when the sailor who kept a lookout from the masthead cried "Land!" could we make out a blue streak on the horizon. We quickly approached the coast, which little by little rose up immense on the horizon. We stared mutely at that region where lay the American mainland and the goal of our travels. Conflicting emotions coursed through the heart of everyone who for the first time neared the blessed ground of the New World. Joy and mysterious apprehension seized the soul: joy, because one finally beheld the long-desired land; apprehension, because stepping onto this land was connected with vital matters of the highest importance.

Two circumstances united to produce these contrary feelings. On one hand lay the inviting quality of the stately mountains, the abundant forests and plains that our fantasies painted, not in vain, with the most beautiful colors, the hope of a good result, and the thought of a rewarding return journey. On the other hand, there loomed the idea of trodding upon a land whose inhabitants, speech, customs, and practices one knows only little, and where pure caprice, anarchy, and the accompanying lack of security prevail, and the wanderer is abandoned to his good luck and providence. This latter thought is sufficient to sap one's courage; but the feeling seldom endures for long if one recalls the splendor of tropical lands, and the traveler persuades himself through the splendor of nature that here as well as in Europe an inscrutable power reigns, should we stand in need of its assistance.

Night had fallen when on November 6, 1845,[2] we passed through many dangerous reefs and came to Veracruz. The anchors fell with a rattle, but despite our longing to go ashore, nothing more could be accomplished for today. For that reason we enjoyed from the ship the magical sight of the world-famous city that now lay submerged before us in a profound tranquillity. Since only a few thought of sleeping, we wandered around the deck for a long time, partly saying good-bye to one another, partly getting our luggage in order or forging plans for the future. For an instant the sight of a total lunar eclipse distracted us; then, however, we gladly abandoned ourselves to intimate conversations with our fellow travelers, who had become dear to us through a long time together on the same ship, and whom we would perhaps never see again. And what is more, it is difficult to part from the ship itself, a ship on which the voyager has so often counted the hours until he abandons it, since he appreciates its worth all the more if it has conducted him safely over so long a journey.

Since during the afternoon we had tried in vain to glimpse the snowy peaks of Orizaba, which can be seen long before the mainland itself, we rejoiced the next morning, hoping we might catch sight of this grand spectacle. Sadly, our hopes were disappointed, since on the following day a shroud of fog enveloped the mountains, and just to the right we saw the somewhat lower range of Antigua, while the city and the port of Veracruz spread themselves before us in the fullest light.

The harbor of Veracruz consists of a succession of sandbanks that enclose a small bay. A few of these sandbanks rise up to create small islands. Of those lying to the left,[3] Sacrificios is particularly noteworthy, and a stout castle stands upon it. In 1838 the French bombarded and occupied this almost impregnable fortification in order to force Mexico to pay its foreign debt.[4] Although soon liberated once more, since that time it has lost its importance in spite of a competent and disciplined garrison. Most ships anchor under the shade of its powerful walls. Nevertheless, during the time of the northers these ships find themselves only scarcely protected in the Veracruz harbor; since neither these walls nor the sandbanks are capable of breaking the frightful power of the waves, the vessels are very often torn loose and dashed onto the coast.

Across from the fortress, which bears the name San Juan de Ulúa,[5] stretches the sandy region in which Veracruz rises with its bare houses and walls, a city in a joyless and disconsolate wasteland. Doubtless Veracruz perfectly suits its current population, which is able to endure the place because it is tied there exclusively by and for commerce. Any other place in Mexico would seem more suitable for a city than this dreadfully bleak coast, and one can scarcely comprehend how the number of inhabitants, which had reached a quite respectable twenty thousand, has shrunk to six or seven thousand. Everything seemed to work against the prosperity of this place. The appalling heat, scarcity of water, the shadeless environs, excruciating mosquitos and other pernicious insects, and finally yellow fever, which on the average carries off two-thirds of the newly arrived Europeans: these factors militate in so hostile and repellent a form against mankind that one considers himself fortunate not to have chosen this location for his residence.

Across a small jetty we reached a lovely gateway into the city, where, despite the fact that we hailed from a European port, we were examined and taxed before everything else. After the gateway a huge plaza emerges, in which I could discover neither exceptional beauty nor the slightest element of cleanliness. Houses are constructed in the Spanish style, in straight lines with flat roofs, on right-angled streets that are populated more by carrion birds and mules than by human beings. Over the mass of houses rise sixteen cupolas, which in their time belonged to luxurious churches. Only a few are now maintained in good condition. The most handsome section of Veracruz is the *plaza mayor*, where reigns the rather impressive *ayuntamiento* (a city hall and law court) and a certain liveliness. Adjoining this is the marketplace, which I will not mention again because it has little that is worth noting, and for that reason will change the subject to my own affairs.

I hurried with Herr Hartweg to the commercial house of Drusina & Company, to which I had been directed to arrange my business, so that I could forget Veracruz as quickly as possible. The director of the house received me most graciously and immediately offered me all the means necessary to set out on my journey the next morning, so that I had to pass only one night here.

Here as well my estimable travel companion helped me immensely, since I was not yet entirely fluent in the language. He arranged our mules and our luggage, and an *arriero,* or muleteer, who would serve us as guide to Mirador. After everything had been thus prepared for the morning, we repaired to the hotel, if in reality one can call it that, in order to have something to eat and to pass the night there. The midday table was a mixture of English, French, and Mexican dishes, to which the uninitiated German palate must accustom itself little by little. On the whole it seemed that in Veracruz people drink more than they eat; rum, together with other spiritous drinks, plays such an essential role that very many Europeans have cut short the thread of life before its time. Never before accustomed to bring so much as a drop of such liquor to the lips, I was startled to see people who had never separated the glass from their mouths. By necessity I grew accustomed to it, but sadly I must confess that Mexico above all lands abuses strong drink.

The enterprising spirit of the north Germans has also attracted many to this place, and in my brief time there I had the pleasure of making many valuable acquaintances. In the company of my stouthearted countrymen, who tried to help me by word and deed, I passed the afternoon pleasantly and then retired to the tremendous heat of my quarters. I had scarcely rested a quarter hour here when a raging pain rousted me out of my bed, a pain whose cause I was unable to comprehend at first glance. I soon discovered that it was a host of mosquitoes that had chosen me as their spoils, since I had forgotten to stretch a mosquito netting over the bed. I cannot describe the pain these gnats produce—a mixture of burning and stinging that reduces one to a state of torment.

I tried to correct the defect by wrapping myself up, but I nearly suffocated from the heat. The night thus passed in a dreadful way, and I had paid dearly for the first experience of small suffering in tropical lands. For that reason I greeted the following morning joyfully. Before daybreak the animals stood ready, so that I could make my first exploratory journey on horseback, something which I, an inexperienced rider, was rather dreading.

Blessed with a favorable breeze, we left the city that I had a multitude of motives to remember and trotted out merrily to the gate. When the traveler has the city walls behind him, he finds himself in a waste of burning sand where no grasses or plants are to be seen. The dunes change their form with every powerful wind, and like grave mounds make only a tragic impression. We rode a good while along the sandy coastline, upon which the waves of the ocean raced inland with arrowlike swiftness, tossed crabs and shellfish onto the land, and together with the powerful rays of the sun produced an unpleasant atmosphere. Just after an hour the road turned to the left, becoming the main road to Mexico. It was covered in deep sand in which our animals often sunk by a foot, and I could not grasp how a post carriage (the so-called *diligencia,* which goes twice a week from Veracruz to Mexico) can travel. After we had ridden for five hours we reached the small village of Santa Fe, where we halted for a moment to refresh ourselves, since I in particular, exhausted by the unaccustomed heat, had begun to long for something to drink.

A few cane huts stand in this spot. We paused in the best looking of these: there we discovered a small store, something one comes across from time to time along the main road, and where in addition to rum one occasionally stumbles upon other foodstuffs. The interior of this house is arranged in a remarkably simple manner. Two or three ordinary chairs covered with oxhides, and at most a table and hammock, make up the simple furnishings. Since I had not yet learned to quench my thirst with cool, clear rum, I looked for water, and since this was undrinkable I had to make the acquaintance of another Mexican beverage. This drink is called *tepache;* it is prepared from fermented sugar syrup with water, has dirty-yellow and opaque color, but tastes rather good and is a quite recommendable refreshment in the hot climate.

Despite my horsemanship and my broken-down mule, things had turned out better for me than I could have hoped, and my courage grew by the hour. Meanwhile, my body struggled with all its might against this unaccustomed form of travel, and a tremendous sleepiness began to overpower me. Half a day's journey still lay ahead when I found myself yearning for our immediate goal. The reader can easily imagine the figure I made as a horseman under such circumstances: although of cheerful humor, I could not resist the notion that I surely resembled Don Quixote of old. A saddle that was beneath contempt sat on the back of my mule, whose inner anatomy one could study without difficulty. My poorly fastened and scant possessions rocked to and fro on the same, and I myself rode armed with saber and pistol, as if in that instant we might encounter a bloody struggle. However, it was frightful for me, and it had to be as well for the spectator, when I set my lazy hinny into a gallop through a stiff punch of the spurs; for he belonged to the so-called *troteros* (i.e, trotters), and with every step I flew three inches off the saddle, so that the sheath of my steel saber caused a dreadful clatter, and I was compelled to assume a gentler gait.

My weariness grew with every moment under the rays of the sun directly overhead. Even though lagging behind would have been pardonable for me as a novice, I would not have been able to reach that day's destination if I had not had the company of Herr Hartweg, behind whom I dared not lag. Moreover, the increasingly rich and interesting vegetation distracted me and cheered my soul. At last toward 5:00 in the afternoon we neared our stop, a place named Paso de Ovejas,[6] and hurried to the best house, where we could expect a bit of hospitality. As it now turned out, this hospitality was somewhat meager and consisted merely of rice and meat; but this dish left us entirely satisfied, since during the day we had eaten nothing and were thus extremely hungry. Since there was no possibility of a comfortable evening camp, I immediately stretched myself out on the bench standing in front of the house, halfway under the open sky, and with ease fell into a profound sleep despite the discomfort and hardness. Here, however, the mosquitoes and sand fleas soon overcame me, so that after midnight I was on my feet again, and we resolved to take advantage of the fresh moonlit night to journey on.

Around 4 A.M. we mounted up once more and set out in the deep, lonesome stillness of a region sunk in tranquillity. The moon wonderfully illuminated the clusters of trees and bushes, the hoofbeats of our animals resonated far into the distance, and even the conversation between my companions and I fell silent. For only a brief time we followed the main road, and at once we turned onto a footpath to the left, which led us into a rather bare region overgrown with mimosas, where the terrain now began to rise. Huge, lone boulders of black stone projected out into this steppe-like land. Beside them stood enormous cactus trees, and in vain I looked around for noteworthy vegetation as the sun climbed forth from behind the high mountains whose snowcapped peaks I had never seen before, however much I had tried, owing to the persistent mists.

At length, after the traveler has already completed fifteen leagues,[7] he comes to a region where nature suddenly begins to reveal itself with tremendous force. The mimosas become less frequent, and trees of powerful build rise up everywhere and are covered with a parasitic plant called *barba española,*[8] which, as the name accurately suggests, hang like a great beard from the branches, and are applied to many household uses that we reserve for moss, something that is rather rare here. In that region I also spied off to the left one of those deep ravines that characterize the eastern slopes of the Orizaba, and which are known by the name of *barranca.*

These barrancas, a number of which are to be found on the eastern side of the *cordillera,*[9] often reach depths of more than twelve hundred feet, and what is more surprising, they often cut through land that is completely flat. One might easily take them for deep riverbeds. But the explorer climbs down them, something that, because of their steep slopes, involves great physical exertion and even danger, and there he at most finds a tiny brook which trickles into that place through the natural incline. This formation clearly argues that the barrancas are simply a product of volcanic tremors in which the water, such as it is, plays a subordinate role. The vegetation in this barranca is usually of endless beauty, and there one can marvel at the splendor of tropical nature. The further we progressed, the more beautiful our surroundings became; and while isolated palms had charmed us earlier, hundreds of things now demanded our attention.

Just before noon we reached a few small huts where we decided to dismount and eat. To the scanty provisions we had brought along we added a few eggs, black beans, and the thin corn cakes known as *tortillas,* which the Mexicans substitute for bread. Still, at the moment I was too surprised and amazed by the novelty of the country, its inhabitants and customs, to even attempt an accurate description of the same. My exhaustion was so extreme that I did not believe that today we could reach Mirador, which lay four miles away. However, the stately oak forests that faced us from afar and which surrounded our magnificent destination, together with the prospect of a friendly perception, was too tempting for us not to make a final effort.

We immediately mounted our animals again and rode on toward those splendid forests. When we had entered the region of oaks, a strange feeling coursed through me at the sight of these evergreen forests where no summer or winter reigned, but rather only an eternal spring. The traveler finds himself at an altitude of nearly three thousand feet and now free from the realm of yellow fever. Here it seems that nature intended to create a second paradise. Only the liveliest imagination could conjure up the eternal greens and blues, the fertility of the soil, the pleasant and healthy climate, and the tranquillity and absolute seclusion that characterize the region. These features possess an irresistible attraction for men, and often, when I savor the memory of that day, a longing seizes me—in fact something more than that, a passionate craving to behold that region again—and everything around seems to me worthless and insipid by comparison. Doubtless it is true that these memories paint the scenes I saw with livelier colors than they in reality possess. But it is there only, and nowhere else, that one finds that grandeur and magnificence, that quiet and yet powerful dominion of nature into which mankind has not yet allowed itself to intrude.

We stepped into those stately forests. Here the soil teems with countless plants; every pace offers something new, and even the branches are covered with luxurious parasites. Animals of every sort roam about contentedly, knowing no enemy; insects swarm buzzing about the flowers. As a result, the traveler can truthfully say that in that region he finds himself where no law other than nature prevails, no right other than common sense, no belief other than that of the individual heart. There man is all at once placed in a world that on one hand seems so charming, and on the other deeply repellent because of its loneliness and solitude, so much so that most of us would sooner read descriptions than visit it in person and have the opportunity to learn to value it.

We had already progressed for a long time in this oak forest without my remembering my terrible exhaustion. Only when we reached a small savannah did I begin to search for the buildings of Mirador. Hills followed hills in an overgrown wilderness until my eye settled on a sparse point that, by the light of the sinking sun, revealed itself in the middle of this picturesque environs. This was the center of the community, which lay a good hour from us. As we drew closer and closer, we found luxurious fields of sugarcane nestled among the oak forests. Superior roads twisted through the plantations, and with every step we became more aware that here the industrious spirit of men had begun to reign. Presently we reached the first huts, which lay scattered about, and we had to ascend only a small hill in order to reach the residences of the town's occupants. This last stretch of the road was conquered as well, and we soon found ourselves at the door of the hacienda,[10] whose owners, stouthearted Germans, received us joyfully. They were the Herren Karl Sartorius[11] and Karl Stein, who had established a new homeland there. In the middle of these most stately regions, surrounded by a number of countrymen and inhabitants, they lived a life I could have envied had they not so richly deserved it.

I cannot say that I dismounted from my mule. We had crossed twelve leagues yesterday and just as many today, and since I was unaccustomed to long rides, the heat, and the other difficulties, I had become so stiff that my companions had to remove me from the saddle. Soon, however, finding myself in the agreeable circle of German inhabitants of Mirador, overwhelmed with questions about Europe and our fatherland, I could no longer think about my exhaustion. Rather, I passed the time chatting sociably with Herr Hartweg, who had already been here on his first journey. The hours sped by so quickly and pleasantly that bedtime, although longed for, still came soon enough.

A single room set aside for strangers accommodated us with all comfort, and ever after I will remember this hospitable reception with feelings of gratitude. It was now November 16, 1845.

Chapter 4

Mirador is rather like Zacuapan, founded by Herr Sartorius, which lies an hour to the east. Excluding the German personnel indispensable to its administration, its inhabitants are mostly Indians or mestizos. They number approximately three hundred and live dispersed in huts constructed of wooden poles, and without exception labor on the haciendas. This tiny colony, situated far from the big city, is exceptionally fit and hardworking; robberies, which happen so frequently in every other part of Mexico, are rarities here. But as everywhere else on Sunday, drunkenness and gambling form the prevailing vices, against which, particularly in Mexico, no authority is able to take measures sufficiently strong. But when Sunday has passed, everyone returns industriously once more to the cultivation of the sugar fields, to woodcutting, to the production of rum, and to other labors.

On a small hill thirty-five hundred feet above sea level stand the stone houses that are inhabited by the two above-mentioned families, and where at the same time is found a store that carries all the necessary articles for the settlement. A small market, of which I will speak later, adds to the liveliness of the place and greatly stimulates the trade with the surrounding region and the commerce in products of the land.

Regarding the Germans of this settlement, their number is greater than I have found anywhere in Mexico, the capital excluded. The fruit of their industriousness will speak on their behalf from first to last. Along with Herren Sartorius and Stein have come a number of young, cultured individuals in search of work, men who are able to offer to the traveler pleasant as well as informative company. Beyond Mirador but still within the circumference of a few miles are found more German haciendas, of which for the moment I will only mention Zacuapan, the property of Herr Baetke; the coffee plantation Mocca, of Herr Eichhorn; and the small hacienda Esperanza, of Herr Ettlinger. In order to once more tie up the thread of daily activities, it is necessary that I refer to Herr Sartorius's hospitable invitation to enjoy long-term room and board with him until I had selected my own residence, an offer I immediately resolved to accept after the departure of Herr Hartweg, who was to set out from here to California.

On the following morning I was still entirely stiff and worn out from the last two days of the journey, and I restricted myself to the nearby region of the estate, from where I enjoyed a splendid sight at sunrise. To the northwest stretched the majestic peaks of the mountains; in their center the snowcapped summit of the volcano Orizaba towered to a height of 16,750 feet and now at last satisfied my long-standing desire to see this colossal mountain. It is impossible for me to describe the impression this majestic scene made upon me. I stood for a long time enraptured, immovable, and lost in quiet wonder, staring out in that direction, charmed by the innumerable colors that the streaks of the morning sun created on the immense fields of snow. I dared not divert my gaze from it, fearing it to be a supernatural illusion that could vanish again forever. He who has not viewed this sublime scene cannot flatter himself to have seen the most beautiful thing that earth can show.

Toward the northwest, approximately straight ahead and fifteen hours away, a second peak, known as the volcano Perote, towered to a height of 14,616 feet. A cluster of hills extend to the east and southeast; they become ever lower and gradually flatten out and allow their borders to be seen clearly against the ocean. In fact, the air is so clear that even with the naked eye one can distinctly make out the walls of Veracruz from twenty-four leagues. Only a very lively imagination can grasp the delight that filled me with this panorama. I can only compare it with the one that inspired me when I enjoyed my first comprehensive view of the snowcapped peaks of our own Alps. My heart rose upon realizing that I found myself in a region that matched my artistic expectations, and from this moment on I yearned to develop an active life here.

When at last all my luggage had arrived, I could seriously think about selecting a place of residence. I resolved to spruce up a somewhat run-down hut that lay a quarter hour from the main building of Mirador. In a short time a few of the Indians, who in their own way are the best of all builders, had prepared the walls from wooden poles, set up a fence all around, and stamped firm the floor of the interior, while the German carpenter supplied them with a crude door. I found it a simple matter to light the interior, for as can be easily imagined, the sun and moon shone through between the wooden poles. For a cot I covered the floor with a few straw mats (*petates*) that in other moments adorned the wall; and used a quite rudimentary table and chair whose feet were hammered into the floor. My possessions hung on the wall, and in the corner stood a small stand made of cane, designed for drying seeds and plants. In less than eight days this agreeable little house, whose construction had required but minimal expense and not a single iron nail, was ready to receive me.

During the period of this construction, naturally, I had little time to think about botanical excursions. For that reason I initially restricted myself to nothing more than small walks with Herr Hartweg, until on November 28 this gentleman departed from us, and I remained alone. I accompanied him to the edge of Mirador, and have to confess that the departure of this, my worthy travel companion, hurt me deeply. Who would have remained indifferent in such a moment? Just like myself, he was hurrying on to a life that did not give the slightest guarantee that we could see each other again! We clasped hands with moist eyes and for a long time took our leave of one another.

On November 30 I entered my little home and for the first time in my life tried to adapt to complete solitude. The evening approached and I retreated to my den, and throughout the night dreamed of countless animals that seemed to crawl around through every seam and crack, and with such animation that I often rose out of my sleep to ward off these unpleasant guests. At first the activity of the poisonous vermin is overwhelming, but little by little one learns not to fear them. However, I believe no one will laugh over this frank confession of my weakness, if he imagines himself taken out of the middle of a populated city and placed in the remoteness of a tropical land. The fact is that after a few days I felt myself so cozy in my home that I easily did without the comforts of the city.

A few days later I took on a servant, whom I was able to employ for 12 pesos monthly.[1] With his aid as a bona fide expert in the region I soon began my rambles, the recounting of which I must preface with a few observations of the land and climate. The terrain, which rises so quickly over sea level to a stupendous elevation, consequently offers a profound variety of temperatures and vegetation, and for this reason the inhabitants divide the land into three regions. The first, the so-called *tierra caliente,* extends from Veracruz until the oak forest, and is a strip of land where cotton, indigo, sugarcane, coffee, and tropical fruits thrive. The second (*tierra templada*) stretches from the oak forest to the firs, where the third region (*tierra fría*) begins and reaches up to the snows.[2] While in the second region many tropical products are cultivated, the third has a climate in which cereals, potatoes, and European fruits prosper. The average temperature can be stated as follows:

First region: 0 to 3,000 feet, 59 to 104 degrees
Second region: 3,000 to 8,000 feet, 50 to 86 degrees
Third region: 8,000 to 14,000 feet, 32 to 59 degrees

Just as the climate makes the vegetation so different, so too the nature of the soil differs. The main body of the mountains is a conglomeration of volcanic elements, and perhaps seldom do mountain landscapes offer so great a variety of soil as one finds here. Red clay soil, kaolin, chalk, sand, lava, porphyry, and slate are frequently mixed together in an extraordinary fashion, and the vegetation varies according to which mineral predominates.

I hardly need to explain that this mixture of soils points to explosive volcanic upheavals, but perhaps I should mention the distinct irregularity of the land thus produced. Huge masses, even entire mountains, seem to have been swallowed by the earth, and in their place one encounters frightfully deep and broad ravines lined with steeply inclined forests, or hills that look as if they had partly sprouted, partly were thrown together. Both geographical formations give the land an odd appearance, and in particular the ravines (barrancas) intersect and crisscross the eastern slope of the mountain peaks in remarkable fashion, like great canals. This scene's centerpiece, the volcano Orizaba, seemed to glow with an inner fire, even though it has not erupted since 1545. But there is no doubt that if perhaps it has already become extinct, it remains linked underground with the active volcanoes of Tuxtla, Jorullo, and Colima; this fact is confirmed through frequent earthquakes that are simultaneously perceptible on the east and west coasts, just as they are at points on the high tableland situated along this line. I hope to be able to speak more directly to this matter in the course of my journey, and I now pass to my departure from the region of Mirador.

In the last days the weather became quite unfavorable, as is frequently the case in the mountains during wintertime. Chilly north winds blow over the heights and drive a mass of fog before them, until a heavy and often long-lasting rain clears things up one day or the next. This weather, which normally lasts until the middle of March, goes under the name "norther time" and is most unpleasant for those who collect natural specimens. The frequent downpours saturate the earth considerably more than do those of the rainy season. On top of this, the terrible roads become slippery and in the end unpassable for someone on foot. The forests drip with perpetual moisture, the plants grow dormant and relinquish their blooms until the beginning of the tropical springtime, and the traveler is frequently held up for several days. Unfortunately, the little he has collected rots or disappears, and he is condemned, as one is accustomed to say in good German, *Trübsal zu blasen.*[3]

Savannas (steppes or meadows) are heaths that in the summer usually sustain a mass of small, attractive plants but on which now stand nothing more than tufts of grass, gathered in clumps and half withered to boot. I roamed among them in all directions without finding anything of particular interest.

I had already gone almost a mile when I reached one of those small ravines where the vegetation appears to have taken refuge during the wintertime. This place was as lush as the heath had been earlier. Trees, rocks, and branches both living and dead were covered with highly unique parasites, among which especially stand out the most remarkable orchids with their luxurious flowers. Delicate shrubs and palms dot the soil, among which stretches a body of common plants.

Although initially dissatisfied, I returned enriched and satisfied to my accommodations, and repeated this excursion on the fifth and sixth of the same month. On December 9 I made a trip to the so-called Tiger's Cave, lying in a small forest of the district of Consoquitla, to which Mirador belongs. It takes its name from a story that a powerful tiger lived there for a long time until being finally hunted down after he had caused immense harm on the haciendas. On its surroundings the hacienda offers that profuse vegetation which I had mentioned regarding the small ravine, but distinguishes itself by a small heath of orange trees covered with fruit. A flock of parrots filled these trees and pecked industriously at the oranges, whose sour taste seemed to appeal to them.[4]

Owing to the discovery of this small forest I had no doubt that sour oranges grow wild in Mexico, something that people have debated for a long time without reaching a definitive conclusion. I confess, I suppose, that the sweet orange tree is imported, a point confirmed to my mind by the absence of an indigenous name. Under the shade of these stately trees, when noonday had arrived I made myself a cheering fire in order to prepare my frugal dinner, which consisted of potatoes and *tasajo*.[5] After this not unpleasant business was finished, I set out on my way and headed toward Zacuapan.

Zacuapan lies five hundred feet lower than Mirador in a similarly lush region. Around the main building stand in rows the few huts of the workers and the refinery for sugar and rum. The highly cultured owner, Herr Dr. Franz Baetke, has constructed a delightful little garden in front of the house, in which he cultivates useful fruit trees and the most beautiful plants of that area with love and success. He himself is more pleasant than the garden, and so too is his cheerful wife, who knows how to embellish their lonely life with spirit and industry. I remember with the deepest gratitude their kindly reception and the many pleasant hours I passed there, where little by little I found everything a lonely wanderer could wish—that is, an upright and sympathetic friend! Later I often repeated my visit, and usually it was on Sunday when I tried to entertain myself in the agreeable company of this family.

Another small hacienda in the vicinity of Mirador is Esperanza, which lies beyond Mirador and for that reason is somewhat higher in altitude. It too belongs to a worthy German, Herr Ettlinger, who specializes in coffee planting, and who served as a better companion for me in hunting and planting than do many servants. He lives more isolated than anyone, yet remains so happy and contented amid his coffee trees and orange fields that I enjoyed passing an hour with him now and then.

The days passed so quickly and agreeably for me in this way that I must frankly confess that I never spent a happier time in the Americas. Each day excursions brought me some new plants or animals, and I could pass the evenings with Herr Sartorius, and Sundays when time permitted at one or the other settlements. The somewhat greater population of Mirador gave me numerous opportunities to observe the assorted peculiarities of the people.

Thus among other things I came to learn how one prepares an ox head in the Mexican fashion. They take it just as it is, with skin and hair, insert salt and spices in the ears and in the mouth, and sew it up in a petate. After that they make a hole in the ground, heat it with coal, and after removing the coal they place the head in the same; they then cover it with earth and build a fire over it. Twelve hours are needed in order to make this tasty dish in its entirety, and since one normally begins the preparations in the evening, the jolly people spend the night there with a small fandango, the beloved dance of the Mexicans.

One such fandango, which I fancied a very lively entertainment, consists of nothing more than men and women stomping the earth in an effort to display their considerable gracefulness with sensual movements. Two small guitars and some rum are enough to spur the Mexicans to a boundless passion for dance, a passion that often seems to not want to end. Characteristic is the singular whirring of strings, which Mexicans know all too well how to bring out with their fingernails and which from time to time they accompany with songs filled with a love of homeland, and with warm voices chiming in confusedly. Quite frequently the Veracruzanos are in the habit of improvising individual stanzas, which, if they turn out well, are usually received with thunderous applause.[6]

The man who attends such a fandango can certainly form for himself an excellent notion of how contented these folk are. For he finds himself in a wretched hut, one that is often illuminated with scarcely more than a pine torch; here a number of persons crowd together, untroubled by life's sorrows and knowing nothing other than joy, and with whom the direst poverty goes hand in hand with the deepest satisfaction. This circumstance can only be explained in tropical lands, where the needs of the lower classes are so extraordinarily trifling.

The foreigner is not unwelcome in such dances, especially if to some extent he knows how to accommodate the customs of the land. Indeed, it even occurred to me when I myself became mixed up in this line of joyful dancers that I had thus won the favor of those present, and that the company reckoned it a special honor if I took a sip of rum with them or exchanged a cigar. Generally speaking, the lower the Mexican stands, the happier he seems when one treats him the more obligingly. Nothing would be more offensive than to want to close oneself off entirely from such company, and this alone can often be enough to pose tremendous obstacles for the traveler in his enterprises.

On December 15 I set out on the road to visit a place that lay in the mountains, where a highly remarkable oak tree is to be found. Travel was easier since I already had a horse, and thus made rapid progress into the higher terrain. As is the case everywhere in the interior of the land, the road is a mere footpath that can only be traversed on foot or on horseback. It leads uphill and down along countless turns, now through small valleys, now through fields or forests, and offers an indescribably profound diversity. Immense ferns join with the stateliest trees and are interwoven with thousands of climbing plants that majestically raise their finely feathered, leafy crowns. Shrubbery reminiscent of European vegetation appears, and the explorer finds places where both worlds come together. After two hours we reached the village Totutla, which lies at an altitude of forty-five hundred feet, possesses five hundred inhabitants, and has a church and a school. A number of houses built of mud and wooden sticks stand in a row; their inhabitants principally grow corn, which prospers at up to nine thousand feet above sea level. For the traveler, however, nothing is more astonishing than a huge tree at the entrance to the village, on which an unusual number of canopy liana wind themselves, and which with their huge funnel-shaped blooms provide an exceedingly charming sight. Further on stands a robust magnolia fifty feet in height; when in bloom it alone would justify a trip to this village.

From there the road leads on through astonishing oak forests to an altitude of fifty-five hundred feet, where stands the small village of San Bartolomé, or as it is usually known, San Bartolo. This tiny spot lies in the middle of the mountains, is inhabited mostly by pure Indians, and is almost never visited by whites. When I arrived there I was not a little astonished to see all the residents of the village assembled at the church; of those residents, a number were to be seen dressed in authentically clownish costume and with masks that depicted dark and hideous faces. Under the colored clothing they had fastened small bells, on their heads were straw hats profusely decorated with feathers, and in their hands they carried machetes.[7]

Soon the boys of the village ringed around and stared at me inquisitively. I

"A number were to be seen dressed in authentically clownish costume and with masks that depicted dark and hideous faces. Under the colored clothing they had fastened small bells, on their heads straw hats profusely decorated with feathers, and in their hands they carried machetes." (Photo courtesy of the Latin American Library, University of Texas at Austin)

communicated to them my reason for being there, and after I had entertained the principals of the village with brandy I asked them to furnish me with a guide. This, however, they roundly refused me, since they tried to persuade me that no one could be spared because the festival of yesterday, which was the feast of Nuestra Señora de la Purísima Concepción, had to be observed today as well. Because I could not hope to accomplish anything against the crowd's wishes, I therefore waited patiently for the fiesta observations as a silent spectator.

They immediately put on the masks to begin their dance, at whose lead was a person who as a mark of distinction wore a wooden crown and an old black coat from God knows where. The music began. It consisted of a guitar and a violin with the usual fandango; but now everyone assumed horrifying grimaces, swung their machetes about, and began to jump around and carried on with one another as though insane. This resembled more a war dance than a religious fiesta.[8] Under monotonous bell chimes they at length produced a figure on a wooden carrying frame, something that was imagined to be the Mother of the Savior but which more closely resembled an Indian idol. Scarcely had this figure been carried into the church door than the dancers themselves cut loose as if they would tear the place apart; thereafter they quickly turned back and formed the advance guard of the procession. Behind them followed two men who burned incense in paper bowls, and next came two other men with rockets, men who understood rather well how to make them and who constantly fired them into the sky (it was just now midday). The frame with the idol followed these, and a crowd of people struck up appalling songs. After they concluded a procession around the church in this manner, each dancer began a furious solo performance, and the sacred ceremony came to an end.

In this manner one celebrates the memory of the greatest moments of the Catholic religion in Mexico, I thought to myself, as I, astonished, contemplated the Indians in their ridiculous activities. The first glimpse convinced me that here we find the mixture of idols with the religious customs of our church. Spanish clergymen created this mixture, for therein they saw the means to bring the Indians toward them little by little. Consequently, I have often suspected that the Indian living in a small, isolated village has as imperfect a concept of the Christian religion as he did before the Spanish conquest.

Generally speaking, one has all too frequent an opportunity to observe the pitiable results of the former Spanish reign. I would like to say, and with truth, how systematically that reign worked to suppress little by little the seed of all that is good and noble among the people of Mexico—who possess capabilities for everything, and in whom docility unites with meekness—in order to force upon them practices whereby the natives were made suitable for slavery. In place of their forefathers' gods, the Spanish gave them a new saint cut from wood, without which one cannot know the true God. Instead of a humane upbringing, the Spanish refused them instruction in reading and writing under pain of death, and thrust them into the deep recesses of the mine, where they languished or became victims to the Spaniard's poison, rum. Only in this way can we explain the fact that a people who before the conquest of Mexico stood on a high plateau of civilization have now sunk to a small heap of squalid creatures, and of whom many seem more akin to primitive animals than to humans. And nevertheless in remote places one again finds remnants of that powerful stock whose muscular build, facial expressions, bearing, and respectable conduct recall a time long forgotten.

Although frightfully diminished owing to the reasons stated above, the number of Indians is nevertheless greater than one believes in Europe. The majority are distinguished by middling stature, dark brown complexion, straight hair, low forehead, and a large mouth full of beautiful teeth. The muscles of their bodies are extraordinarily less visible than is the case with the Asiatic or European stocks; nevertheless, an unbelievable strength resides therein, one that makes itself known by how rapidly the blood replaces muscle tissues. One sees examples of horrifying wounds of which a European would have perished, but which here they heal simply through washing with brandy.

Their nervous system is all the more sensitive, since what for us would be an altogether trivial nervous disorder for them almost always brings death. They live happily among themselves, are closed toward strangers, and in spite of all efforts, one cannot coax from them the slightest knowledge of historical traditions. However, the respect toward the offspring of their *caciques,*[9] something they always demonstrate, clearly indicates that they are aware of their tragic past. Many of that place belong to the famous swift runners who astonished the first conquistadores. I have seen Indians with hundredweight burdens trot all day long behind the horses. Similarly, they wander with terrible loads through the dangerous barrancas in all weather, and easily lend themselves to any sort of labor.

When at last the fiesta was over, I returned to the road to that place where that lush oak tree[10] was to be found in a barranca. It was evening when I had reached the object of my journey, and since I felt little desire to spend the night with the Indians, who were flushed with brandy, I therefore set out on the return journey in pitch darkness. Uninjured and duly instructed, I reached my residence astonished at how my horse stepped with such tremendous dexterity over that dangerous road.

Chapter 5

I had already spent several weeks in Mirador. My diverse pursuits, the different excursions, and the ordering of collected items consumed all my time—a great relief to me, as the first months of residence in the Americas are a time of the greatest trials for the traveler. He has to struggle partly with the climate, partly with the novelty of the customs and with the unusual difficulties and dangers, all at the same time. Moreover, there are still many hours when in his loneliness he is often moved to sadness through the fresh memories of his homeland, of his circle of friends, and of the convenience of European life. This sadness derives from the uncertainty over the outcome of his enterprise, the thought of whether he will ever see his homeland again.

One of those days in which I reflected so vividly upon the past was Christmas Eve. I found myself alone in my hut, remembering countless friends and the many religious customs of my homeland, and I imagined the hurried steps wandering through snow-covered meadows to the church. The more I thought back on my former life, the more I felt lonesome. I stepped out of my house and looked upward at the dark blue sky, which arched in a splendor I had never appreciated before. Only the call of a few night birds broke the lofty silence; otherwise there was no sound all around, not a living creature to be heard. A gentle breeze wafted through the leaves of the annona tree[1] that stood before my hut, and I became aware, as never before, of my loneliness, which in every expression was more immense, and moved more deeply, than ever before. It was a sublime sight, one that I will never forget, and which perhaps comes but seldom in a person's life. This much is certain, that I had celebrated my first Christmas Eve in Mexico, meditating in a way that only a lonely wanderer, whom holy bonds still chain to the fatherland, can do.

The next day I set out on horseback to undertake a small excursion to the town of Huatusco, five leagues away. The road carried me through the village of Totutla, described above, at which point it veered to the left and led to the spot after winding hither and thither through countless ravines and tiny villages. One has to pass fourteen valleys and for that reason just as many mountains when going from Mirador to Huatusco. The first and most interesting point is a small barranca through which flows a splendid clear stream, and over which two small bridges extended. They call this barranca Dos Puentes.[2] The difference in vegetation is evident above all through styrax trees, hawthornes, and bloodtwig dogwood.[3] Greenery of the European variety reveals itself between the forests therein, until one comes to a final promontory from which one catches sight of the charming town of Huatusco in the valley below. There are stupendous mountain ranges all around, and in the background towers the gigantic Orizaba, the whole forming a profoundly enchanting picture.

Huatusco, which lies approximately four thousand feet in elevation, has two churches and five thousand inhabitants. The well-to-do engage in commerce, while the poor occupy themselves with cultivating corn and excellent tobacco. The number of stone houses is trifling; the number of stores, however, is so extraordinary in proportion to the size of the town that one cannot comprehend how one could exist alongside the other. In the most recent times it has also become the site of a subprefecture, which gives the place more importance.

On this excursion, which was intended more as a reconnaissance of the region than for scientific ends, three mountains of middling height in particular caught my eye. Lying at a slight distance one from another, they distinguish themselves through their strictly geometrical form. They resemble oblong, truncated pyramids, and their four sides are so sharply delineated that one cannot criticize the popular belief that they are the graves of great caciques. However, subsequent examination of the same has shown me that they are burned-out volcanoes, on which the craters can still be clearly recognized.

The region so delighted me that I resolved to change my place of residence there in a few months, and I will provide a greater account of this area further on. On the following day I returned to Mirador and resumed my earlier life unhindered, so I will mention only the most essential items and excursions. To those categories belong, among other things, the account of different market scenes on Sunday in Mirador.

Herr Sartorius quite prudently knew to attract the inhabitants of the region little by little through the merchandise of his store. This market has now become rather important, and is much more interesting than what the Indians, who do not even speak Spanish, manage to come up with by themselves in the mountains. The items one finds among the merchants are highly diverse; there, products of the tierra fría are brought, just like those of the tierra caliente. Thus, according to the season, one finds anonnas, mangoes, bananas, oranges, papayas, custard apples, granadillas, pineapples, pinguins (timberiches), pine nuts, cahoon nuts, avocados, wild pinguin bromelia, peanuts, and even apples and pears, which are sold with the aforementioned fruits. Beyond these, one finds vegetables, among which are the so-called *mafafa,*[4] yucca, arrowroot, camote, jícama, chayote, beans, and yams which are still enclosed in their skins; fronds of chameadorea palm, and the flowers of the mound-lily yucca, which are enjoyed as salad. Even the hard fruits of the macaw bactris palms are eaten. Beyond this, the people bring salt, corn, rice, fresh and dried Spanish pepper, tasajo, poultry, eggs, lard, and so forth, items that they partly sell, partly barter. Toward noon the plaza is already abandoned, and only a few Indians gather in order to enjoy brandy, which they mutually offer to one another with many and endless ceremonies. It seems that a few of them habitually remain in the plaza, overcome by the strong drink.

Clothing on this day is clean and simple. Over white linen trousers men wear a short shirt, and over that an ordinary blanket whose richness of color varies according to one's prosperity. The most beautiful of these blankets, here called *sarapes,* which are produced in Mexico and are worn by the richest Creoles, range in value up to 35 pesos, depending on their quality. The women mostly have white or highly colored skirts, a small and daintily sewn blouse that covers the bosom only sparingly, and over the head a long, delicate shawl (*rebozo*), also produced in Mexico, and whose ends they cast gracefully over the shoulder. The altogether impoverished lower class is perhaps not always so respectably dressed, but rather, often covers its naked body only scantily.

It always gave me the greatest pleasure to visit the plaza or market, since there I had opportunity to hear the Aztec language[5] and to observe the people who, although there is little to be said about them, still greatly fascinate the traveler. These markets are quite worth seeing for another reason, because according to the differences of place where they are held, so too differ the products and the people who come there. Thus the market of Huatusco, to which I made a second journey on January 18, 1846, is far more opulent than that of Mirador. To this place come not only all the fruits and vegetables mentioned earlier but also first-rate potatoes, the bulbs of sweet potatoes, animal skins, and so forth. In that same place I occasionally found highly striking skins of jaguars (*Felix onza*) on which, to my deepest amazement, I could discern no bullet wound.

After I had lived for a long time in that region I had the opportunity to learn how one hunts this animal without shooting it. The Mexican's dexterity in handling the lasso is world famous.[6] It is usually those people responsible for protecting livestock (*vaqueros*) who exceed all others in this skill. They

"The women mostly have white or highly colored skirts, a small and daintily sewn blouse that covers the bosom only sparingly, and over the head a long, delicate shawl (*rebozo*), also produced in Mexico, and whose ends they cast gracefully over the shoulder." In this scene, Veracruzan women fetch water from the San Juan River. (Photo courtesy of the Latin American Library, University of Texas at Austin)

throw the noose of the rope, whose end is fasted to the saddle horn, for several body lengths[7] with unbelievable accuracy. I have seen vaqueros who lasso the head of a beast some eight to ten yards away while riding at full gallop, and it is remarkable how through a dexterous toss of the rope to the forelegs they often bring down and subdue the most ferocious steer. The jaguar is also there caught, and one goes about it in the following way. A skilled *lasero* tracks the jaguar with a number of dogs and stalks him until the beast hides in a tree. The pursuing hounds now assemble at the trunk, constantly barking upward, while the jaguar, in the manner of all cats, trains its gaze unflinchingly upon them. After this small maneuver has succeeded, the lasero ties the end of his rope to a high branch and warily throws the noose over the head of the animal, which sometimes shakes it loose again but does not give up its place for fear of the dogs. At last the repeated application of the noose agitates it too much and it risks a desperate leap, in consequence of which it hangs itself. In this way jaguars, pumas, and even small tigers are overpowered and one has the great advantage of being able to remove the skin undamaged.

Here too a huge number of Indians had again made their appearance. They drank up their scanty earnings in brandy, and a number of them were already waltzing in the streets. I observed with wonder what care, what cooperation, I might even say what respect the remaining Indians manifest before a drunk. With countless gentle words they try to persuade him to move along, or if he is not inclined to do this, something he gives to understand with a perpetual *no voy,*[8] then they lift him up and carry him to his house. More than anyone it is the women (who play a subordinate role, and who are little given to the enjoyment of brandy) who with tender words try to coax their men out of the ruinous *tiendas,*[9] where spirited liquors are always sold. It is also the women who above all others cling to the old customs and usages, for their husbands handle them in the crudest way if they come into contact with whites or even speak with them. This is especially true in remote settlements. Having reached a certain age, however, women begin to wield great influence in the community. They take the place of doctors, know a body of herbs and miraculous cures, become prophets, exorcise angry spirits, and so forth, enjoying the respect of all younger people. Generally speaking, the Indians are still forever entangled in prejudice and superstition. If they also believe in God, in whom they fully revere the Good Spirit, so too do they still place that spirit alongside their old gods of wrath, whom they fear more than anything else.

I have seen how an old Indian woman found the greatest pleasure in the lovely blond child of a German, a child whom she tried to protect through an exorcism formula mumbled in incomprehensible language before the Angry Spirit. She turned her hideous old face toward the sun, clasped her hands, and repeatedly touched his cheeks and eyes, as if to say that neither blindness nor smallpox, which she greatly feared and which raged terribly among them for a few years, would ever be able to come over the child.[10] It is characteristic how at such affairs the Indians standing nearby suddenly grow silent and listen with respect to the words that are spoken. I often ask myself of the good consequences of the Christianity spread with so much exaggerated zeal by the Spanish, and I have no answer.

When I returned to Mirador I met the governor of Veracruz, a certain Señor Serapio, who had fled to Jalapa and from there had made a journey to Mirador and Zacuapan. He was a handsome man of approximately forty years, seemed rather well educated, and conducted himself with that studied etiquette which still adheres to the highly placed Mexican from his Spanish forefathers. He brings me to relate a brief episode over the conditions of Mexico at that time.

Mexico, whose history from the time when its independence war began until the present day can be called a very sad one, was already in circumstances fraught with danger when I arrived. Since 1824,[11] when it stood as completely independent, no government could maintain a firm footing. With the end of Spanish authority, only the flaws of the ancestors had remained in the country, while the benefits had vanished, so that there was self-interest instead of patriotism, deception and theft instead of lawfulness and stewardship. In consequence of this, presidents were appointed and through intrigue removed once more, carried in triumph and then exiled, so that only the scum of the earth managed to hold on to the presidential chair for any length of time. In 1845 the head of the republic was Herrera, a brave and esteemed man, but his administration had long faced opposition that festered in different places. Finally, on December 23 the revolution broke out in Veracruz. One made what is here called a *pronunciamiento,* namely, a procession in the street, which proclaims the change of administration and to which, as everywhere, a mob of the lowest rabble attaches itself. The city, whether it wanted to or not, had to adhere to the new plan, since the revolution emanated from the real ruler, the military.

Only a few individuals in the fort San Juan de Ulúa opposed this uprising, but the remainder joined immediately, after a brief skirmish left several dead. This revolution seemed to have originated with General Paredes, who on the very same day rebelled in San Luis Potosí with his forces against the government.[12] Initially, it appeared that the cities of Orizaba, Puebla, and Mexico would uphold the old administration, to which end they made extensive arrangements; but they soon joined the opposition, and Herrera had to resign. For a few days a triumvirate took his place; a so-called *junta* of twenty generals followed this, at whose head stood Paredes, and in which, in the usual fashion, new fissures quickly arose. However, this administration prevailed for a brief while, during which time it changed nothing, and its leaders troubled themselves to live remarkably well at the cost of the nation. Soon, however, General Arista proclaimed in Tampico against the junta, while the North American ambassador (Minister John Slidell) left Puebla for Veracruz, and everywhere people said that a war with the United States of America was inevitable.

Thus stood the affairs of Mexico after my two months' residence, and I mention this revolution all the more as it was the beginning of a sad and for this land highly destructive era, one that I was sadly compelled to suffer to its conclusion. Consequently, I will have still more opportunities to digress into the political sphere, and will be happy when the reader can draw for himself an accurate picture of the condition of the Mexican republic.

For now I return once more to my daily activities and my excursions. February 1 was the eve of the feast of La Purificación de Nuestra Señora, and like all other feasts it was celebrated through gambling and dancing. The former in particular exerts an undesirable fascination upon the Mexican. In moments of entertainment a game of chance is seldom lacking; the people are given to these in such a way that I almost want to doubt whether one could find a people so addicted to gambling. From the richest to the poorest, all gather according to their rank, in order to be able to attend their favorite game, "monte." Sitting in, the magistrate forgets his office; he does not move, and if the village goes up in flames, the father of the family forgets his house, wife, and child, the subordinate his duty. In fact, this gambling mania goes to such an extreme in Mexico that I will almost be persuaded that the tragic circumstances of the land in part find their basis therein. The following passage will allow me opportunity to explore this topic in more detail, and to call attention to its evil consequences.

A crowd of people had assembled under the porticos of Mirador. The game they began there is called *la polaca* and is still one of the better ones, since it is more a type of lottery than an actual game. On a table improvised from a few boards stood glasses, plates, bowls, and other knickknacks; ringed around the same sat and stood men and women of lusty glances, counting out their few *medios*[13] or smoking their *cigarritos* and forming an interesting group. At last the raffle for which they had waited so patiently began. Each one now bought for himself two cards of a deck, whereupon the raffler took cards from a second deck, and whoever's cards matched those of the second draw came away the winner. After a few hours most lost their money there—an occasional win excepted—and they arranged a fandango in order to spend the rest of the night in joy and celebration.

Naturally, I had left my hut unoccupied in order to attend this celebration eve, but was not a little surprised the next morning when I noticed that the evil consequences of the game touched me in an unexpected way. As I have previously mentioned, my house was built merely from wooden poles, and with the well-known honesty of the poor inhabitants of Mirador I had not thought of locking it further. To my horror, however, I now found a hole in one wall next to the floor, through which someone had broken in. I quickly cast my eye around to discover what he had taken from me, but for a long time failed to discover anything, until at last I realized that a small satchel was missing, one in which I had the beginnings of a modest coin collection. My loss was not great in comparison to the remaining items that could have been taken. It amounted to 12 guilders, and since among them were a few Austrian coins, I therefore hoped to be able to track down the thief, something that sadly did not happen.

I had hoped to have him placed for a few days in the stocks, a punishment that is employed quite frequently and in the following manner. The *cebo*, or stock, consists of two stout beams lying one over the other, and held together on one side with a hinge, on the other with a lock. In the middle of these two beams that, when placed one on top of the other, form a circular hole that extends from one side to the other. The criminal is placed on the beams and his two feet in the holes so that he can neither move nor turn around. Twelve hours are passed in this position, a justified but still difficult and dreaded punishment.[14]

Toward noon of the following day many people had once more gathered to attend yet another game and, of course, the ever popular cockfight. The majority split into two groups, which for a long time prepared their roosters for battle and then wagered significant sums of money against one another. After they had brought in the cocks and the head of each party had determined that his animal was sufficiently valiant, the tip of one spur was sawed off and a sharp knife two to three inches in length was fastened. This struggle is called *pelea de gallos a cuchillo,*[15] different from the *pelea de gallos a pico,*[16] wherein the cocks merely fight with their natural weapons. A thick circle closes around the place of combat, into which enter the elected deputies of the parties, the roosters under their arms. They seize the animals by the tails and, inclining toward the ground, excite the same by these means, that they hold them toward each other and pull them back again, while they pluck a few feathers out of their backs and hold the same between their teeth. This done, they get up again and put them down at the edge of the circle. The roosters go here and there for a while, without betraying anger or bloodlust, until they suddenly set upon one another furiously, and try to wound their adversary with the supposed spur. In most cases the sharp blade brings the contest to an end quickly, since seldom is more than one well-aimed blow necessary to kill the other. Often both end up dead, or else one cock flays the other with a strike at the head; a rooster seldom abandons the arena of battle, something that matters as much to the gamers as if he had been defeated. But the valor of these animals is indescribable and especially horrible in the case of a battle *a pico,* or with beaks. Not infrequently such cockfights are repeated in the afternoon ten or twelve times, until one party is completely vanquished, and occasionally force a loss of 200–300 guilders. It frequently happens that a single rooster wins two to four battles. Today the inhabitants of Zacuapan went away the victors, although with trifling winnings.

During my frequent visits to the aforementioned hacienda I met a young German, Herr Hugo Fink, who occupied the role of overseer, and who demonstrated quite an intense passion for the natural sciences. The goal of my journey frequently brought us into contact, and I granted his request to accompany me for a little time, all the more gladly as he, through his many-year residence in the state of Veracruz, was intimately familiar with the land and the customs of his people. He came to stay with me in Mirador, where we lived for a while in the very same hut. I had found a fearless and true companion. In the course of a few weeks we made countless excursions, of which I will related only a few of the more outstanding.

On February 15 we set out for the so-called El Fortín, which stands beneath Zacuapan between two barrancas, on a strip of earth. This altogether narrow ridge is inaccessible, since to reach any side one has to pass a deep valley. It takes its name from the lonely ruins that lie scattered there from the time of the ancient Indian kingdoms. When the explorer has climbed the ridge, he comes to a place in whose center a steep rock stands, on which he discovers a few walls with rifle holes, steps, and various components of a mighty structure. This point is extraordinarily well fortified for defense, since there exists only a single road, and it leads through the Fortín; to the left and right, awe-inspiring barrancas stare at the wanderer, and thereby a powerful enemy can be halted with minimal force.

Once the explorer has climbed up this rock, he finds himself on a narrow plain, which at present is covered only with grass; upon examining the soil more carefully, however, he finds that in earlier times it was covered with heavy deposits of chalk, sand, and stone, according to the style of the Italian *terrazos;* although it appears that the entirety would have formed a defensive position where at the same time religious ceremonies were held. Even now in that same place one finds a huge body of fragmented obsidian arrowheads[17] and a thousand small sherds of earlier pottery lying scattered about. Somewhere in the middle rises another breastwork, on which are clearly recognizable the form of a pyramid consisting of more terraces. It is, without doubt, one of those Mexican *teocallis,* which were used for sacrificial duties, since human remains were discovered a few years before in its vicinity.[18]

A bit further on this ridge narrows even more, until finally it ends in a stone point that juts out directly over a place where two barrancas intersect, and the visitor gazes down timidly into an almost bottomless depth. On the outermost point stands a small altar or rather a block made of stone of approximately four cubic feet, which might have served as a place from which to hurl the unfortunate victim into the frightful ravine. Beyond this we discovered still many tumbled-down walls and tombs, whose intended purpose can no longer be recognized. These and still other ruins in the barranca of Consoquitla suggest the dense population of the region, of which, sadly, only little remains.

On this journey we had fatigued ourselves considerably, and since the heat was frightful, for the first time I myself felt such tremendous torments of thirst that in the truest sense of the word my tongue had dried up in my mouth. Not a drop of water was to be found until we had again reached the bottom of the barranca, where a pure stream gently flowed under the shade of colossal trees, and at which we satisfied our intense craving. However, the yields of this day were rich, since we had never before seen such splendid vegetation as in the barranca of the Fortín.

On February 23 we stood ready for a journey to explore the Los Baños, or baths, which travelers had very seldom, or perhaps never, visited. The Baños are the name for sulphur springs that lie six Spanish miles below Mirador toward Veracruz, and which bear the Indian name Atliaca.

The norther season, which here lasts from the beginning of November until the end of February, was fairly over and the dry season had begun. Day by day the sun burned down ever fiercer and with relentless intensity on the level savanna, so that the soil burned almost red-hot. We slowly pushed on through this joyless steppe, equipped with provisions necessary for a few days therein. The thermometer showed 122 degrees in the shade of a bush on the savanna,[19] and I feared, perhaps not unreasonably, for evil consequences to my health. Indeed, when toward evening we had finally reached the barranca with the spring, a headache that had seized me had worsened to such a degree that I collapsed almost unconscious under the shade of a tree. Luckily, there was fresh water here, and a pleasant bath restored me little by little; I found myself recovered the following day, after a restful sleep.

As soon as I felt better, we began to investigate more closely our nearby surroundings. The barranca of Baños was one of those ravines in which the vegetation of the hot country surpassed all others in splendor. *Cereae* cacti and dracaena, euphorbia, and a countless number of other small plants grew on the rocks as if firmly glued upon them. In the background stand immense trees of wild pea flower, sassafras, ficus, pictum croton, crepe jasmine, and lively ceiba, which are partially sown with flowers and exhale an almost stunning perfume. A body of Mexican rubber trees, which furnish the so-called *hule*, was also on hand. A mass of luxurious winding plants, among which more jungle weed and sweet potato stand out, everywhere covered the branches of trees and bushes.

Moreover, the tropical animal kingdom seemed to have found a haven here, where the foot of man seldom treads. Everything was present, from the tiger to the tiny, irksome gnat and still tinier tick. We feared the birds of prey less than we did the latter, which inflicts unexpected tortures upon the wanderer. It is scarcely larger than a small pinhead and lurks in large numbers on the leaves of low-lying plants. At every opportunity, whether the victim be human or animal, the tick falls and digs its way into its victim with unbelievable swiftness. This bite is not all that painful, but its consequences are highly unpleasant. Whether one extracts the tiny creature or whether one allows it to sit, a painful pustule always forms, often giving way to the most dangerous abscesses. When the reader considers that one has scarcely to walk five steps to be covered with thousands of these tiny creatures, he will thus understand that I feared this tick, which here one calls *garrapata* or *pinolillo,* more than all the ravenous beasts of Mexico.

To be certain, the mosquitoes tortured us a great deal as well; however, since we built a hearty fire every evening before our small hut, which Herr Baetke himself had constructed in that same place, the smoke tended to keep them from our skin. The hut was not nearly as good as a typical Indian hut; on the contrary, it was a mere roof held together by a few poles ringed around. We had prepared for ourselves a rather soft place out of barba española. Our provisions—chiefly dried beef, or *tasajo,* but also the lard jar, sugar, salt, and corn—hung from the rafters in order to protect them from the destructive fury of the ants.

In this manner we had settled, so to speak, in that wilderness, and lived a life that only a genuine writer of novels knows how to paint with a hundred lovely colors. I cannot do this in equal measure, but must insist that the place has a charm that resembles nothing else in the world. Nature is splendid here. Trees and bushes seem to grow untouched from time beyond memory. The profound stillness is interrupted only by the distant calls of wild animals, by the croaking of birds of prey, by the cheerful song of tiny feathered songbirds, or by the buzzing of a thousand insects. Here one can truly say that he finds himself in a region that corresponds to the expectations of art.

In the middle of this small but remarkable world, which is bounded by a mass of rock, runs a fine mountain brook rushing over the stones. Tiny, delicate fish[20] swim about in the clear water, and charming plants line the banks. The most important of these provides a handsome bath place and is a warm 102 degrees. Analysis of the water reveals that it is absolutely identical to the sulphur springs of Baden in Vienna and for that reason, since healthful in the highest degree, merits greater attention. Indeed, many years will yet pass until the entrepreneurial spirit of the Mexican hits upon an opportunity that will be of immense use to the healthy as well as to the sick.

The name proves that these springs were not unknown to the Indians of old, and I even found hieroglyphics engraved on a rock wall. They belong neither to the Aztec nor Toltec nation, and I reproduce them here in faithful copy, without having so much as an inkling of their meaning.[21]

". . . these springs were not unknown to the Indians of old, and I even found hieroglyphics engraved on a rock wall. They belong neither to the Aztec or Toltec nation, and I reproduce here in faithful copy, without having so much as an inkling of their meaning." This illustration comes from original text of *Reisen in Mexiko,* and was presumably drawn by Heller himself.

The time passed for us so quickly in zealous investigation, climbing up and down while following the barrancas in all directions, that our provisions were nearly exhausted, and we were still far from completing our work. It would have been a sin to separate ourselves prematurely from this place, believing our mission to be completed. For that reason we seized the corn destined for our mules, cooked it with some lard and sugar, and lived a few more days with this simple food and one or another animal that we shot, until we had finally exhausted our supplies as well as our investigations. After we had spent eight days pleasantly and unpleasantly in the wilderness, we returned to Mirador loaded down with treasures. Only a few points in the vicinity of this settlement still remained for us to visit. In the following days we made the necessary excursions; I dispatched a shipment of fourteen crates to Europe, and thereupon relinquished my small entourage in order to definitely establish myself for a brief while in Huatusco, which I have already described above.

When I reflect back on the time I spent in Mirador, I have to confess that it was the finest of my life. The inhabitants of the settlement who became my true friends, the magnificent region, the lush vegetation, the success of my work, the indescribably lovely climate: in short, everything united to bring me to a state of satisfaction, indeed, I would say bliss. The scene of that district impressed itself on my spirit and will remain forever fresh and lively until the end of my days. I revel in the memory of that time, and the wanderer who has this in his burden-filled life will look back with satisfaction on his undertaking!

Chapter 6

On March 12, 1846, we found ourselves in Huatusco. In the vicinity of this charming place there is a pleasant valley through which flows a lovely mountain brook; many years earlier on the banks of this brook, in the shade of a small forest, the Belgian natural scientist A. Ghiesbrecht had built a thatch-roofed house that now stands abandoned. Since he was in the capital at this time, I received his permission to occupy it, a favor he most readily granted me.

One cannot easily conceive of a place more suitable for the naturalist than this. With little effort and loss of time, someone living here could travel from the beautiful valley to the forest lying nearby, and without being interrupted in his various labors by the curious inhabitants of the place. I lived alone, of course, but in the middle of a resplendent nature. Here I settled in perfectly, and as in Mirador, made excursions in all directions. My principal attention, however, was focused on a journey to the volcano Orizaba, a journey I launched on March 23.

We followed the road that led to it and soon reached the barranca of San Juan, stretching uninterrupted from the peak of Orizaba to the plain of Veracruz. At the place where we had to ride through it, the barranca may have reached a depth of perhaps twelve hundred feet. An extremely dangerous road leads downward, twists around the rocks, and is so ghastly that one looks toward the end goal with great apprehension. Fortunately, we made it down and were pleasantly surprised to come upon a sturdy bridge in this vast ravine, one that led over the Jamapa River. On the rock walls, which drip with moisture, grows a mass of achimenes and gesnerias standing in full bloom. The rich vegetation of the barranca was splendidly represented here and resembled earlier specimens.

We climbed to the other side without particular incident and reached a small, high plateau at the foot of the cordilleras, in the middle of which the market San Juan Coscomatepec stood invitingly. This place lies five leagues from Huatusco, and like most Mexican villages from afar it resembles a grove of trees in which houses lie scattered. The visitor comes nearer, however, and steps upon straight-running streets whose small structures are surrounded with gardens for the most part encircled by a hedge of coral tree and custard apple, a stately fruit tree that is quite common here. The Mexican's fondness for flowers, a point of which Hernán Cortés speaks, still flourishes in the present day through the cultivation of stunning orchids on these trees, and often a village such as San Juan is a living compendium of the handsomest plants of the area.

San Juan is a significant community of four thousand inhabitants. It lies on the upper boundary of the *tierra templada,* and for that reason neither sugarcane nor lichen prospers there, no more than do avocados or oranges. More than other villages it lies on the fault line of earthquakes, which very much make themselves felt from the volcano Tuxtla on the Gulf of Mexico to Colima on the Pacific Ocean. As a result many buildings are frequently destroyed, and the rather handsome church has already collapsed many times. At the time of my journey it lay in ruins, and the public service was held in an atmosphere of great fear.

I stayed only a brief time there, and found lodging with a hospitable Spaniard. But I did have the opportunity to experience an earthquake. During a withering heat at 4:00 in the afternoon came a powerful tremor, so that all the people ran into the street and implored the Creator for mercy. Luckily this earthquake was brief, and remarkably no harm was done. The following evening, however, a second tremor erupted, so strong that all the glasses and bottles in the house clattered and we leapt up terrified where we sat, even though the earthquake did not last long enough to cause serious destruction. But I agree with all travelers who experience similar moments, that there could be nothing more unpleasant than losing the very ground under one's feet; there remains no other salvation than to hurry as quickly as possible to a large, open plaza, where one is safe from collapsing buildings.

We set out on our journey the next day, following the road toward the peak of Orizaba. Climbing for a stretch of two leagues, we reached the village Santa María Alpatlahua, which lies six hundred feet higher than the previously mentioned location. Beside the earlier vegetation appear new varieties characteristic of the region, and because of the now significant altitude they recall European flora. For example, the alder tree grows here, together with oaks, while the parasites become ever rarer. The village Cacahuales is separated from Alpatlahua merely by a *barranquita;* it lies quite picturesquely on a small elevation, from which one enjoys a deeply panoramic view. Although consisting of a few unsightly houses, both villages have charming churches that are made of stone and date from the time of the Spanish, and in which one can recognize the Spanish-Byzantine style.

The road quickly rises from here, and the spruce forests begin at an altitude of seven thousand feet with white pine, which pleasantly startles the wanderer with its long, supple needles and its elegant form. The path leads for a good distance through these woods, and many trees 10 feet in circumference and 100 to 150 feet in height astonish the observer. Although it is presently the dry season, the traveler progresses arduously along many lonely huts, or *ranchos,* which are inhabited by shepherds living wretched lives. These, in turn, are surrounded by small, sparse cornfields, which are found at up to nine thousand feet despite the fact that the harvests often turn out badly. Sheep and goat herds graze here, for in the aromatic mountain grasses they find excellent pasturage, and the lowing of these animals and the chiming of bells interrupt the deep quiet of the primeval forest in homespun fashion. From time to time in some unobstructed location the wanderer manages to catch a glimpse of the peak of Orizaba looming ever nearer, or of some land spreading out below. The landscape gains infinitely in charm when contemplated from such heights. Seen through the tropical heat, and shaded by the dark green of the firs, the dun-colored plains appear deeply picturesque, while on the mountain pastures in the neighboring region, small, charming plants like potentilla, ranuncula, strawberry, and others rise up playfully; to my mind they bore an uncanny resemblance to our mountain lands.

Here we found ourselves far removed from the domain of the villages, in a place where the elements manage to create and destroy unobserved. So we were not a little surprised to see our entire strip of forest to twelve thousand feet frightfully devastated. Trunks that might well have resisted the centuries lay uprooted and shattered on the ground, barricading the road; others had all their branches broken off, and they towered like barren mastheads, high up to the heavens, blasted away in the middle. Moreover, we found still others, called *ocote*, which, owing to their resinous wood, are used for torches; trees cut down by the Indians; and the shepherd huts that have been destroyed and never again rebuilt . . . in short, everything united to complete a picture of horror. We frequently had to make laborious detours in order to work our way around the trunks that blocked the road. Often we were forced to climb over them with great difficulty, and we could make but slow progress. A dreadful storm had caused this destruction, and as we later learned, it was the same one we had experienced in Mirador on January 5, 1846, although far more powerful here. Even if we had not been enchanted by the region's low-lying flora, this scene of destruction would still have mesmerized us.

By this time we had climbed nine thousand feet and little by little were beginning to tire; but the road was still passable by horse, all the more so since the Mexican steed possesses an extraordinarily safe and agile footing. Alongside the spruce we now saw the stately Mexican fir tree, whose tip sways at a height of 160 to 200 feet, and which often has a trunk 20 feet in circumference. The undergrowth steadily diminishes; the woods grow thinner, until one finally steps into a small meadow on which lie more wretched huts scattered about, and which in turn are surrounded by small fields of corn and potatoes. We had reached the highest inhabited point of this cordillera. It is the rancho Jacale, ten thousand feet above sea level.

Warily one nears these pitiful and remarkably secluded homes. They would be appropriate scenes for robbery and murder, if travelers were not so rare an occurrence and the inhabitants not such thoroughly honest people. I look back with anger on my mistrust, when I recall how genially and courteously they received exhausted wanderers such as ourselves. Soon we were glad to recognize the lean, over-six-foot-tall form of Juan Gómez, overseer of this rancho. I now wonder how men who live in the greatest poverty and are only occasionally visited by tobacco smugglers can be of so hospitable and upright character, certainly a rare occurrence in Mexico! In a hut consisting of a few boards we found meager lodgings, on the floor a hard bed. But what else would the traveler, worn out by hardships of the road, have wished for himself? We wanted only to sleep, and would have slept peacefully and tranquilly had the thermometer not dipped to 41 degrees after midnight. With the ice-cold morning breezes this translated into a penetrating cold, so that we were only too happy to welcome the sun at our little camp. However, we had to get up and try to warm ourselves by running up and down in the open air.

After we had enjoyed the marvelous spectacle of the sunrise with endless wonder, I trained my good telescope[1] on the peak of the volcano, wherein no man had ever set foot, at least to examine it more closely. The sun projected its first rays on the extensive snowfields and walls of ice. Those rays burst into a thousand colors on the different peaks, in some places begat clear shimmers of silver and gold, in others casting deep shade that strengthened little by little in the crevices to the deepest black. This play of darkness and light offered manifold contrasts and lent to the whole such a splendid appearance that no words can describe the splendor of the scene.

Gray clouds gathered over the estates that stretched at the foot of Orizaba; because we stood far above these clouds, they obscured the sight we had a right to expect from so high a vantage point. Sadly, I have always found that at a height of ten to twelve thousand feet one is seldom able to enjoy a vista of the region lying far below. I therefore contented myself with the summit of the volcano lying before me, and concentrated on the scene from where I stood to the direction of the crater. Past the area where pines still grew in sufficient numbers I glimpsed another region with mutilated trees, and on top of this were mostly rocks and lava thrown out by the volcano. Above that, piles of ice and snow extended all the way to the summit. The crevices that showed themselves here and there led one to suppose them several fathoms across. Of the two peaks, the westernmost seemed to be the higher; it constantly sent up a column of smoke, but owing to its prodigious height (16,750 feet) I could clearly discern this column from my vantage point.

We remained in Jacale for the day in order to attempt another climb, and with restored strength, on the following day. The third day of my travels in the mountains had already dawned when I set out on my way. The sky above me was clear, while the east had concealed itself in clouds that quickly gathered there. The light breezes of the mountains blew briskly through the pine needles, stifled our breath, and made the unaccustomed cold freeze against our limbs.

A path scarcely three feet wide ascends the volcano vertically, running in an endless zigzag through the rocks. To be sure, the traveler seldom comes across a living creature at such altitudes, but unfortunately I met with a team of mules carrying bundles of snow down to the cities in order to chill drinks. In the place where I came across this team, a high rock wall rose to the left of the narrow path; to the right gaped a frightful chasm, so deep that it was impossible to make out the vegetation at its bottom. As soon as we had come upon on another, I climbed down from my horse and pressed myself against the rock wall. The passing mules, however, brushed so hard against my extremely temperamental horse that I was scarcely able to hold him steady. The team had passed; nevertheless, I still had to contend with the considerable task of mounting my almost crazed horse in this dangerous place. But the instant I set foot in the stirrup, the horse rushed up onto the rocks. The swiftness and the large bundle behind the saddle prevented me from mounting firmly. For that reason I hovered for a few seconds, literally between heaven and earth, and fearing that a misstep on the animal's part would bring certain death, I preferred to jump off. I spied a favorable spot and tumbled down; however, because I fell so swiftly I landed on the edge of the ravine, face down. Still, with all my force I grabbed a stone that lay within the reach of my hands, then opened my eyes and saw that my head and chest hung over the abyss. The moment was tremendous: slightly less presence of mind, and I would lie shattered in the ravine of Orizaba. Perhaps never in my life did I feel such rage; I tore my long knife from my side, and would have run it through the animal, who now stood peacefully. The beast's tranquillity, however, and the thought that without the horse I would never again be able to descend, soon calmed me. Later, when I was sitting peacefully in the saddle and pondered what had happened, I gradually came to realize in what immense peril I had hovered, and what an important warning I had received.

The road turned toward the right, passed not far from the source of the

Jamapa River, and climbed to a height of fourteen thousand feet. All vegetation stopped here. Sand, obsidian pieces, and stones of volcanic origin covered the road. A fearful storm blew ice cold upon this mountain edge, breathing became ever more difficult, and the nearby stretches of ice left all life frozen. We inched forward slowly along the frightful abyss, and scarcely dared to cast a glance into the horrifying depths. Whole skeletons and isolated bones of fallen mules lying about provide sufficient warning of the perils and difficulties of the road. Finally, after two and a half hours we reached the highest pass (La Cuchilla, at 14,000 feet). A rough-hewn wooden cross is fastened between the stones, and few, I believe, will push along without thanking the Creator for having come so far without harm.

This far and no further, it meant for us; it showed quite well the futility of attempting to climb higher, an idea we could not consider, since until now even the most daring efforts to reach the summit had remained fruitless. We therefore contented ourselves with this height and rested for a long time while we contemplated in silent wonder the sight that loomed before us. To the west stretched an immense high plateau that runs from Puebla and which is bounded by the two mountain chains that cut through Mexico. The yet higher snowcap of Popocatépetl rises to 17,081 feet; to its right stands the 15,139-foot Nevado de Iztaccíhuatl, and on both sides lie mountains that become proportionately lower as they stretch into the vast distance. This luxurious sight held me fast for a long time, and the more I contemplated both these gigantic snowcapped mountains, the greater became my longing to know them more closely . . . even while I still found myself on the peak of Orizaba, and had clearly witnessed the perils of such mountain travel. Of course, I could in no way satisfy this desire at the moment, since I was not prepared for so long a journey (85–115 miles), but could not resist the allure of visiting the high plateau that lay beneath me. Suspecting that this would be the case, I had already inquired at Jacale regarding the way there, and learned that it carried me past the silver mine La Fundación, lying to the northwest, if I wanted quickly to reach the small high plateau Los Derrumbados, which I would describe as rich in cactus.

I therefore descended the west side and had again arrived at the pine forest of this slope, where I still sought, though in vain, plant species that would have been worth taking along or at least observing. Nothing was to be seen, absolutely nothing other than trees I have already related. Instead of the red, fertile loamy soil of the east side, here lie volcanic ashes and rocks. Instead of stately bushes, here stand huge, scraggly looking clumps of grass scattered about. Indeed, the only bush I saw was further down, and also only once, was the flowering currant. The water-laden clouds of the east cannot pass over the high cordillera; for that reason, the rainy season excepted, not a drop of water falls here, and the blazing sun of the tropics allows not a single weed to sprout up. The inhabitants of the high plains must repair to a gully clear of pine trees in order to use the much needed water of that place, where said water collects in the sand.

Shaded by the monotonous vegetation, exhausted and worn out by the arduous ride, I longed for the goal I had set for that day, the hacienda of Tepetitlán. Although I lacked a guide, a man quite opportunely passed by, and I endeavored to learn from him how far away the hacienda lay. I was not a little surprised when he told me that I had passed the road to La Fundación a long time back and had already crossed a good stretch of the road to Puebla. What to do now? To return was impossible for the animal and myself, so I had to try by circuitous means. Luckily I succeeded, but traveled five leagues to do so.

First I had to try to reach Tlachichuca, and for that reason set out on my way according to the account I had received, since even the newest and best maps of Mexico (published with Arrowsmith in London) fix the position of places so incorrectly that the map offers the traveler little use. Still descending, I finally came upon a few oaks at an approximate elevation of eighty-five hundred feet, but here were absent the splendid parasites that always cover the trunks on the eastern side. No orchids, no ferns, no resinous plants, not one lichen adorned the trees of the western slope, and what will say a great deal about variation in the tropics, not a single clinging vine was to be observed.

I had already ridden downhill for five hours, and wandering through the dry pine forest had grown tremendously tedious when I reached Los Derrumbandos on the high plateau. In fact, the plateau was the most intimidating I had ever seen: an endless expanse of nothing but sand, lava ash, and volcanic rock. Moreover, the harshly burning hot winds that come out of the south, and which drive enormous dust clouds into the sky, cover the traveler and scarcely allow him to open his eyes. The road grows so indiscernible as to hardly be recognized, and is so full of mole burrows that with almost every step the mules sink a foot deep. A few cedar woods and cacti excepted, there was almost nothing to be seen that one could call vegetation. In short, during the dry season the plain resembles my idea of an African desert; and yet it is anything but barren when the rainy season comes here, for then one cultivates cereals, corn, and beans with very good result.

At length I reached Tlachichuca, a small village that is planted length and breadth with maguey. From this plant they prepare a beverage called *pulque* here, and in the following manner. Cultivators select the oldest specimens

"From this plant [the maguey] they prepare a beverage called *pulque*. . . . Every morning it is doled out with a long ladle made from a gourd, and fermented in a sheepskin bag, whereby it forms a distinctive intoxicating beverage that initially tastes rather disagreeable to those not accustomed to it." (Photo courtesy of the Latin American Library, University of Texas at Austin)

(many six feet in diameter and all on the point of sending up their flower stalk), cut out the crown in the middle of the shaft, and hollow out the plant. This hole, so large that it can hold almost five liquid measures, quickly fills with juice (*agua miel*),[2] which when taken fresh has a quite pleasant taste, rather like apple cider. Every morning it is doled out with a long ladle made from a gourd, and fermented in a sheepskin bag, whereby it forms a distinctive intoxicating beverage that initially tastes rather disagreeable to those not accustomed to it. A plant handled in this manner often furnishes a daily measure of pulque for three months, until finally it dries up and perishes.

We had already ridden on for three hours, and were sunburned and completely exhausted when we came to the foot of more limestone mountains at the hacienda of Tepetitlán, some 7,814 feet above sea level. A few of these limestone hills rose up scattered about the plateau, almost like mountains in ruins or like rock reefs of the sea. The vegetation itself consists of cacti, a few *Mammillaria* and aloe, and a form of yucca. The two highest mountains, which may rise a thousand to fifteen hundred feet over the high plateau, have given this stretch of land the name Los Derrumbados because of their stone rubble.[3] A low mountain lying northwest of Tepetitlán stands out for the fact that steam and smoke climb up constantly out of its peaks, which at night spread a bright light from afar. This is a lively and easily visited crater, and the people of the region frequently go to it because of its low height. Here the hot steam causes sweat to break out immediately, and thereby provides relief for many rheumatic and arthritic illnesses.

Residents had assured me that a certain hacienda owner would receive me hospitably, and I rejoiced at the prospect of resting well for a night. How very greatly I erred! Instead of providing a friendly reception, the owner answered my request to spend some days collecting Mexican barrel cacti with few words; he informed me that there was no such thing here and that I would do better to go to a certain village lying nearby, where he believed to have seen the same. All the while, several plants standing nearby utterly contradicted his statement. He also scrutinized my arms with many curious questions; he grew quite nettled, and only my letters of security and my arms permit seemed to quiet him somewhat. I saw that the man believed nothing of my assurance to have come solely because of the plants, and made clear that in no case could I remain here a long time.

Although his hostility was highly unpleasant, nothing in the world would have brought me a step further that day, and for that reason I asked him that at least I be allowed to be able to spend the night here. And behold! His indulgence extended so far as to direct my animal and myself to the nearby sheep barn for evening quarters, while his spacious home would have been able to accommodate not one, but rather twenty strangers. The poorest Mexican joyfully offers his hut to the visitor, yet this man had the heart to refer us—whom he could clearly see were exhausted—to the barn, in order to sleep on the cold floor, where instead of resting, one's limbs would stiffen and weaken!

I did not know at that time that I was in a district where numerous robberies have bred a deep mutual mistrust; even with all necessary documents, the traveler will probably be considered a dangerous highwayman. Later I came to understand through my lad, whom he tried to pump for information, that he had initially taken us for suspicious people, but later decided that we were prospectors who had come to look for silver mines, and as the owner of such a mine, he feared harm. That there might be men who traveled about merely because of plants and animals seemed to him utterly incomprehensible.

The fourth day dawned and I once more mounted my tired horse at sunup in order to push on. Again the road stretched into the sandy desert, and I pushed toward the direction of a few of the limestone mountains in order to fill the still rather empty chest that my lone mule hauled along behind. We arrived after a few hours; I climbed and explored, but found nothing beyond a large number of unusable cacti and aloe, a mere two branches of *Mammillaria* and a few other not particularly important plants. Since I could find nothing else, I rode off to another hacienda which in fact lay closer to the cordillera and is called La Capilla. I inquired about the second pass over the mountain range, and fully informed I again began to ascend the slope.

On the same day I reached the rancho Canoitas, at an altitude of ten thousand feet. We were hospitably received by the poor people, who cultivate potatoes and the so-called horse beans (*habas*).[4] The place was half vacant, for their rancho was almost entirely destroyed by the storm mentioned earlier, but they prepared us a place using the straw they always had as fodder for the animals. Moreover, the woman of the house was eager to offer something to eat, which consisted of tortillas and beans.

Since until now I have not described the Mexican hut, I will take that of Canoitas as a model. A room of at most four yards square is surrounded not so much with walls but rather a fence built of sticks or beams bound together with the vines of climbing plants (*bejucos*). A few sticks crossing overhead form a pointed roof that here is covered with the leaves of agave, in other villages with sugarcane leaves or other grasses (both called *zacate*). A fire burns in one corner, around which the small children play about half naked. The housewife immediately fills her pot with beans or meat and grinds or mashes corn on a stone (*metate*), forms thin flat cakes, and then on a clay griddle produces the tortillas. Mexicans can never do without these tortillas, which take the place of bread, knife, fork, and spoon. In another mortar crudely hewn from stone are Spanish peppers, here called chiles, ground and made into a sauce that to the people of Mexico is as indispensable as salt to the European. They are able to enjoy this dreadfully strong broth in unbelievable quantities, so that one may justifiably attribute the frequent stomach disorders of these people to excessive use of the same.

Outside of a few pots and bowls that are arranged on poles, no further household furnishings are to be seen. No table, no chair, no bed: nothing is present other than the bare ground. People eat with their fingers while sitting in the corner, and among the poor folk meals consist principally of black beans, which are never lacking, even at the most elegant Mexican table; of tortillas; and on rare occasions of a small piece of boiled meat or baked chayotes.[5] On the whole the Mexican satisfies himself with very little, and his supper would not sate the European stomach, which has been weakened by its climate. In the evening they spread a few straw mats, or *petates,* on the floor, and one's bed is ready.

The next day I had almost reached the highest point of this pass, accurately referred to as La Cumbre,[6] which is twelve thousand feet high. And here once more begins the descent into the gloriously plant-rich region of the eastern slope. Already at an altitude of ten thousand feet I once more came upon barba española and stonecrop, and further, below nine thousand feet in elevation, I found many beautiful shrubs, among which stands out in particular a night jasmine covered with flowers, something I recognized as a new variety, and which I named *H. abelii* in honor of my brother-in-law Ludwig Abel, who indirectly lent me brotherly support on my journey.

Following different paths I reached Achilchotla, a little-known Indian village that lies in the center of a highly fertile mountain valley. The houses lie scattered among charming groves of fruit trees; encircled by pine-covered mountains, this place resembles a tranquil refuge for this oppressed tribe. Old and young stared at me with curiosity, but without providing for me along the way. Perhaps I was the first European ever to touch upon this village! The fruit trees were studded with flowers, and a heartfelt surprise seized hold of me when I spied the union of tropical and European features. Here are agave and lichen, there apple and cherry and apricot trees that grew handsomely at this elevation (9,000 feet) and which so vividly called to mind the homeland. Delighted, I must confess, I pushed through this village and set forth in good spirits over countless small mountains and valleys that rivaled one another in beauty. I soon reached the village of Quizmistlán, and toward evening the ranchería of Ahuayeca (8,000 feet), where that profoundly important medicinal plant known as the jalap weed, like other wild and cultivated plants, finds its true home.[7]

We spent the night here with extremely poor but friendly people, sleeping on the ground as usual, and began our final day's journey before the first light had broken. The initial sunbeams wonderfully illuminated the snowfields of the north face of Orizaba while slowly and quietly we trotted along in the half dark toward our final destination. At six thousand feet we reached Chichiquila, and in order to come to a decent road there remained no further difficulty to pass other than the deepest of all barrancas, that of Chichiquila. This, in turn, is a branch of the Jamapa barranca.

It is impossible to adequately describe this path or the perilous task of riding through it. Briefly put, it is something truly horrifying, and whoever has passed this barranca once will certainly not test the gods twice unless it is absolutely necessary. A narrow rock footpath advances into the immense depths, downward along the sheer stone wall, and upward again on the other side in the same way. Even our dexterous animals, from whom we had dismounted, often trembled throughout their entire bodies through instinctive fear, and on occasion resisted so that we had to push them onward with force. We had to jump over steps of three feet, and a single slip at one place or another would have brought certain death.

We had spent three hours reaching the village Elotepec on the other side, from where we then hurried over San Diego (5,000 feet) to the valley where the town of Huatusco, my residence at that time, peeped up at us, cheerful and inviting, out of the dense greenery. We reached it in the daylight hours of March 28, 1846, and then refreshed ourselves for the remaining difficulties in the heartening circle of our few but sincere friends.

Chapter 7

Before I move on to the account of a new journey, I would like the reader to know something more detailed about life in my little house in Huatusco. As I explained in the previous chapter, it lies secluded in a charming valley, a good quarter hour from the village to which a narrow stone path leads. I frequently wandered this path in order to visit some friends whom I will mention here.

The first whom fate had thrown here was a German, Herr Wilhelm Ziehl, who with zealous industry had opened a small store and maintained his residence there. He knew most of the naturalists who had explored that region earlier, and I turned up at his house as often as I wished. I cannot sufficiently praise his extraordinarily pleasant personality, his highly honest and upright character, his kindness and hospitality; I will never forget them. I passed many pleasant hours with him, and in the process of my later return home we shared many small adventures.

One afternoon it rained frightfully and the night was damp. Since I knew my narrow footpath well enough, I decided to make the trip without lighting. Concerned, however, Herr Ziehl forced a lantern upon me, and with this and a walking stick I took up my evening journey. The path, which led through a few deep ditches among dense undergrowth, was especially dirty and more than anything else slippery. I slowly climbed up the hill; unable to maintain myself on the extremely sheer place, I fell, tossed my beloved lantern on the ground, and sat in the ominous night on the road without knowing how I could have been reduced to such circumstances. At length I picked myself up, seized what remained of the lantern, and tried to set out on my way. But since I was at times in the underbrush, at other times at the edge of the road, I had reason to fear a dangerous fall. Moreover, I could see nothing at all, so that everything depended on my sense of touch, and as it happened I came down the hill more on all fours than on two legs. But my difficulties had by no means ended; for I had to pass a mountain stream that surged tempestuously near my house, and over which lay nothing more than a tree trunk, which served as a bridge. It was hard enough to balance on this trunk in the daytime; at night it was nearly impossible. There remained no other option, therefore, than to sit on the tree trunk and ride over it, something that was a very safe but extraordinarily comical manner, over which we later laughed quite heartily.

I recount these small adventures in order to show how often, and unexpectedly, one can find oneself in a highly difficult situation. I would need many pages to cover all these trifling episodes I experienced in the Americas. However, I cannot leave unmentioned a remarkable phenomenon that caught me by surprise. It was once more a gloomy night when suddenly the entire horizon lit up, and a fiery ball, which seemed to spit flames, traveled through the air from south to north with unbelievable speed. For a moment all things stood before me in a clear light. Such phenomena are not unknown in the tropics during the rainy season, and as it moved along with tremendous power, this heavenly occurrence seemed to me an altogether natural event.

Beyond the family of Herr Ziehl, there were a few others of Spanish descent in that place, individuals whom I sometimes visited, and by whom I was well received. In particular I must praise Huatusco, since it is still one of the few Mexican towns that for the longest time has maintained lawfulness and a sense of integrity, something that seemed to be very much facilitated by its isolated location in the mountains.

We now turn to the affairs of my own small household. The hut in which I resided lay in the midst of these tobacco fields, so frequently cultivated in Huatusco, and Herr Ghiesbrecht had earlier encircled it with a fence in order to be able to plant something different inside. Although it was now quite neglected, I spared no pains in decorating the surroundings as nicely as possible. In my free hours I planted palms, treelike ferns, small flowering beets, and banana groves. I hung lovely orchids on the trees, and a path led through the vegetation to the river, where I had a cozy place to bathe. Inside the house I was all things: master, servant, and cook. Concerning this last role there were initially many hard nuts for me to crack, since I had no cookbook in hand and had to prepare my own food according to my own notions. Nor was I in a position to defend my provisions against ravenous ants, which, although I had taken all imaginable preparations and precautions, hotly disputed all of my possessions. They are a veritable torment, and one is exposed to countless stings of the army ants just like the painful bites of the small black ones, which fall particularly over the meat and the sugar. Another sort altogether is a horrifying fiend that can completely defoliate orange trees in a few nights. Only the American traveling ant can be regarded as highly useful.[1] They come marching unexpectedly in huge swarms, then disperse themselves throughout the entire house with unbelievable speed, and the tranquilly sleeping resident often finds himself forced to leave at midnight in order to allow them free latitude. They spare some provisions, but at the same time hunt all the more voraciously for insects. They do not even spare the smallest worm, and drag everything along with them. When they are completely finished with this work, they push on again in a disciplined hoard, and the delighted owner enters into a well-cleaned house. But regardless of this struggle with the ants, the art of cooking, and with limited ingredients, involved such difficulties that since that time I have had no small respect for it.

In this manner, as the reader can see, there was quite a bit to manage in my small household circle, and the only time that remained for me to write was in the lonesome stillness of the night. And yet I lived happily in my own way here, and the time passed for me with unbelievable swiftness.

The fact of the matter is that in this region there were no mountains, valleys, woods, or meadows that I had not already explored in great detail. So on April 27 I resolved to make an enormous journey once more and to an Indian village lying far away. No European had ever visited this place before, because its inhabitants had a reputation of stubbornly refusing the company of whites. Since an opportunity presented itself for me to meet the cacique of that place, I therefore believed it was not incorrect to inform him of my purpose. But he had declined to accept me, and this was enough to make me all the more determined to go there. In the company of Herr Fink and another German by the name of Runkel, together with my servant, I set out exceptionally well armed on the road to that place.

First we came through splendid oak forests to a lovely waterfall that is formed by the Río Huatusco and bears the name La Cascada de Tenexamaxa. After running over a stretch of rocks to this place, the brook tumbles downward thirty-six feet with tremendous force into a rock basin where the water, scattered in a million droplets, comes together again and then flows tranquilly into a small ravine. It is with difficulty that one climbs down into this basin, but however arduous the scrambling down, just as rewarding is the sight one finds below. It was an authentically splendid scene. All around stood rocks luxuriously adorned with handsome plants like ferns, club moss, begonias, centradenium, and other small shrubs. One might have taken the place for a masterpiece of tasteful gardening. When illuminated by the sun, the dark green leaves, already damp from the mud of the atomized water, give off splendid rainbow colors that compete with the bright red of the flowering begonias. Streams of water fall among them, forming a bright silver band down over the rocks and producing an uproar that is doubly frightful in this narrow space. Nearby, two other small brooks enhance the beauty of the scene. They form enchanting cascades whose waters, after they have washed over the stony path, unite with the principal stream. Further down from here many ardisia bushes, bamboo, and above all plantains adorn the bank.

After we had enjoyed the stately tableau for a long time and had refreshed ourselves in its stimulating coolness, we again climbed to the burning heights and set out on our way, uphill and downhill, mostly through lovely woods, until we came to the barranca of Jamapa. This blocks the path for the traveler like some dreadful monster. We came upon a seldom traversed road in the depth of the densely overgrown ravine . . . seldom disturbed by foreign intruders, but for that same reason a dangerous place, for it is inhabited by every species of animal. A serpent at least twelve feet long and an arm thick flew with arrowlike swiftness through the grass, while parrots raised an authentic hue and cry. The royal pheasant, startled by the selfsame visit, passed majestically through the air. The white-headed eagle circled around us at limitless heights, waiting, as it were, to see whether a meal might not turn up. Even a jaguar, startled by the crack of our shotguns, hurried over the facing rocks with audacious leaps.

Although the barranca serves as bed to a huge brook that comes from Orizaba, the visitor observes no runoff outside of a single lake, itself in the deepest place of the same. Soon, however, he goes upstream a few hundred paces and the mystery becomes clear. The right side of the barranca here reveals a rock wall five hundred feet high, which seems to form the retaining wall of Matlactliahuatl, a mountain that rises overhead. At its foot opens a mouth formed of rock, fifteen feet high and eighteen feet wide, which devours the river with frightful thirst. Such caverns are highly interesting, but it would have been foolhardy for us to venture into this narrow, water-filled tomb without the necessary preparation. At its entrance the cave is so narrow that with the torrential downpours it is unable to take in the newly swollen current, a fact to which the now partly dry riverbed downstream attests. Careful investigations have shown that the river that descends into the earth here is the same river that, after it has run underground through the entire mountain for three hours in a straight line, springs forth again with full force on the other side near Chicuhuite, three hundred paces upstream from the first stone bridge on the road to Córdoba. At the second bridge on the same road the Cotaxtla River comes forth in identical fashion. Thereafter, just like the Jamapa on the left side, the Cotastla River on the right side descends into the barranca of Tomatlán, into the mountains, and flows through it underground in a straight line for four hours.

This nature scene not only fills the traveler with wonder but also forces upon him a mass of speculation and questions, whose answer is of importance in determining the formation of this mountain. The first of these questions is perhaps this: how does it happen that the river does not follow its riverbed, and how does it happen that it should have found its way on the rocks and under the mountain? In any case it must be accepted that the river existed before this mountain range, for even if one supposes that the mountain range was formed earlier, it is still inconceivable, on account of the flexibility of the water, that the river forced its way through the rock over time, for it would have followed the natural incline of the riverbed. The only remaining explanation is a powerful volcanic upheaval. Clearly, this is the only theory that explains both the mountain rising *and* at the same time the creation of immense empty spaces in the mountain's interior, spaces through which two rivers can pass. What speaks still more for this sort of origin is the fact that this small mountain chain shares no connection whatsoever with the cordillera lying to the northeast, but to the contrary rises to the east, on the line formed by the volcanoes Orizaba and Tuxtla. And further down, volcanic stone lies in deposit, while overhead lies the older limestone.

I myself have never doubted the Matlactliahuatl, with its adjoining mountain range, to have sprouted up; and I think that with their creation these rivers in fact filled the nearby subterranean spaces and perhaps had now flowed through them for centuries. He who knows the origin of Jorullo, in the year 1759, which Alexander von Humboldt describes in his *New Spain,* volume 2, page 145, will find my hypothesis not only unobjectionable but rather on the contrary corroborated.

Out of the barranca and uphill to the other side leads a stone path so steep and narrow that our mules, who went freely while we climbed up almost on all fours, were close to tumbling backward. In addition to this difficulty came a frightful heat of more than 97 degrees in the shade, so that we were completely exhausted when we arrived at the top. We were not a little pleased to find a decent road to the village there, areas that led along the right edge of the barranca, in the refreshing shade of huge trees. However, we were more surprised still by the fact that the road was partially paved, something that suggested the greater importance of this small village in olden times. In reality, during the days of the first Spaniards, Pueblo Viejo was a considerable city; it later declined, and fell into the hands of pure Indians who live shut off there in patriarchal style, in approximately twenty homes, and who maintain themselves with plantings of corn and tobacco.

The location of the small village is splendid. Its houses, scattered among trees and shrubs, stand on a small plain at the foot of the mountain, while scarcely a quarter hour away begins the undefiled virgin forest, to which more than anything one might justifiably apply the Spanish name *monte virgen*—that is, virgin woods. The Mexican tiger and lion, tapirs, monkeys, pheasants, wild hens, and parrots, all of which have withdrawn from the populated regions, still enjoy unrestricted freedom in these woods, since the inhabitants of this village are poor hunters for want of shotguns.

The reception in the village was quite frosty, as we had foreseen, and would perhaps have been hostile had not our arms, with which we intentionally showed our preparedness, inspired so much respect. The alcalde, or ruler of the village, also called cacique, assigned us a tobacco-drying house (*galera de tabaco*) as residence; nothing was to be found in it that would have justified this name, that much goes without saying; moreover, the alcalde, full of mistrust, did not make a move on our behalf, until finally an unfortunate incident brought us closer together.

In Mexico all travelers are taken to be doctors, and the same thing happened to me as well. On this assumption an old Indian cautiously approached me and asked me whether I knew no cure, or *remedio,* against the bite of a venomous serpent, since that morning a young man was bitten by a *palanca* (an extraordinarily poisonous snake), and in fact was doing quite poorly. Since the *alcali* (*Ammoniacum causticum*) always worked well for me, I therefore answered his question in the affirmative, and immediately repaired to the patient's hut. On a bark mat, huddled up in a corner, lay a young Indian who had silently endured his terrible pain for eight hours, death written on his face. I inspected his foot, and in the vicinity of the ankle found the bite resembling two pinpricks. The entire foot was tremendously swollen. I immediately removed the toad that they had laid upon the wound as an antidote, slightly opened the wound with my knife, poured a drop into it, gave him as well a drop of it in water, and prepared a salve of *alcali* and oil, which was meant for application on the foot. After this we went away, uncertain as to whether the medicine had not perhaps come too late.

After this small assistance, however, the people were much friendlier. As the patient felt himself far better the next day, and I could promise him his recovery with certainty, we were now treated as honored guests. The very same day we had to relocate to the home of the alcalde, and similarly when we paid for anything, then everything was gladly afforded to us, and we became the masters of the village.

The next morning an Indian went with us through the virgin forest, which consisted of magnolia, myrtle, and other beautiful trees on which crept an enormous mass of climbing vines. We advanced with immense difficulty, for we were constantly busy cutting these vines apart. For a long time we pushed on without path into the forest around us, and I can scarcely imagine how we ever found our way out again. The acute senses of the Indian, however, took care of that. With his naked legs he slipped through leading the way, everywhere scarcely touching the ground in his dexterity, a fact that astonished us greatly; only from time to time did he stand still, at places where the sky peeped through, looking at it attentively and then hastening on again. I could only imagine that he was observing the movement of the clouds in order to orient himself. Even in the shaded woods the heat was ghastly, and already we were pining for a drink of water; but since neither a river nor a spring was to be found, we thought we would wither away. Then the Indian pointed out a thick shoot and made us understand that this was fresh water, something we would not have grasped earlier, until he had cut down a piece of the same and out trickled a clear liquid with which I filled my cup eight or ten times. I recognized this climbing vine as cissus and as a result made use of this experience on frequent occasions.

Many times over I convinced myself that the actual virgin forests are poor in parasitic plants like orchids, bromeliads, and so forth.[2] They are all the richer, however, in handsome trees and small palms, especially parlor palms, a few of which reach a height of twenty feet. Indescribably beautiful, however, are the wild fig trees, which through their highly peculiar growth and their thick aerial roots reaching to the ground sometimes seem to form Gothic doors, windows, or even small colonnades, and in no small way surprise the wanderer.

As we collected specimens we were thus charmed and astonished by the inexhaustible power of nature that manifested itself at every step. Without knowing where, we had followed our guide as he returned us to a good road and shortly after that to the village. Already a crowd of people awaited me there; a few of them had come here hours before in hopes that I would give them a cure for this or that malady. I satisfied them as well as I was able, and when I left Pueblo Viejo on April 29, I did so against the wishes of the inhabitants, who would have liked to keep us in their area for still longer.

Next we traveled to the rancho of Tres Encinos ("three oaks"), whose owner, an Indian, likewise belonged to my coterie of patients. It lay an hour southeast of the above-mentioned village and is surrounded with plantations of sugarcane, out of which the people prepare a form of sugar syrup with extremely crude apparati; here the syrup is called *panela,* in other provinces, *pa nucha.* We were well received beyond expectations, put up free of charge, and roamed through a great part of the woods, which entirely resembled those described above.

On the same day we rode through deserted and rather bleak estates—for the climate in this place is highly feverish and quite prejudicial for settlements—to Chicuhuite, a way station for mule drivers (*paraje de los arrieros*) on the main road from Veracruz to Córdoba. Since this region is really far superior to that of Mirador, its few houses have a different form of construction. Like most of those of the tierra caliente they are assembled from cane; their owners hang hammocks, are far more lightly dressed, and worry themselves far less about agriculture than is the case with those in the mountains.

At the same time a mule train numbering into the hundreds and laden with wares for the capital city now arrived here, and the formerly deserted plaza now sprang to life in an extraordinary fashion. The arrieros wore unique clothing, consisting of white underpants, over which they don wide leather trousers (*calzoneras*) slit down the side and decorated with many small buttons on a red waistband. In addition to that they sported long knives and their bright gold- or silver-trimmed hats. These arrieros now moved about the plaza to load their mules, something they accomplished with unbelievable speed. Others hastened to prepare corn as fodder and to drive the animals to the watering place, while still others were busy lighting fires in order to prepare their own meals. With night falling these different groups made an interesting picture, and I regret only being able to hint at it with my pen.

Of all Mexicans the arriero is the most industrious, and as such is the most honest man. One must come to terms with them over freight and over the time of the delivery, but having done so, one can trust that merchandise to them with confidence. They transport it scrupulously, if nothing particularly unlucky comes upon them, like an attack of great bandit gangs, to whose power they must yield on the spot. The arriero is the sole representative, I would say, of the working class in Mexico, and his life is a constant wandering upon the road.

One usually counts on six to eight mules to an arriero; if the animals' number is very large, they form a *chinchorro, recua,* or *atajo,*[3] which again are led by certain head arrieros providing supervision. These teams depart very early, and after feeding usually make five to six leagues on a day's journey without stopping for a single meal, a method the Mexican for the most part observes regularly on his journeys. The mules are laden with burdens of three hundred to four hundred pounds, but cannot easily travel the abovementioned distance under this circumstance. On journeys where the mule must follow a trotting horse, the weight cannot exceed two hundred pounds or eight Mexican *arrobas.* With the heaviest saddles, which consist of a form of large cushions laid upon both sides, the animals suffer tremendously from the pressure of the cargo, and often when they are unbridled one can see the red flesh of the abraded hide. Consequently, however, the arriero knows an abundance of native herbal remedies, and in the absence of these he perhaps takes advantage of tobacco ash or dust to dry the wound, or rubs it with lard. As long as the journey is not complete the muleteer will not spare the mules at all, and his only concession is to see to it that the loading on both sides be as equal as possible. For this reason arrieros only reluctantly accept voluminous objects, because for want of a suitable counterweight they must fasten them onto the middle of the back, something that is all the more unwieldy since the arrangement of the packsaddle is scarcely appropriate for that purpose. As soon as the train is in motion, then begins the arriero's true worry; for the shouting to drive on the mules is endless, and here the cargo has to be bound down, there an animal that has fallen has to be put right, or otherwise some disorder in the train must be cleared away.

Even from afar one recognizes the approach of a chinchorro through the ringing of the bells that garland the mules in the front of the line, and the arriero must be truly cautious not to allow himself to be injured by the heavily laden animals, who pace continually. In this manner the arriero makes an uninterrupted journey of one hundred or more leagues, and only then does he allow himself and his animal to rest a bit.[4]

When we set out the next day, nothing more was to be seen of the arrieros for a long time. We followed the second main road from Veracruz to Mexico, which leads over Córdoba, and which must still be called a very difficult one for us, in order to reach the national capital. But compared to previous hardships we found it not only comfortable but in fact quite lovely. Immediately after Chicuhuite we came upon two stone bridges that I already mentioned in connection with the river. These extended over two small barrancas, on which the road stretched onto an elevation from which we enjoyed the most splendid view of the tierra caliente spreading gently outward toward the ocean in the most varied hues.

Since the road stretched almost level from this elevation to Córdoba, we made the remaining seven leagues in four and a half hours, and for that reason arrived at this small city at 11:00. Córdoba occupies one of the most enchanting places I know, reposing on a small ridge over the highly fertile soil of the hot country. It was founded in the time of the Huatusco florescence by the wealthy inhabitants of this city, and in those days such prosperity reigned in the city that it was ranked among the richest of the colony. Now it numbers only slightly more than five thousand inhabitants, with four churches, a few schools, and a prefect. The streets are paved and straight, and throughout bear the names of different flowers: for example, *calle de rosa, de jasmín, de amistad* (cotton rose), and so forth. A huge plaza with lovely houses stands in the middle; behind it tower two royal palms, whose height so greatly astonished me that I did not spare myself the trouble of measuring them. I found that they reach 150 feet, and I am inclined to consider them the tallest palm in America.

It was already market day, and I managed to see a great many fruits that were new to me, among which the zapotes, mameys, small coconuts, and

"It was already market day, and I managed to see a great many fruits that were new to me, among which the zapotes, mameys, small coconuts, and even apricots figure prominently." This photo—actually from Tuxtla Gutiérrez, Chiapas—illustrates the abundance of wares and faces that so captivated Heller. (Photo courtesy of the Latin American Library, University of Texas at Austin)

even apricots figure prominently. Two inns furnish a suitably tolerable and cheap lodging, but the traveler does not think of them as being on the same level as a European inn, since in the rooms of a *mesón* he finds nothing more than four walls and a wooden bed.

Córdoba pleased me endlessly. However, since I had never had the opportunity to be able to collect much in that place, I soon returned to Huatusco, setting out on the road over San Juan Coscomatepec, which is a stretch of twelve leagues or fifteen hours,[5] which we traversed in one trip, even though we had to pass two barrancas, of which the first is called Tomatlán, and is where the previously mentioned Cotaxtla River descends. The second was San Juan, which we had passed earlier on our trip to the volcano Orizaba. On this day we were in the saddle eight hours without rest, and the reader will thus discern that I was already broken in to riding, far more so than when I had left Veracruz a half year earlier.

The sinking sun of May 1846 pleasantly illuminated our small house in Huatusco as we arrived there.

Chapter 8

After completing this last journey I seriously contemplated making my way to the interior of the nation. However, two circumstances delayed the execution of this plan: in the first place, of course, the political conditions of Mexico; and secondly, an illness that held me prisoner in my house for a long time.

In chapter 5 I already hinted a bit over the looming war with North America. What one feared in those days had not truly come to pass. Mexico, which wanted to prevent Texas's annexation into the union of North America, had issued a declaration of war, in consequence of which in the month of March an American army of three thousand men had already approached the boundary of the disputed land in the vicinity of Corpus Christi. This force had divided itself into two parts, of which the weaker, under General Zachary Taylor, had established a position near Tamaulipas, and the stronger, under General Worth, along the Río Bravo near Matamoros. Opposite them stood the Mexican General Arista with approximately four thousand infantry and a thousand cavalry. For a long time the two forces sat there facing one another without attempting anything beyond reconnaissance parties, until finally on March 22, 1846, the American troops occupied Tamaulipas on one side and Matamoros on the other, and with that the invasion of Mexican territory had begun in earnest.

Initially, Arista conducted operations well, and managed to cut through the enemy forces with his cavalry, under Torejón. Failing to make sufficient use of this advantage, however, he had to surrender said position, and when a battle erupted between the two armies on May 7, Arista had to evacuate the field of Palo Alto defeated after a desperate resistance and begin his return journey. At this point the Americans formally occupied Matamoros, and thereafter Reynosa and Camargo, thus placing themselves in control of three cities of the Mexican adversary. Almost at the same time, on May 20, all Mexican ports were placed under a blockade, to which end American warships passed to all points and on June 5 closed down the maritime trade for the appointed time.

Under these circumstances I hastened to send to Europe everything I had collected before the blockade was complete. But since we still awaited a peaceful resolution, I therefore decided to pass some time in Huatusco, in order to be able to anticipate the outcome of the matter, when a second mishap suddenly befell me in this place. Namely, at the end of May a form of diarrhea seized me, an illness that soon became a mucous dysentery and brought me very near to death.

Abandoned as I was, without the assistance of a doctor, I mixed the most effective medicine possible. Only large quantities of laudanum quieted my suffering for a short time. The disease always broke out again twice as strong, and no treatment seemed any more effective. Fourteen days had passed without relief, and since I could not bear any form of food, my strength was so diminished that I could scarcely drag myself to the medicine chest. The end of my life seemed near. For that reason, and as far as my strength allowed it, I put all my papers and all my worldly affairs in order, so that in the most extreme case I could cross over peacefully to another life. The illness persisted a few days more, until on June 20 the symptoms were so severe that I had no hope of surviving the night. I called my faithful Pancho (a diminutive of Francisco) to my side. To me he was a trustworthy lad. I had selected him in Mirador, and during the time he was my apprentice he became accustomed to rigorous discipline in performing many services useful to me. He cleaned, fed, and saddled the horses, had understood perfectly how to load the mules, was himself like all Mexicans a first-rate rider, knew how to quickly prepare chocolate (the most customary evening and morning beverage in the land), and had the advantage of not drinking to excess. However, it was necessary to treat him like almost all Mexicans, that is, either with great severity or with great kindness. In the course of time we had become so attached that his only wish was to be able to serve me always, and in fact he accompanied me until the moment I set sail from Veracruz to Yucatán. I told him with a broken voice: "Pancho, I'm going to die. For that reason, take my black horse with the velvet saddle as a keepsake for yourself, since you have served me faithfully. But after I am dead show a little respect and bury me under the great sycamore tree where I have so often sat. Take these papers to Veracruz and give my final farewell to my friends in Mirador!" Pancho wept and kissed my hand, and again swore that he would do everything. I felt, however, that my heart bled with the thought of having to leave a world upon which I had only just begun to tread; but with sadness I tranquilly looked death in the face, and every breath seemed to me more difficult until instinctively I closed my eyes.

When I opened them again the morning was dawning. Pancho slumbered at my feet. "You still live, then!" I called to myself, and like an echo it chimed again joyfully within me: "You live, you live."[1]

The sun pleasantly illuminated everything around me; Pancho now awakened, dared not to speak until I cried, "Oh, take me out into the open air; let me once more behold Nature in all her splendor, and then, if it is the will of God, I will die." Pancho did as instructed. But what a wonder! In deep gasps I inhaled the fragrant breezes of the scented flowers, and with every breath I felt that my life force grew stronger, at last the thought awoke in me with lightning speed: "No, you are not dying, you must live—you are saved!" For the first time tears rolled down my cheeks onto America's soil, tears of joy and thanks that it pleased heaven to extend my days. And so it was, the crisis had been surmounted and from that unforgettable moment onward I was better. Thereafter, whenever I think of that time a strange feeling of deep emotion seizes me, a sensation of joyful astonishment over the almost miraculous recovery of my life. Dear reader, may you never come to so bleak a predicament as that which befell me, the lonely and abandoned wanderer. May you never experience how difficult it is to say good-bye to the world in a place where no tear can fall on your weathered grave, indeed, where perhaps you must even consider yourself lucky if there is a kindly soul who buries you.

After a few days, during which I quickly recovered, I ventured onto the horse led by my trusty Pancho, but in spite of my cautiously chosen diet, which consisted of nothing more than water and sago flour cooked in some red wine, I still felt the consequences of this disease quite palpably for a long time, and only fully recovered when I had lived for a longer period on the high plains of Mexico. In the belief, therefore, that only a trip to the interior could fully heal me, I hastened to abandon Huatusco, even though the epoch unfavorable for traveling, the rainy season, had been coming on since the beginning of June.

The rainy season in Mexico begins at different times, shifting between the months of May and August according to the elevation of the land over sea level. At an altitude of three to six thousand feet on the eastern slope of the cordillera it usually commences in June and lasts a full three months. During this same period the morning heat is tremendous, but white clouds appear early on the horizon, clouds that gather with force and around noon begin to discharge themselves with fearful power. The elements then seem to engage in the most terrible struggle. Countless lightning bolts cut through the air, the thunder resounds a thousand times in the mountains, and the water comes down in such torrents that brooks turn into rivers, and rivers into rolling masses of water that threaten to destroy all things. The wanderer often finds himself in great danger when surprised by such downpours, since the water is capable of sweeping him away altogether. After this discharge has lasted three to five hours, however, a lovely evening usually follows and a still lovelier morning, in which the damp air pleasantly cools the heat.

When I felt myself sufficiently strong, I made preparations to depart. All unnecessary items were left in Huatusco, and only the indispensable was taken along in order to make my cargo, which consisted of two medium-size trunks of identical weight, as light as possible for the mules. We shod the hitherto unshod horses, polished and sharpened our weapons, and selected for ourselves clothing that was appropriate to the nation. Most prominently this included the huge, broad-brimmed hat of the Mexican, which is useful against both sun and rain; enormous spurs; and a waterproof blanket that is pulled over the body and is called the *serape.* Before I abandoned this place that had grown so dear to me, however, I made one more visit to Mirador, Zacuapan, and Esperanza in order to say farewell to my esteemed friends there. Indeed, it was highly doubtful that I would ever see them again, given the political conditions of the country and the extreme danger of the journey. For me parting was terribly difficult, in part because I had here realized my most audacious dreams, in part because a secret misgiving told me that from now on my luck in the Americas had run out. The course of my travel narrative will show how right or wrong I was.

On July 2, 1846, the team, consisting of myself, Herr Fink, and Pancho, were all mounted and well armed, and my loaded mule ready for travel. Each of us showed that deep inside we were steeled against whatever might come, and we set out on the road to the city of Orizaba. We silently pushed on at a trot over the difficult road, parts of which the rain had once more rendered bottomless mud, when suddenly my mule sank to his ears in a hole. It cost us no little work to get the animal out again, even though we instantly cut the cargo loose, and only the beast's prodigious efforts saved me from losing him. We passed without further incident through the barranca of San Juan, which I have mentioned so often, and reached the village of Tomatlán, where a road on the left leads to Córdoba, and another on the right to Orizaba. The rain came down in torrents, and the bad road was exhausting, thus limiting us to no more than six leagues for the day.

Tomatlán is a small village in the mountains. In earlier times it had a greater importance, as one could recognize from the decayed *casa constitorial.*[2] The scanty population lives freely among the mountains and occupies itself chiefly with cultivating corn. We found meager lodgings in the house where a small store is located, and for beds we had to content ourselves with the ground.

Early the next morning we rode out from there and soon reached the barranca of Tomatlán, upon which followed a small altiplano that stretched almost to Orizaba. It lies approximately four thousand feet above sea level, is surrounded by stately mountain ranges, and owing to poor drainage would have been almost entirely underwater during the rainy season had providence not carved out the huge barranca of Metlaque. If not for the inundations, the road through it would have been one of the most pleasant imaginable. But we rode on thus for half an hour until ankle deep in water, and as we reached the barranca we came to realize that the river within it had grown so furious that we could not pass it without great danger, even if we had known the pass in precise detail. In fact, several mules had perished in that river in recent days. Since we had little choice, we named an Indian as guide in order that he show us the way.

Soon we had reached the banks of the raging mountain stream. With our horses Fink and I plunged waist deep into the river and made it to the opposite bank, struggling successfully against the current with all the horsemanship we could muster. From here we pulled across the mule laden with his cargo to the other side, using a rope we had not forgotten to bring along; even so, the animal came close to being knocked down and carried away. At last followed my lad (or as the Mexican say, *mozo*). As I said, after we had this danger behind us, the road was more level, but covered so thick with mud that we approached the town of Orizaba quite slowly, and only reached it at 1:00 in the afternoon. Twelve leagues separate Huatusco from this town, and the vegetation is almost the same as in that aforementioned city.

Orizaba is a town of the third rank[3] and is situated in the basin of a limestone mountain range, through which a second highway leads to Mexico. But as poor as this mountain range might be for the botanist, it is just as rich for the landscape artist, since the immense masses, whose highest ridges are covered with conifers, form a picturesque scene. Orizaba lies four thousand feet above sea level, has five thousand inhabitants, six churches, a public school, and given its size demonstrates much commerce and liveliness. Since many travelers are accustomed to pass through here, we found a splendid lodging where we greatly enjoyed fare offered in the European style.

The factory of Cocolapan, a huge cotton mill, distinguishes itself among the sights worth seeing. This building is outstanding not only for its handsome construction but also for the splendid machinery inside, and constitutes one of the most stunning shops of the new era in Mexico. It was founded by Legrand and Company but was never finished, and was left almost entirely unused. Later this factory passed into the hands of Count Juan de Dios Pérez de Gálvez, a descendant of the immensely rich Gálvez family, of which so many anecdotes endure. In fact, their wealth was so great that in Havana they had built two enormous and fully fitted warships of mahogany and cedar, and gave them as a present to the king of Spain. Under the auspices of this wealthy heir the factory was completed; during my visit it only worked at half capacity because one of the huge waterwheel engines was broken.

The other half, however, afforded me the great pleasure to be able to see the entire processing of wool from its unrefined to finished state. This process in its totality is carried out by thoroughly ingenious iron machines that were manufactured in New York, and to be sure function so rapidly that they yield a vast body of white woolen cloth that enjoys a strong market within Mexico. At the present they have 12,000 spindles (*malacates*) and 240 looms in motion, with which they produce 730 pieces of *manta* at 32 yards weekly. When the factory is again in full operation, it will employ 1,800 men and produce on average 1,200 pieces weekly, and therefore close to 15,400 Mexican yards (at a width of 2.75 feet) monthly. The managers are mostly British; the second director, Franz Schmidt, is a German Swiss. Besides this textile plant, Orizaba has saddle factories and lumber mills that are even more famous.

I delayed my departure from Orizaba until the morning of June 5, which was a Sunday, for different reasons—principally, however, because of the many bandit groups that make the road from here to Mexico so extraordinarily unsafe. In order to elude them as much as possible, one must employ different stratagems. For example, the traveler tries to pass through dangerous places on a Sunday, when for the most part the bandits are accustomed to attending church.[4] In addition to this it is best to make an unexpected departure that one keeps in complete secrecy. In the same way, continually false declarations of the travel route can protect against many dangers.

Since my company was very modest, I had to take appropriate measures. The cruelties of the bandits in Mexico had started to multiply everywhere in consequence of the wars that had now begun and which had caused the security guards to disappear. Still, in those days I was constantly prepared to defend myself. It was hard to believe that the situation had reached such depths so soon after Mexico's declaration of independence. In particular a certain Gómez perpetrated the greatest cruelties, of which an Englishman named Dickson gives a frightful account. He was overtaken by many bandits under Gómez, and two of his company were murdered; he himself was left on the road with sixteen wounds. After many hours, some passing soldiers found him there near death and brought him to Puebla. Here he fortunately recovered, although he had a bullet in the abdomen and one of his hands was cut through nine times.

When I left Orizaba I was splendidly outfitted with three eleven-gauge shotguns at our disposal, not counting the sharply honed swords.[5] A well-paved street led from here through a sporadically swampy ground to the second mountain pass of the cordillera, which in any event we had to cross in order to reach the high plain of Puebla.

Although we now had no difficult terrain under us, on the other side of Orizaba we were in danger of being set upon by bandits at every moment. But since as I say we were firmly determined to defend our belongings, we therefore trotted along the road in good cheer. It led almost always through natural paths of pepper trees and thickets of Mexican juniper, among which splendid nightshade, verbena, Mexican poppies, small bulbous plants, and camote displayed their flowers. In the forests lying close to the mountains we glimpsed a cheerful hacienda here and there, or a village whose church steeple projected white as snow above the trees or the individual houses, things that gave winsome character to the landscape. In short, the road in the valley is splendid and greatly recalls many parts of the European Alps. It wound its way among the mountains, climbing gradually until it reached Aculzingo, a village at the foot of the same ridge that links the high sierra of Orizaba and the basin of Oaxaca. Its edge forms the boundary between the states of Veracruz and Puebla. A zigzagging road eases the difficulty of crossing the highest point (6,500 feet above sea level).

On this same day we came to Puente Colorado, a small, shabby-looking group of houses that lies in the valley on this side of the range, and which takes its name from the nearby bridge leading over the river. We had to pass the night in a wretched hut, and one whose inhabitants offered none of that hospitality to which we were accustomed in the region of Huatusco. We therefore lay down to rest with the greatest caution—our saddle as pillows, pistols in hand—since we did not believe we could completely trust these people. Such fear was not entirely unfounded, since this place had no small reputation for skulduggery. But the night, which we had deliberately cut short, ran well, and already at 4:00 the next morning we were once again under way, even though we had traversed nine leagues the day before.

We first reached the Cañada de Ixtapan. This is a level-bottomed valley, notorious on account of bandits, and in reality if there is any good place for such, this is it. On both sides of the road Mexican junipers form an undergrowth so dense that the wanderer's gaze cannot penetrate it; these woods serve all the better as an ambush for bandits. Although repeated attacks had taken place in recent days, we fortunately managed to get through, and soon reached the small village of Ixtapan, which was situated on the high plateau of Puebla. A crowd of people flocked toward the hamlet Tlacotepec, which lies to the left of the range and where a huge church festival was being held.

This lucky coincidence might have protected us from an unpleasant encounter, and we accordingly rode care-free on the high plains.

Since we entered it in the rainy season, the altiplano was now entirely transformed, and the picture I paint of it here is one quite different from that which presented itself when I visited Los Derrumbados. The vast, barren sandy waste was changed into a cheerful-looking flatland covered with splendid green. Field upon field lay in rows; corn, wheat, barley, and beans stood partly blooming, partly with fruit. The loose sand, which when stirred up by the wind in the dry season covered the traveler with every puff of breeze, was now held fast by the moisture and through the roots of the plants, and only had free room to play on the road itself. On the edge of the same, stately trees and flowering plants such as camote, Mexican poppy, cinnamon, and nightshade emerged unexpectedly. Where there were no fields there arose a mass of yucca and cactus, while in the grass the astonishing forms of *Mammillaria,* together with barril, melon, and *Cereae* cacti, commanded the traveler's attention. Everywhere, however, one notices immense numbers of agave, which in part grow wild, in part are routinely cultivated for the extraction of pulque, and very much give to the landscape its singular character. Beside the agaves stood hedges of crested cactus, which with their high, stiff trunks form a row like organ pipes and by means of their thorns create an impenetrable palisade.

On this day, shortly before it began to rain as always, we reached San Agustín del Palmar, a sizable village in the middle of the boundless plain. A handsome church and a huge plaza adorn this place, which lies twenty-nine leagues from Huatusco and where we found rather good accommodations. The significant change of our location manifested itself here in many ways. Instead of water, which here has a rather salty taste owing to concentrations of soda, the people universally drink pulque, which initially we could only swallow in drops owing to its unsavory aftertaste. Instead of the horse fodder common on the eastern side—corn, corn husks, and sugarcane—here one uses straw and cereals, which taste as unappetizing to the unaccustomed beasts as does pulque to the traveler.

On July 7 we pushed on once more. The plateau remained more or less the same, and vegetation such as barril and *Cereae* cacti appeared more frequently only in the vicinity of the village Chula, so that one cannot easily ride through without exposing the horse to wounds from its thorns. Between this village and San Simón the traveler passes another spot notorious because of banditry. This is the small Barranca Honda (that is, "deep ravine"), which we fortunately passed, and straightaway reached Acatzingo.

In the distance there rose a few small mountain ranges; these too seemed to be limestone, and break up the monotony of the landscape to some degree. However, while the region itself is one of the most beautiful parts of the limitless high plain, it nevertheless seems to me quite poor to the botanist. On a small excursion I made into the region the very same evening I found nothing more than a few flowering maples, maurandia, evening primrose, climatus, begonias, and the above-mentioned cacti.

Acatzingo is a considerable village thirty-nine leagues from Huatusco, with six churches and a lovely plaza that is surrounded by houses with corridors set at right angles. Sadly, the inhabitants of this village also enjoy no very good reputation because of the many bandit raids that take place there. But since I had come so far without mishap, I therefore began to doubt very much the correctness of the bad reports of this road, although I remained completely faithful to my system of giving out a false travel route.

The room of the mesón where we had spent the night was the essence of simplicity. Beyond the door, the four empty walls had no opening whatsoever. A form of broad wooden bench constituted the bed, without anything that could have given it any semblance of a resting place. Not even a table was found in the same, and in order not to have to set the light on the floor, the wall included a small shelf on which lamps or candles could be placed. The fare was bad as well, so that we received nothing beyond a few pieces of cooked meat and beans, which moreover we had to consume in the presence of many suspicious faces that watched us closely. But the night passed well, without any mishap. Just when we saddled up our horses the next morning, a troupe of travelers appeared, consisting of a Mexican with his wife and servant. Since in this region it is not customary to join company with persons one does not know well, it thus happened that we let these same folks push on ahead, and when we looked out the doorway they were already out of sight.

The road ran along small ditches formed of scarcely more than a foot of water. The trees of the altiplano, already described earlier on many occasions, formed a perfect hiding place by the side of the road, and for that reason bandit attacks are frequent in that area. We had already ridden a good stretch further without meeting anyone, when the road ran uphill slightly and concealed the view from us. We redoubled our caution, and scarcely had we reached a small elevation when we glimpsed a group of men who at a distance of a few hundred steps appeared to be occupied with something. My lad immediately cried out, "Son ladrones, esperamos, esperamos!"[6] Doubting the matter, I swore to him that we would go forward in any event, and ordered them to hold their weapons ready.

We approached almost unobserved to within gunshot range, and by the sunlight glinting on Toledo swords I now recognized five bandits on horseback, who were at that moment busy robbing a group of people. Suddenly they spotted us, and one of the thieves, who also saw our swords shimmering, cried "Aquí vienen señores con armas!"—"Here come men with arms!"—and in that same instant threw themselves against us with force.

Fearing that I could not shoot securely enough on horseback, I quickly dismounted, laid the gun over the saddle, and tranquilly waited for what might come. After the bandits saw this they halted and called out a "Párense!"—"Surrender!" But I replied to them with a ball from my gun. Perhaps it was my anxiety or the unforeseen nature of this attack: this much was certain, that not one of them tumbled to the ground. In spite of that, something had to have happened, for the frontmost two abandoned the field of battle and did not return. Three more still remained, and since the battle was now a bit more even, I quickly mounted my steed and leapt to the company of Fink, raising a six-barrel pistol and the sharp, polished sword flying freely over the remaining three. Crafty as they were, however, these bandits seemed to recognize that our powerful weapons were dangerous, and tried to intimidate us through an audacious maneuver. They sprang just as quickly at us, and since this quickness prevented us from taking accurate aim, one of them got to within saber's length and fell upon me. However, I stepped aside in a lucky moment and the point of his sword penetrated my left knee only slightly.

All this was the work of a moment, and in fact seemed to have been calculated to intimidate us, so that they could quickly carry off what they had robbed from the other travelers. And in reality they made no second attempt against us, but rather abruptly seized their victims' pack animal and rode cross-country with it. A pursuit was now in order, and as strongly as possible Fink and I urged that we hasten after these wicked individuals. The bandits, observing that step by step we came nearer, now abandoned the pack animal and disappeared behind a group of trees. Since pursuit was strongly inadvisable, we therefore contented ourselves with the recaptured mule and returned to the plaza, where the victimized travelers, the same who had left before us in the mesón in Acatzingo, still sat with altered faces in the corner. It cost no little trouble to convince the Mexican and his wife, who had almost been rendered speechless from horror, that we were not robbers, but rather had arrived to save them. Only when we returned the previously lost animal to them did they recover little by little and begin to trust us. Nevertheless, in their haste the bandits had taken the rings of the woman and a beautiful shawl, or *mantilla,* and one of the robbers had mounted the travelers' handsome old horse, upon which he rode away when chased from there. But the poor people were joyful to have kept their freight and their lives, poured out their thanks to us, and begged to be allowed to travel to Puebla under our protection, a favor we were only too happy to grant.

When the entire retinue was again in order we moved on, keeping up our guard as much as possible, since a second and fiercer attack was not impossible. Luckily we reached the hamlet San Bartolo and then in an hour Amozoc, even though the woman did not tire of reminding us of all the dangerous characters about, and of seeing every person who came across us as a bandit.

Amozoc is a large village where two main roads from Veracruz to Mexico converge, one passing through Xalapa and the other through Orizaba. It is famous for the production of handsome Mexican spurs and horse bits, which enjoy a vaunted reputation throughout the entire republic. From here there are still four leagues to Puebla, and we fortunately reached this city at 3:00 in the afternoon. From the *garita* (gate and customhouse) a splendid new street and bridge lead into the city, on which now labors a gang of prisoners loaded with chains. At this same place our adventure was placed on record, and in consequence of our heroic deeds we marched into the street untaxed and unquestioned for passports.

Chapter 9

After Mexico City, Puebla is the largest city of the republic, and bears the name "de los Angeles" because legend holds that angels helped build the Cathedral. In many respects Puebla is almost more beautiful than the capital itself. The streets run at right angles, are well paved, and are provided with sidewalks. Thoroughly charming flat-roofed houses constructed in medieval style rise to multiple stories and now and then form splendid lanes—such as, for example, the Calle de Mercaderes, de Mesones, and others.

Puebla is estimated to have sixty to seventy thousand inhabitants, and in spite of the fact that two-thirds belong to the poorer classes, luxury reigns in the stores, icehouses, and cafés, a luxury almost like that of Europe. Just as common is a huge number of idle dandies who roam the streets in European clothing. What the foreigner finds most ridiculous, however, is the fashion that prevails in every Mexican city, of going about with Spanish cloth overcoats; often, to be sure, this also serves to cover up the remaining bad clothing. Still, it is a fact that otherwise respectable people make no exception to the practice.

In proportion to the other cities Puebla has very few foreigners; moreover, the common folk also stand in an ill repute, proof that in spite of the crowd of churches and clergymen and the religious fanaticism that follows, morality is not highly developed. To the contrary, the inhabitants live in luxury just as do the other offspring of the Spanish. The rooms of the larger houses are mostly tiled with porcelain and adorned with fresco paintings or stucco-covered walls, which enclose a plaza with corridors.

In Puebla there are different inns of good quality; some are furnished as much as possible with European art. I selected the mesón El Cristo, which is rented by a Frenchman, but I certainly found nothing of that comfort which I had been led to expect. Nevertheless, I still considered it very good, for I was accustomed to bad lodgings and for that reason was easily satisfied.

In the short time of my stay I hastened to visit the notable sights of the city, and among them I identify the following. The huge plaza (*plaza mayor*)

"In spite of the mass of silver that has been carried away, there remain many altars crafted entirely from this material. Its construction involved extravagant and almost unbelievable sums." The Puebla cathedral still retains its grandeur. (Photo courtesy of the Latin American Library, University of Texas at Austin)

is an extended square surrounded by houses with corridors (*portales*) that allow protection from the rain and sun and are filled with stores of all conceivable objects. In the middle of this same place rises the Cathedral, a structure that in its style belongs to the most handsome and most opulent in the world. It was completed in 1540 under Charles V, and inside is so overloaded with silver that its aesthetic beauty is almost lost thereby. In spite of the mass of silver that has been carried away, there remain many altars crafted entirely from this material. Its construction involved extravagant and almost unbelievable sums; out of a total of 3 million pesos used to decorate the nave, then-bishop Juan Palafox y Mendoza used 1.5 million of his own on the project. He used all the varieties of marble in the state of Puebla. In the middle of the church Palafox constructed the Temple, or the so-called Cypress, where bishops of Puebla are buried, and which surely cost so much that one might well have constructed it two times over from pure silver. The statue of the Madonna that stands upon it, and which was poured from massive quantities of silver, alone surely weighs 320 *arrobas,* or 8,000 pounds, so that in case of emergency one can therefore mint from this single figure 128,000 pesos. This same luxury also reigns in all forms of sacred vestments and carpets which contain the costliest gold embroidery. Moreover, the church possesses such an important treasure of pure gold that during the 1834 revolution the Federalists broke into the same and carried away the pesos in wheelbarrows.

Outside the church stand two stately towers, one of which bears a clock weighing ten thousand pounds and from which the traveler enjoys an unusually lovely and interesting view. At his feet he finds the houses of Puebla built at right angles; above these, more than one hundred towers rise from seventy-two buildings where religious services are held, and among which are counted forty-three huge churches. From there the gaze passes over the fertile high plains to the east. At its sides stand the cordilleras, while the volcano Orizaba looms in the middle, toward the west; together with Popocatépetl and Iztaccíhuatl, these features form the plateau's boundaries. The visitor gazes in astonishment at the three snowcapped giants, and this magnificent sight allows itself to be felt, certainly, but not described.

In addition to the Cathedral, noteworthy churches include that of San Felipe de Neri and Espíritu Santo (the latter of which was connected with a lovely Jesuit college) and the cloister of San Agustín and Dominico. Another splendid building is the spiritual sanctuary where repentant persons can atone for their sins in a brief time. It enjoys considerable revenues and is used by more than a thousand persons each year; they are received in that same place free of charge throughout the week, and through prayer and fasting prepare themselves for the holy sacraments.

Puebla possesses good educational services, among which the Palafox Museum with its abundant public library, the theological and medical school, and additional small colleges stand out as the best in the republic. Here too one finds a top-notch law court, two textile factories, and one for soap; the *teatro principal* is also worth mentioning. Finally, for the inhabitants' pleasure a small promenade decorated with trees and flowers lies outside the city, but despite its proximity to the houses of residence it is not infrequently visited by bandits.

After I had taken in all the sights of the city, I used a lovely morning to make an excursion to Cholula, where looms the famous pyramid of the same name. It lies only two leagues away, and the road is level, so that we soon reached it. Cholula is presently a small place, but before the Mexican conquest it was one of the largest cities of the Americas and the cradle of ancient Mexican civilization.[1] In the modern day, with the cultivation of fields in the entire expanse from Cholula to Puebla, one finds remains of structures, so that in agreement with the letters of Cortés there is almost no doubt over the earlier connection of these two points. More than anything, the pyramid hints at a dense concentration of people that existed here, and it belongs to the greatest works of ancient times. In fact, the form can no longer be easily recognized. Since it is overgrown with bushes and has a small church built on top, the structure is more likely to be taken for a hill than for a Mexican pyramid or teocalli. Closer inspection, however, soon shows it to be the work of human hands.

Alexander von Humboldt describes this antiquity in detail in his work on New Spain, volume 2, page 133, and says that it consists of four terraces, on top of one another, built out of sun-dried bricks (*adobe*) and covered with a variety of mandelstone.[2] In spite of my detailed inspection I could only make out three terraces. I am convinced that in reality the entire mass is built of adobe, for I could determine nothing mandelstone; doubtless this latter is nothing more than a layer of plaster, which even today at different places I have seen made out of sand, water, and unslaked lime.

Presently the height of the pyramid comes to 170 feet, the horizontal length of the base 1,388 feet, and the platform has a surface area of 13,285 square meters. The four sides of the same are perfectly aligned to the four cardinal directions, a circumstance that was observed with all monuments of similar form.

The small church is a very neat construction where services are still held daily, but the panoramic view is unrivaled. At not too great a distance rises the Sierra de Malinche,[3] far to the west the Nevado de Popocatépetl, and in the far east the Nevado or eternally snowcapped ridge of Orizaba. At one's feet stretch the rich and fertile high plain, cultivated with agave and grain fields—in short, it is an enchanting vision! One reflects upon the fact that the entire region was one of the bloodiest stages of the wars of conquest, and Cortés, the glittering star of that era, might often have stood on this point, as still thousands more crowded around. So too, it was here where the great Toltecs had preserved their blessing, bringing knowledge that they imparted to the Aztecs. A certain tingling thus seizes the wanderer as he stands on this consecrated soil, where every mountain, every tree, every rock, every stone recounts to him something different from the book of history. Swept away by the force of such an impression, he believes himself to be cast back into that era!

Still another object in Cholula calls the attention of the traveler, and that is the church of San Francisco, which was built by Cortés himself. No more services are held in it, since the altars are destroyed, but the entire structure is perfectly preserved. First of all the main door commands the wonder of the visitor. It is hobbled throughout with large-headed nails, each of which carries its own seal on top. Also remarkable is the design of the church itself, which consists of a number of equally high, flattened cupolas that rest on four columns each and thus intersect the interior in avenues.

I have later seen this structure in other churches in Yucatán. I know with certainty that they were over three hundred years old,[4] and for that reason it appears not unlikely that San Francisco originated from the time of Cortés. I could obtain no sufficient explanation, however, concerning the symbols on the nails of the main door. I returned satisfied to Puebla, since I had seen many and great things that day.

I had made the journey to Puebla in such an uninterrupted effort that both my horse and I were completely worn out, all the more so since my former illness temporarily made itself felt. For that reason I selected the so-called *diligencia,* a post carriage connection that crosses between Veracruz and the nation's interior in order to continue on to Mexico City. The coaches of this diligencia are quite sturdy and well built according to the English style, and the transportation is conducted by North American postilions and with the help of very good mules, which in spite of the poor roads are changed in appointed stations with unbelievable swiftness. The diligencia from Veracruz to Mexico, for example, thus travels some three hundred miles in one night and three days.

Sadly, the traveler never risks more danger of being robbed than when he uses this conveyance, and in the last three days it was assaulted daily and the passengers forced out. In vain the newspapers raise their voice to the government to portray the fear generated by these highway misdeeds. No institution will be found to remedy this immense nuisance; in fact, justice in Mexico goes so far as to free the captured bandits again after a few days, either because disguises used during the attack conceal the culprit's identity or because judges fear the revenge of the bandit's associates who still remain free, an entirely possible turn of events.

However, in order to avoid the appearance of aiding and abetting criminals, they have recently stationed a small cavalry escort at the most dangerous points between Puebla and Mexico City, a strategy which at least for a time made this road somewhat safer. But that escort generated its own problems. Indeed, at every sentry point the traveler is forced to give copious presents to the four or six returning men, something they demand with arms in hand.

But the traveler gladly complies, because he prefers to settle with these legitimate bandits over a few pesos than let himself be formally robbed by others. In a word, he is compelled to choose the lesser of two evils.

After I had sent out my mozo in advance with the animals and luggage, I departed Puebla on July 11 at 4:00 in the morning. In order to reach the valley of Mexico, one must necessarily climb over the second cordillera. This climb begins with the notable village San Martín, seven leagues beyond Puebla. The road from here onward is quite good and remains so for the rest of the journey, even though at one point it climbs 11,835 feet into the Sierra Nevada. This road has to overcome enormous difficulties, just as in the stretch from Veracruz to Perote; it is certainly one of the greatest works of the modern era in Mexico, and had already preoccupied Alexander von Humboldt, in whose presence it was planned more than forty years ago.

From San Martín the road leads almost constantly through immense pine forests that offer countless hiding places to highwaymen. The bandits so well know how to use this opportunity that the traveler could not identify the most dangerous spot were it not indicated by the greater or lesser number of crosses the religious Mexicans place to commemorate murders.

The traveler's breath becomes extremely short near the highest places in the road, at the Río Frío, where the air is already quite thin and the climate almost European. Here a German by the name of David has built a lodge that provides a good table and warming drinks of the best quality. I could not help but ask him how he conceived the idea to settle down in a place that stationed him practically in the center of Mexico's bandit hordes. He answered, however, that the business was so profitable that he had to live on good terms as much with the bandits as with the travelers, so as not to risk being slaughtered by the former in a moment of anger. And in reality he has now resided for years in Río Frío, is known as an honorable character, and has made advances of money and clothing to many travelers in need. His inn is truly one of the most charitable in the world.

With the help of the above-mentioned escort we came without attack through the forests and the infamous Barranca de Juanes, traveling downhill for a long time already without having enjoyed anything in the way of a view. Only at the small hamlet of Venta de Córdoba, 9,345 feet above sea level, on the other side of the mountain range, did a wonderful scene present itself. To the left we beheld Lake Chalco on the plain of Mexico, to the right Lake Texcoco surrounded by green fields and ringed around by high, picturesque mountains. Small hills pleasantly interrupted the view and concealed the capital from the inquisitive wanderer until he has advanced a league further, at which point he comes upon immensely large dams (*calzados*) simultaneously serving as streets. These intersect the drainage land that grows larger from year to year as Lake Texcoco recedes, and ultimately lead into Mexico. This point is Peñón de los Baños, of which I will speak later. Handsome avenues led from here to the city gates, where we arrived at 5:00 in the afternoon. I stepped across the threshold with a joyful sensation, for I had now once again placed a huge multitude of dangers behind me.[5]

Chapter 10

Mexico City,[1] the republic's capital, lies 7,198 feet above sea level, numbers approximately 210,000 inhabitants, and is the home of the president and an archbishop. It has a university, several *colegios,*[2] many churches, two theaters, and a huge arena for bullfighting (*plaza de toros*). The streets intersect the city at right angles and are often six thousand to nine thousand feet long, well paved, and furnished with drains and sidewalks. Everywhere the buildings have a stately appearance and are mostly built from mandelstone or quartzless feldspathic porphyry. Its teeming multitude lends the city the appearance of imposing grandeur and points to the immense wealth that was assembled here in earlier times.

This new city of Mexico, which the Spaniards built in 1521 in the place of the destroyed old Mexico, will seem beautiful to everyone, even to someone accustomed to the greatest cities of Europe. The long and direct streets mentioned above, the lovely buildings, the stately plaza, the colonnades around the same, the luxurious stores, the animated hustle and bustle everywhere, the cafés and icehouses, the horses and carriages: in short, *everything* unites here to conjure up a European city.

Perhaps one who knows Mexico only through descriptions will be unable to imagine such a city in this republic, all the less if he has previously wandered through its areas of wilderness. And conversely, who can form an accurate notion of the condition of the country if he merely follows the main road and has come directly to Mexico City from Veracruz, via Jalapa and Puebla? I doubt that the republic would manifest such conditions if it had not earlier been built on Spanish wealth and luxury, nor would it profitably receive the huge multitude of foreigners, mostly salesmen and businessmen, who animate it in the present day. Such facts notwithstanding, foreign influence is insufficient to meet the commercial needs of the current regime. No improvements, no beautifications, no suitable arrangements for peace and security have been undertaken since the republic came into existence.

The cities and lands are without legal supervision, and an arrogant impunity reigns. The capital swarms with thieves who if necessary will also murder, and no day passes without at least one corpse being found on the streets. I regret to say that in spite of the Mexican's fanaticism there is perhaps no city as morally tainted as the capital. The hand of Spain once rested most heavily on this land; the self-interest of the motherland was clearly detrimental, but at least a certain law and order prevailed, one that reached to the furthermost province. These days, however, the Mexican government knows no more about its provinces than what it has learned from the works of Alexander von Humboldt—a man whose good advice it anything but obeyed—and it is sufficient to know that the state has made no effort at a census for fifteen years, despite a great deal of concern about the outlying provinces. For that reason it happens that Mexico, a country extraordinarily favored in its physical geography, a land that even under Spanish rule was in full bloom, at present deteriorates from year to year owing to the weakness of the government, and will soon collapse altogether if the necessary changes are not undertaken. I say once more that I sincerely regret the condition of the country, all the more since there are many men in whose breast true patriotism lives but who cannot resist the powerful alliance of greed and lust for power, men whose well-intentioned councils will be trampled upon, and whose love of truth will be held as treason to the fatherland. How can Mexico hope to win the present war with North America, when even now the undisciplined troops, as they advance on the Río Bravo, rob their fellow citizens instead of protecting them, and when they are everywhere more to be feared than the enemy himself?

Over the past four years Mexico City has in no way improved, for the reasons cited above, and if I give a description of the different points of interest it is in order to show what has changed for better or worse in most recent times. I begin with the huge plaza. This is one of the greatest and loveliest in the world; it forms a well-proportioned, beautifully paved rectangle 520 steps long and 330 steps wide, and is bounded on the north by the Cathedral, on the east by the former palace of the viceroy, currently the national government. Opposite this we find lovely buildings with colonnades, among them that of the Cortés family, while on the south side stands the former Casa de Cabildo, now the seat of the governor of Mexico. In earlier times the plaza was adorned with a masterfully realized bronze statue of King Charles IV of Spain on horseback, but it was removed in recognition of Mexico's independence, in order to erect a freedom pillar in its place. They placed this famous masterwork in a corner of the university building, with nothing more of that planned column, which was to form the new centerpiece of the plaza taking its place than the base, and in all probability it will never be completed.[3]

The Cathedral is constructed in the purest Doric style and comes rather close to the opulence of Puebla. From its many towers the visitor enjoys a first-rate panorama. But what greatly arouses the wonder of the traveler is the stone calendar of ancient Mexico positioned on the western side. It is cemented into that place and offers a key of extraordinary importance to the learning of ancient Mexican.[4] The church is built in the same place where the main temple of the Aztecs stood. The former was begun in 1553 and completed in 1657. The construction costs must have reached 3,504,000 florins in our money. The portals are everywhere adorned with reliefs and statues. On both sides of the same rise the towers, which were only fully completed in 1791, and in one of which one finds a clock weighing 15,000 pounds, in the other a clock of 14,900.

Beyond the Cathedral the most noteworthy buildings are the exclusive cloister of San Francisco, that of San Domingo, and the church of the cloister of the Profesa. Other buildings that astonish the visitor include the former Palace of the Inquisition, the Casa de Moneda, and the Acordada, an immense structure wherein are located the jails, in addition the Hospital de Jesús de los Naturales, which is dedicated to taking in poor children and elderly of the Indians, and was founded by Cortés. It is quite spacious, with a plaza in the center; the sickbeds are clean and well ventilated. In the chapel belonging to the same are found the earthly remains of the great conquistadores and founders of this institution.

Among the scientific institutions, a few deserve to be mentioned because of their former greatness, despite the fact that they have been in continual decline for some thirty years and I might even say are nearing their collapse. The Minería, or College of Mining, a splendid building by the famous master builder and sculptor Tolsa,[5] which in former times included collections on physics, mechanics, and mineralogy, is now worth seeing as little more than a monument of consummate architecture. The collections, once so outstanding, have by now fallen into a wretched state; and although a few first-rate individuals are found among the faculty, this institute has lost its brilliance and its importance.

The botanical garden, at the palace of the viceroy, was likewise a very interesting spot in earlier days, because there one rarely cultivated useful plants for private uses alone, but rather for the human race as well; but it now scarcely merits the name. The rudiments of isolated shrubbery are still found, to be sure, but of all the scientific layout nothing more remains, and everything appears so neglected that the visitor could sooner take the whole thing for a courtyard than for a botanical garden. A showpiece still remains, however: the huge *arbol de las manitas* (Mexican hand plant), which is noteworthy not only for its flowers but also for the fact that it is the only tree of this sort known to grow wild in the republic.[6]

The Academy of Bellas Artes surely gives the most tragic proof of the decline of the arts in Mexico. This institution was once so excellent in models and copper engravings, which have cost the Spanish government more than 80,000 florins, that even in Europe one could have found no better school for drawing and sculpture. Here, where rich and poor, white and Indian once trained together to produce so many noble and handsome works, one finds neither a school for drawing nor one for sculpture. The stately gypsum figures are mutilated and the collections generally neglected, like the entire building. To be sure, given the current condition of the country, one hopes in vain for a new florescence of this institute.

The university, a less handsome building, includes a library and several different faculties, which likewise are not very well represented. In addition there is a collection on which they have bestowed the name Museum of Mexico; it contains old and new artworks that I will here recount. In an entryway in the courtyard to the left, one first glimpses the huge sacrificial stone that was discovered on Isla de Sacrificios, and which is decorated with bas-reliefs that depict the triumphal procession of a Mexican king: the statue of the god Teoyaomiqui, an enormous stone mass nine feet high; a statue that depicts an anthropomorphic figure wrapped around with serpents, equipped with a necklace of human hearts, hands and skulls; and still other sculpted idols of two to three feet in height, which lie around covered with dust.[7] From here one comes to the first story, where the following objects are preserved in two galleries, partly in cases, partly on tables and on the walls.

1. Products of modern-day Mexico: silk textile, plaster impressions, coins, medallions, artwork in wax, models, a few sculptures and busts made in Rome from Mexican marble, and more artful counterfeits of precious stones.

2. Products of old Mexico: the *tambora,* a huge drum made out of a hollow tree trunk. The Teponaztlis, small drums of wood, which are more like a small, elongated case, one side of which consists of a gap of three different thicknesses, in order to be able to draw out three different tones.[8]

Enormous urns of clay for preserving the ashes of the dead, more with magnificent work and peculiar painting; bows and arrows, whose poison tips are made from slate/shale. War clubs of bone and serpentine, very much in the style of the New Zealand Indians; in addition, a huge collection of larger and altogether tiny arrow and lance heads of quartz, shale, and obsidian. A mass of cone- and hatchet-shaped instruments of serpentine, opal, chalcedony, quartz, basalt, and copper, with which they carried out all their reliefs and sculpture work (since they had no knowledge of iron), in a fashion inconceivable to us in the present day.

Oars and long clubs, carved in handsome fashion from wood, spindles, like a number of wind instruments of wood or clay, and many small, crude idols of basalt, porphyry, and sandstone.

A collection of delicate works consisting of idol-sculptures, pitchers, cups, rings, and other ornamental items, here and there extremely tastefully and artistically fashioned from white marble, serpentine, opal, chalcedony, bone, and shell. What elicits the greatest wonder, however, is a mask that is fashioned and burnished out of obsidian with such perfection that one cannot recognize the slightest trace of a tool on it![9] Even more deserving of attention is a mirror made of the same material, a few of which are also produced from polished copper.

Finally, a collection of kitchen and household utensils of clay; the visitor has the opportunity to marvel at their magnificent work and indestructible glaze of different colors. Near them are found still more collections of clay models, and many smaller and occasionally quite lovely masks and heads. Many of these masks were laid in the grave of the dead and represented the multitude of family members left behind, principally children.

3. Old manuscripts. A collection of maps, pictures, accounts, and plans, among which in particular the ground plan of old Mexico, a present of Moctezuma to Cortés, deserves special attention, just as much as the pictures painted by Indians, depicting scenes of the conquest, the illustration of the Aztecs wandering from the north to Anáhuac, an ancient tally of tribute that was rendered to the Mexican leader, and a genealogical tree that begins with two men standing under a fruit tree and which includes all the rulers of Mexico, ending with Charles V. A number of chronological hieroglyphics chiseled in sandstone, which are of the greatest interest, occupy the chamber to the left.

In the second room we find a few unimportant natural history collections, which are neither scientifically arranged nor especially well preserved. A few fossils and the remains of a mammoth are the only notable items. Among the diverse objects worth seeing is a display of the arms of Cortés and Alvarado,[10] together with a number of portraits of famous Spaniards and kings.

The caretaker of this museum is Herr Isidoro Gondra, an exceedingly well educated man who received me quite hospitably, and I am deeply grateful to him for his instruction concerning the antiquities of Mexico.

Regarding the noteworthy sights of the city, those which redound to the material use of the citizenry, the following deserve to be mentioned. The marketplace (*plazuela de voladores*),[11] located to the east of the university building, is of considerable size, and in the morning is the most popular place in the entire city. The traveler also finds a mass of stalls in which vendors offer everything imaginable. Here too is an infinity of Indian men and women who bring the natural products of their areas in extraordinary quantities; they mostly come via the canal that leads from Lake Chalco to Mexico City, and they sell their wares with a noisy hubbub.

This market offers everything that I had in fact seen earlier in Mexican markets, and with whose recitation I will not tire the reader a second time. However, I must mention that here in particular are to be found European fruit in superior quality, along with the southern fruit of the tierra caliente. The loveliest grapes, excellent pears, apples, and peaches were to be found daily in the market when I was there. No less splendid are the vegetables displayed in the vicinity of Mexico in the *chinampas,* of which I speak later; these same goods are brought for sale to the capital.

As luck would have it, meat dishes are common here, while in the provinces they are expensive and rare. The market for animals in Mexico City not only equals that of precolonial days but actually surpasses it owing to the crowd of cattle, sheep, goats, and pigs that are now brought here.

The liveliness of the plazuela de voladores could scarcely be exceeded at a European market. The cries of the fiery Mexicans, the different languages of the Indians, and the haggling of buyer and seller create such a din that one could believe the welfare of the entire world was at stake here. Moreover, the *léperos,* a class of persons resembling the Neapolitan *lazaroni,* conduct their not entirely honorable business here. They are the only people who surpass even the English pickpockets in cunning and dexterity. Locals tell countless anecdotes of their thievery, yet the léperos employ violence only in the most extreme case, for in addition to their skill they also demonstrate great cowardice.

From this place the wanderer follows the road that leads along a small canal and soon finds himself on the Paseo de la Viga, or "passage of the beam." It consists of double avenues of handsome trees and extends a considerable distance to the point where a small stone bridge leads over the canal from which this promenade takes its name, since the passageway of the barges, where one charges the toll, can be closed off by means of a beam. The promenade is frequented quite a bit at certain times of the year, especially in the months of April and May, while in autumn, to the contrary, it is abandoned. The canal is always popular. Barges of all forms pass through the waters of Lake Chalco:

"Gliding down the canal, one soon reaches Santa Anita, a small village that lies in the marshland of the lake and which is surrounded by the so-called floating gardens, or *chinampas*." (Photo courtesy of the Latin American Library, University of Texas at Austin)

from gondolas of the well-to-do, equipped with all comforts, to the Indians' small, narrow canoes fashioned from a tree trunk, and which float here and there laden with fruits and vegetables. Songs accompanied by guitar quite frequently ring out from one canoe or another, while a young pair of sweethearts who have strayed from the city into that undisturbed solitude of the lake flirt under the vessel's canopy.

Gliding down the canal, one soon reaches Santa Anita, a small village that lies in the marshland of the lake and is surrounded by the so-called floating gardens, or *chinampas*. These chinampas have their origins in the ancient days of the Aztecs, who crowded together on the lake. In order to remedy the poverty of the soil, they laid huge latticeworks four hundred to five hundred feet long and thirty to fifty feet wide, made of tree trunks and covered with soil, and there cultivated their corn and other essential vegetables. Many of these chinampas do not really float, but rather are fastened to the ground in shallow places. They jut out above the water's overflow and are washed over and so permeated with moisture that the most splendid vegetation flourishes upon them.

I have sailed around many of these chinampas, but saw no authentically floating gardens, although such still exist. I found all the more charming, however, the mass of flowers that bloom everywhere upon these same, and among which a small house, that of the owner, often peeps through in picturesque fashion. In spite of everything, an excursion to this region ranks among the most pleasant that one can make in Mexico.

The Alameda, or main promenade, consists of rectangular plazas surrounded with trellises and equipped with gates, and is located opposite the Acordada. Paved walkways and the dense shade of immense trees make it the most pleasant and frequently visited place of the capital. A few poorly done statues and a fountain in the center of the same supposedly serve as its centerpieces. While the Mexican truly believes his Alameda to be something splendid, the European finds nothing exceptional here, excluding the shade of the trees and the resulting scene. What far more commands his attention is the quite solidly built aqueduct, which is 33,646 feet long and whose third part rests upon arches. It brings high-quality water from the spring of Santa Fe into Mexico City, and ends at the bridge of La Mariscala, in a part of the city called the Traspana.

Not far from the Alameda one finds the Paseo Nuevo, also a promenade, which was built upon an earthen elevation over the marshy ground. Although the avenues are not very shady, the riding public still visits it eagerly. Two fountains rise up in the middle of the street, of which one, the older, is not without taste. To the left of this promenade rises the old citadel, a flat-roofed, one-storied building with bombproof vaults, which in the time of the Spanish empire housed a tobacco factory. It is now used more or less as a barracks.

At the end of the Paseo the second aqueduct runs toward Mexico City, bringing in water from Chapúltepec's so-called Salto de Agua. The aqueduct is 10,825 feet long and rests on 904 arches built out of stone. But the water of this conduit is less clear than that of Santa Fe, is strongly impregnated with carbonated, calcareous earth, and is consumed only in the suburbs of the capital.

Among the theaters the Teatro Nacional is above all worth seeing. This is certainly one of the loveliest theaters in the world as far as graceful construction, size, and elegance are concerned. It admits comparison only with the Teatro Tacón in Havana, and has no peer in Germany, France, or England. The lovely building front opens toward the Calle Bergare and encloses two lobbies, which are covered with glass and surrounded with galleries. From these one accesses the private boxes via two luxurious stairways, and through the middle to the public boxes and orchestra stalls.

The greatest comfort and elegance reigns in the interior. The lower boxes are lined with marble, while the galleries rest on thick and rather elegant columns of mahogany. The performances themselves are quite good, mostly presented by Spanish artists; moreover, shortly before my arrival they presented a rather choice Italian opera, in which the role of prima donna was performed by Mlle Borghese, who is well known in America. Since that time it does not appear that a second opera has materialized.

It seems strange to the foreigner that one smokes universally before and during the performance, in which matter women, who appear in their finest, form no exception. Since the theater is particularly spacious, however, and has excellent ventilation, the smoke does not bother in the slightest, and one finds this custom of the country not as unpleasant as it might seem.

In this same building is found also a fine hotel with elegant rooms, *table d'hôte*[12] for travelers, a coffeehouse, and billiard room. After this theater, the older Teatro Principal is the only one worth visiting. In earlier days it must have been authentically magnificent, since even now one can recognize the great luxury throughout with the silk-upholstered seats and many ornamentations.

Mexico has countless guest and gaming houses that, depending on whether they are managed by Englishmen, Frenchmen, Germans, or Italians, bear the name of the nation represented. In general the guest eats superbly, but in comparison to Europe quite expensively; the wines in particular carry a high price, since almost none are produced in the nation itself. A recently erected English brewery provides a modest alternative. The capital also displays a striking wealth of small shops, and one might more easily be at a loss for consumer goods in a small European city than in Mexico, where commerce can yield so high a profit that it will long remain the El Dorado of merchants.

In the vicinity of Mexico the village of Tacubaya is noteworthy. It consists of the country homes of wealthy Mexican families and is highly popular in the summer months. These country homes are usually enormous buildings furnished with gardens, and for the most part are rather simply arranged. Since many foreigners have their summer residence in that same place, here and there one finds handsome if small public gardens; I mention only that of Herr Schneider, a German merchant, whose garden is adorned in the most lively fashion with flowers of the country as well as of Europe. Greenhouses are extremely rare in Mexico, and the only one I have seen is that of Herr Kubli, a Belgian commercial gardener. Tacubaya is famous for its olive tree orchards, which flourish splendidly there and yield a rich harvest.

The archbishop's palace is one of the handsomest buildings to be encountered in the city and valley of Mexico.

In the area of Tacubaya, a mere hour from the capital, are found the hill and the castle Chapultepec, the latter of which was built by the Spanish viceroy Gálvez and at great expense.[13] In the present day it is run down, but it is

"The largest of the bald cypress trees that stand there is a mighty specimen whose trunk is forty-six feet in circumference. The branches of the same are covered with barba española and press still more firmly upon this old man the seal of age." (Photo courtesy of the Latin American Library, University of Texas at Austin)

noteworthy as the residence of the last Mexican emperor and for its huge cypress trees. It has won historical attention as well in most recent times as a hotly defended point during the war with the United States.[14] The largest of the bald cypress trees that stand there is a mighty specimen whose trunk is forty-six feet in circumference. Its branches are covered with barba española and press still more firmly upon this old man the seal of age. Yet more trees of the same sort are found in the vicinity of the hills, and the visitor wanders through their rows with a feeling of respect. The castle now serves as a military academy and is likewise visited by locals and foreigners for the splendid view one enjoys from there.

To the north of this place lies the famous cloister and church of Our Lady of Guadalupe, the patron saint of Mexico, the most famous pilgrimage site of the country. One arrives here on an avenue that is surrounded by handsome trees. The splendid church stands at the foot of the small hill Tepeyac and is one of the richest in Mexico. For its vast reputation it has to thank a wonder-working image of the Mother of God, to which is attached a legend concerning the apparition of Our Blessed Mother in 1531 on the hill formerly a temple of the idol Tonantzín, who was goddess of the earth and fertility. The Virgin appeared three times before a newly converted Indian and called upon him to go to the bishop to have a church constructed in that same place. As a sign she filled the serape he held with roses, and on this serape emerged her miraculous image. Now protected under glass, this image adorns the high altar, and subsequently is said to have worked very many wonders, so that in the modern day countless persons come here in order to implore this or the other favor. I myself have seen how a man who had been brought here dragged himself with a broken leg before the image of grace and requested of the Mother of God nothing less than that she make him well without any surgical assistance. I cannot confirm whether this cure took place, since nothing manifested itself during my stay.

Quite noteworthy and healthy is the mineral spring near Guadalupe, which bubbles up near the church and over which a small chapel is built. The water is rather warm (68–73 degrees) and contains muriatic soda, carbonic acid, and some iron. The taste is quite like that of seltzer water. Similar springs are found at Peñón de los Baños ("rock baths"), which I mentioned in the previous chapter. This water too contains muriatic and sulpheric soda, as well as some calcium and carbonic acid, but it has a higher temperature than that of Guadalupe and is frequently used as a curative.

Finally, in the region of Mexico are two other important sights: the ruins of the two pyramids of San Juan de Teotihuacán, northeast of Lake Texcoco. They are surely the work of the Toltec and have served the Mexicans as models for their teocallis.[15] They are consecrated to the sun and moon, and the length of their base amounts to 645 feet, their vertical height 170 feet, and therefore rival the pyramid of Cholula. Their age may well run to nearly a thousand years. Moreover, one can perfectly recognize them as works of the human hand, since their interiors consist of a composite of clay and stone. The traveler can also make out the features of a hill superimposed upon this structure, features which for a long time led people to believe that nothing lay to be discovered within.

These were the noteworthy sights of Mexico City, and if in the description of the same I have deviated only a little from that of other authors, so may the kind reader attribute this not to me but to the responsibility of the Mexican government, which for four decades has made no improvement and no innovations.

In conclusion will follow a few observations about my residence in the capital. During my stay I selected as my quarters in Mexico the hotel of the great theater, whereas my lad and horses were economically put up in one of those so-called *fondas* of which Mexico has an enormous number to show and which are destined for arrieros and similar people.

The numerous letters of introduction that I carried allowed me many amenities during my residence in the capital, and I consider it an altogether pleasant obligation to thankfully mention here the hospitable reception of Herr ex-Conde de la Cortina,[16] one of the most cultured men in the country; of Herr Drusina and of Herr Schneider; no less the displays of friendship of the nation's people whose acquaintance I had the pleasure to make, and whom I will always remember fondly. These acquaintances made it easier for me to come to know the capital in the shortest time possible. The visit to sights of interest and access to different company allowed me to convince myself that Mexico possesses all those privileges and faults that one otherwise finds in the great cities of Europe. But what comes into consideration here is the peculiar character of the Mexicans, their passion for play, love of boasting and luxury, and their so-to-speak anarchic union; it stamps upon them a distinctive tone that is strange to the European.

Mexicans of both sexes love idleness as much as the foreign merchant loves industry and activity; and they are never happier than when they sit on a handsome steed or in a carriage, at the gaming table or the theater, and are able to give free rein to their ostentation. I was particularly struck by the women who, like all southern females of cheerful temperament, better than anyone seem to understand romantic intrigues and extravagance, jewelry and ornament in general. There are unbelievable stories to be told in this regard, and in spite of the kindliness with which I was received in Mexico, love of truth allows me to pass no milder judgment upon them. I could in fact say a great deal about the power of the clergy, much about the heads of state and the army, much about the hustle and bustle of the streets and promenades. But since opportunities to touch upon these matters offer themselves in the course of my travel narrative, I do not wish to tire longer with my description of the capital.

I had passed three weeks here, and in the latter period much in the company of Herr Ghiesbrecht, a Belgian naturalist who then resided in Tacubaya. However, I began to think seriously about continuing the journey. The citizenry still hoped for a speedy settlement to the discord between the United States and Mexico, even though in political terms nothing had changed to the favor of my undertaking. In any event I believed that I could venture into the interior. Already gossip was circulating furiously that Mexicans would once more recall Santa Anna, banished in complete disgrace, a man who with all conceivable fanfare claimed to wish to rescue his fatherland.[17] Santa Anna was waiting for a circumstance that might restore to him the dignities of high office that he had lost upon his expulsion, but to the impartial observer this seemed the safest way to ruin and destruction. I therefore departed from the capital on July 30, 1846, in the company of my cheerful lad and of Herren Fink and Ghiesbrecht, who accompanied me on a jaunt for Toluca.

Chapter 11

Just as we had earlier abandoned our residence in Huatusco, so too we now set out on a narrow road leading to the gate of the capital. This road is called "Lerma Highway." It is one of the most beautiful in the country, and was constructed at considerable cost over the mountain range that borders the Valley of Mexico on the western side. It leads over Chapultepec through the village of Tacubaya, behind which it begins to climb.

Initially the land is quite infertile and reveals only scant vegetation, since few plants find nourishment in the rocky soil, or *tepetate.* Only after Santa Fe does the vegetation begin to grow richer, and from Venta de Guajimalpa almost until Lerma the traveler encounters the most stupendous forests of fir and oak on both sides. Since the rainy season had not yet ended, the road was adorned with many delicate flowers.[1] Solitary, uncultivated romantic patches delight the eyes. The road from Mexico to Lerma is really the loveliest in the highlands, and to be certain would be abundantly visited were it not, like so many others, feared because of the bandit gangs. No one tells stories about its beauty, but rather of the robberies and murders that take place there almost daily. Sadly, it turns out that almost everyone forgets the beautiful scenery because of evildoers. In the mountain range the traveler comes upon only a few huts that are able to offer an evening's lodgings, and since generally speaking it is not advisable to spend the evening in isolated rancherías in this disreputable region, I was therefore compelled to reach Lerma that same day.

The rain was already pouring down in sheets when we were still on the Cerro de las Cruces (Ajusco), which was so famous during the independence war, and which at its highest point reaches 13,800 feet.[2] Often the water pelted our faces so fiercely that we only went forward with difficulty, and in this struggle with the elements the road seemed to climb up and down endlessly. We were already wet through and through when at 6:00 in the evening the valley of Toluca lay before us. To be sure, nothing was to be seen of the snowcapped volcano of the same name, for it had concealed itself in the dense clouds, but at the foot of the mountain range from which we descended lay the inviting hamlet Lerma, which we greeted ever so joyfully, since we needed a protective shelter in the worst way.

Without anything unpleasant befalling us—the bad weather excepted—we reached the fonda of the village at 6:30 in the evening. Lerma, which lies twelve leagues from Mexico City, enjoys considerable fame because of its production of outstanding spurs and horse bits. Almost the entire population lives from this trade. Immediately the people crowded around us. They offered us a rare opportunity for commerce, and I bought a very handsome pair of spurs there for the low price of 1 peso.

The lodgings of the fonda were poor, but as tired as we were, a hard warehouse would not have bothered us as much as the mistrust-provoking faces of everyone around us. Something so suspicious hung upon their exteriors that I am not able to describe it, and the tremendous insecurity in the entire region between Mexico City and Toluca, and again toward the south, speaks clearly enough to the truth of this seemingly unfounded suspicion.

The climate there is splendid; the valley and the mountain range surrounding it are lovely and rich in beautiful and rare vegetation. Still, I could never make myself entirely comfortable, because it turned out that the people were so corrupt, dishonest, and suspicious that to me they seemed to play the lowest roles among the creatures of that region. Isolated as I was, I thus had to avoid them all the more, rather than seeking out companionship.

We set out on our journey the next morning at 7:00. The limitless and beautiful high plain stretched out before us, while in the morning light we beheld the startling image of Toluca, Mexico's fourth snowcapped volcano. Green flatlands of corn and agave fields extended up to its foot and connected with the dark forests of the mountain range. Many haciendas lay scattered among the abundant pastures, on which the eye of the wanderer rests with pleasure, and through which a straight road leads to Toluca. This road is partly built up by dams in those places where it leads through swamplands (perhaps the remains of a great lake), and is partly covered with fine sand that whirls up into great clouds of dust. Ever since we had left Lerma, the city of Toluca lay constantly before our eyes, even when we were still more than three hours away.

Toluca is sixteen leagues from Mexico City[3] and lies at 8,502 feet—therefore 1,304 feet higher than the capital. It rests upon the lower porphyry range of San Miguel de Tutucuilapilco. In former times Toluca was the capital of the province of Mexico, but owing to the dissolution of the federal system,[4] whereby Mexico City became the capital in the former Federal District, it has declined to an extraordinary degree. Toluca is a lovely city, with straight, paved streets, more pretty churches, and splendid *portales* or corri-

"The limitless and beautiful high plain stretched out before us, while in the morning light we beheld the startling image of Toluca, Mexico's fourth snowcapped volcano." Here we see the area of Metepec, just outside Toluca itself. (Photo courtesy of the Latin American Library, University of Texas at Austin)

dors, which on one side are 220 paces long with 38 arches, and on the other 275 paces long with 45 arches, and which cost 300,000 pesos.

Market day excepted, this otherwise inferior city belongs among the most lifeless I know, and the streets are so desolate that grass grows on most of them. They tell me that in the last two years more than two thousand people have migrated to the capital. Many houses stand completely abandoned, while perhaps as many as half within the circumference of the city are dilapidated. Because of its position on Mexico's highest plateau, incidentally, and because it is equidistant from both of the American coasts, Toluca is even better suited as the center point than the capital itself. Formerly Toluca was famous on account of many industrial concerns; but the industry, like the renown, has disappeared, and perhaps will never return. Presently the city has not even one well-maintained inn, and I had to be content with one of those wretched fondas, of which I have already spoken.[5] Of course, I lived in the same extraordinary frugality, for even with the most prodigal intentions I could spend not more than 2 reals for a noon meal in my inn, and daily paid only as much for four empty walls, between which I had taken up my residence.

The city's ten thousand inhabitants include so few prosperous people that even the place of diversion, a form of coffeehouse, is but seldom visited. Since the bulk of the inhabitants consist of the lower classes, which possess no very good reputation, the visitor therefore lives in Toluca more isolated than in any of the wild regions of the country, where he at least finds highly profuse vegetation and much diversion and entertainment in the adjoining environs.

I took up residence in that place, however, because I nursed the intention of setting out from here to Colima[6] on the Pacific Ocean. For that reason I attempted to investigate as thoroughly as possible the environs of the city, as well as the volcano of the same name. My resolve to stay in Toluca deepened on August 4, when General Don Mariano Salas,[7] the commander of the troops that had remained behind in Mexico, rose up against Paredes; Salas championed the Constitution of 1824, the recall of all exiles, and the restitution of General Santa Anna as commander in chief of the Mexican army. The weak people unquestioningly granted these demands, which were to have such tragic consequences for the country.

Naturally, Toluca, which through this revolution once more acquired the right of capital of the province of Mexico, quite happily attached itself to the new movement, and on the morning of August 5 the dignitaries of the city marched through the streets and proclaimed their support for the new government, with a military band leading the way. They were followed by a mob of poor folk, who incessantly broke out with the cry, "Viva Santa Anna y la Federación, muera Paredes!"[8] Few individuals opposed this new order. As soon as the procession had abandoned the street, everything was once again quiet as if nothing had happened, and yet with this cry, which was first raised in the capital and then echoed in most cities, they had toppled Paredes from the presidential chair, called back the exiled Santa Anna to highest office, and changed the centralist government into a federalist one.

I could not with any certainty foresee what the consequences would be, but I had a foreboding of nothing good, and because I needed to leave open for myself the option of returning I dared not risk traveling to Colima. This consideration loomed all the more important, for if the blockade continued any longer my residence in the country would become not only more dangerous but in fact impossible.[9] It was a very painful situation, but as unpleasant as it was, I tried to make the most of it until I could arrange a new travel plan for myself. For that reason I lived in Toluca several more months and toured the circumference of the city, something which despite everything I could only describe as profitable to my objective.

Almost every day I climbed the near-lying mountain range of San Miguel, and found the vegetation to be poor—something akin to European, and anything but tropical.[10] One botanical oddity here is the ancient arbol de las manitas, which grows on a small porphyry range eighty-seven hundred feet above sea level, and which is surely the sole tree of this sort growing wild. Even the inhabitants of Toluca honor this withering old man of the plant world as a great curiosity, and collect its Christmas flowers with much care, although no medicinal value can be attributed to them. Beyond this tree are found near the city only a few ancient cypresses on a small elevation, or a few willows planted in avenues on the barren-lying Alameda. Everything else is rich with agaves, from which one makes first-rate pulque here, or else is covered with lush fields of corn and cereal.

In general, the view of the valley of Toluca is an extremely pleasant one. The plateau stretches approximately four hours in all directions from the city until reaching the surrounding ranges. Field follows upon field, among which lie lush meadows with herds of grazing sheep, or horses and cattle. Here too are found small, charming villages of inhabitants who work the soil; and in the background the highest peak of the mighty volcano, partly covered with snow, towers up into the sky.

The same cultivated cereals and especially the pulque of the villages San Bartolo and Jocotitlán are the principal industries of this region. European fruit species also thrive superbly there, and they make as many uses of corn as possible. From corn the locals produce a drink called *chicha,* which is analogous to beer and tastes quite pleasant. Another comes from the fruits of the guayaba, which is called *pulque de guayaba,* and finally a drink from the stalk of the corn plant, analogous to tepache, which is called *pulque de mais.*

The descendants of Spaniards excepted, the greatest number of inhabitants of this valley are Aztecs;[11] however, in the western region many Indians speak Otomí. They frequently visit the market of Toluca and distinguish themselves both through their evil-sounding language and through their attire. The men of this tribe, just like the women, wear their hair in long, braided tresses and frequently sport raincoats prepared from densely woven dried grass. In their clothing the women display a tremendous poverty, and often scarcely cover their nakedness. Especially unpleasant, however, is their language; despite all effort, I could scarcely recognize a word of it that was not snorted out through the nose. The Otomí appear to represent a distinctly inferior level of civilization, and they all wear more or less the imprint of great neglect upon them. Sadly, they belong to those who incessantly squander their miserable wages on intoxicating beverages, and thus sink to that point where one can find only profound compassion for these poor creatures.

The market of Toluca is amply visited, and in terms of fruits one of the finest in the nation, since to this place farmers bring products of both the temperate and tropical regions. Especially good and handsome are the apples and apricots, along with guayabas, mangoes, and bananas; here too one finds lovely vegetables, among which potatoes, sweet potatoes, and chayotes stand out before all else.

Since the last political upheaval elevated Toluca to the head of the province of Mexico, the residents have again tried to establish the dramatic arts there, and in a small theater they began with a series of presentations which, in spite of the poor execution, nevertheless found a well-disposed public. More than the theater, bullfighting attracts the multitude, since the bulls of the hacienda Atenco, in the proximity of the city, are considered to be the bravest and most furious.

In the course of time I visited the latter, in order to get some idea of this entertainment. It was on a Sunday when I hastened to the *corrido de toros* (bullfights); the most magnificent bull from Atenco was selected for battle today. I entered. The plaza was spacious and was built like a bare circus, only much larger and with ramparts installed in a circle around the arena for the benefit of fleeing combatants. Behind these the seats rose like an amphitheater, and in the middle stood a box for the *alcalde* (magistrate), whose concern it was that nothing unlawful occur in the fight, and who summons and recalls the different combatants. It was already 4:00 in the afternoon, the hour set for beginning. The crowd, which filled up the entire space, either waited quiet as mice in taut curiosity for the beginning of the contest, or else broke into a loud uproar from impatience. Twice the music began and ended, and already the hubbub was limitless when the sign of the deadly drama's beginning was sounded by means of a trumpet from the magistrate's box, and loud cheers from the crowd.

The doors of the arena opened and two riders in stately Spanish costume appeared to the left, while to the right a magnificent bull, brown in color and with curly back hairs, stormed furiously into the plaza. The two riders, who are called *picadores* because of their lances equipped with short points, now have the business of warding off the rushing bull, a function that requires not only all the tremendous cleverness of the fighters but also control of the horses, since they must proceed against the bulls with full force.

The first approach of the bull was so extraordinarily quick and bold that in an instant he had gored one of the horses, and even tossed one of the riders a few feet into the air. The old horse fell quivering to the ground, while the picador luckily came away with a trifling injury, since another had momentarily distracted the bull from his victim. For me it was a ghastly spectacle, but the remaining spectators broke out in jubilant cries over the bull's triumph, an outburst that did not end until they had dragged the horse from the arena between two richly decorated mules.

The second picador was more fortunate, since he held the animal back several times with his lance, whose point penetrated its skin only slightly. For a good while the rider and bull had moved about in this fashion, when the trumpet called the combatants on foot, the so-called *banderilleros,* to the ring. These provoked the bull in the most frightful way, principally by means of a red cloth, and tried to fasten ornaments and fireworks to his hide by means of a small iron barb. To every skillful turn, like the fastening of a decoration (*banderilla*) in an instant of seemingly great danger, the public responded with loud signs of approval; or else it openly manifested reproof if the fighter had to flee from the arena through a daring leap over the wall. After the bull is thus set in a fury, partly through these lit rockets, partly by the other appendages tormenting him, then bellowing and foaming at the mouth he kicks the sand into the air with his fore and hind hooves, or bores his horns into the ground with destructive force. The trumpet calls the banderilleros away from the ring, and there appears completely alone the *matador* (literally translated, "the killer"), a red cape in the left hand, a sword in the right, to begin the final struggle.

The matador must dodge the bull's attack three times. Then, however, at the first opportunity he thrusts the sharp sword into the broad neck, and if he is to be met with approval, the bull must collapse instantly; if this is not the case, then the matador is reviled with the most horrendous insults, and abandons the arena under scorn and derision. But the matador of Toluca performed his business with the utmost dexterity and to the satisfaction of the public. This cruel scene repeated itself five times; one more horse was killed and another picador wounded, until at last they left a tamed steer in the plaza, one that had rubber balls fastened to the tips of his horns, with which he could cause no great harm, while he was selected for the purpose of being chased by anyone from the public. A crowd of scamps and young fellows usually makes its appearance in the ring; they put up a sometimes crude *bouffe,* and I must confess that this concluding fight is not a little entertaining. Otherwise, however, I find that there can be no crueler spectacle than this bullfight, and it greatly astonishes me to spy the finest ladies of every age among the audience, since it seems a singularly poor school for the formation of gentle sensibilities and noble souls, as much for tender and feminine spirits as for sensitive people generally. For my part, I could never bring myself to make a second visit. In fairness to the Mexican it may also be said that their special predilection for the bullfight seems to be on the point of declining. What is certain is that bullfighting was imparted to them since the year 1528 and could not have come earlier.[12]

All in all, I lived reasonably contented in Toluca, although it made an unpleasant impression on me to have to go out armed even into the nearby environs. This necessity impressed upon me such a dislike toward Mexico that I would happily have left this land, if only it had been possible for me to set out quickly to another nation of Central or South America.

From here I made many long excursions, among which the trip to the volcano of Toluca and another to the region south of the city were of the greatest interest, since those regions had almost never been visited in recent times. On August 10, 1846, I set out on my journey to the volcano in question. Early in the morning I rode out of the city, and initially I headed north to cross through a part of the high plain before the climb began. The meadows were richly covered with flowers,[13] and the eye of the wanderer rests on the plants that recall the lively fields of home. Moreover, the morning was wonderful, the air pure and fragrant; insects buzzed in high spirits around the flowers, birds resounded in cheerful song on all sides, and the soul of the lonesome traveler exalted in marvelous fashion. On long rambles there is certainly no more splendid moment than when in the middle of tranquil and powerfully moving nature one is, so to speak, touched by the heavenly breath of the Creator, and is shot through by a feeling whose grandeur the person confined within the walls of the city never has the opportunity to know.

On our way we came upon the small hamlets San Buenaventura and Cacalomacan with the hacienda De Abajo,[14] with which the climb proper begins, and already a few firs (*Pinus russeliana* and Chihuahua pine) made their appearance, without the profuse flora changing a great deal. In general, the climb up the volcano Toluca by no means presents that startling change found on Orizaba, where one goes uphill from zero elevation to the highest point, passing step by step through all climates and vegetation. Toluca's high plateau of eighty-five hundred feet forms the base that completely excludes the hot and temperate regions.

In a few hours I reached the hacienda Cocustepec, nine thousand feet above sea level, to which point the fields of corn, barley, and wheat extend. I was quite hospitably received there, and since I expressed the desire to stay a while they furnished me a room with the utmost readiness, a room that afforded me an indescribably stunning view of the entire plateau, from Sierra Ixlahuacan and De las Cruces to the south side of the volcano. The only problem was that the room to some degree felt the effects of the damp cold and thin air, for at the highest position of the sun the thermometer never climbs above 59 degrees, but perhaps falls to 52 degrees.

Since the rain in the mountain range begins daily at noon, the climb up the volcano presents many hazards, which we nevertheless had to ignore, since it was a matter of either visiting now or never. But I selected the day that, because of heavier-than-average rain falling for one or more days, offered the hope that it would come later or perhaps disappear altogether. For that reason I passed three days on the hacienda and in the meantime collected plants for my herbarium.[15]

On August 12, long before daybreak, we stood ready before the volcano. Our guide, who was quite familiar with the route, led us along the narrow path that winds among small thickets, now running along abundant meadows, now losing itself in the darkness of the woods, and progresses up the mountain over roots or stones. The moon illuminated the landscape with its pale light, and the huge trees often cast nocturnal shadows upon our path. An almost ice-cold morning breeze blew through the trembling needles of the immense pines, the birds remained fast asleep, and far and wide everything lay in the most profound stillness.

We pushed forward at a brisk pace in order to ascend as quickly as possible, and when the day broke we found ourselves in the unvaried pine forest at an elevation of ten thousand feet. The huge limbs of these trees clutched at one another like giants and kept the ground in almost eternal shadows. Only here and there were sparse plants to be seen, including pentstemon richly covered with flowers. Among them were others decorated with blue bells resembling gentian, along with tiny potentilla, geraniums, or lovely grasses.

Our horses performed astonishing feats, and already at 8:30—that is, after approximately five hours—we reached the first alpine meadow. It spread out before our eyes like a green velvet tapestry, and for a short time a mass of tiny plants gave us a not unpleasant pursuit, since we had resolved to collect as much as possible in the brief period.[16]

In isolated, shady areas, small patches of snow could already be found, and little by little the path began to climb ever higher, while the rock masses of crumbled basalt and porphyry crowded together. Around 9:00 we reached the crater, and not without exertion. Before us we glimpsed a small crater, approximately one hundred feet deep, and in it, to our utmost astonishment, two pools with seemingly azure blue water, a lovely color I had only seen in the middle of the great ocean. All around rose majestic rock masses, mountains of tremendously varied height, the tallest of which was that of Pico del Fraile. We scrambled down the crater and found the water, once ladled into a basin, to be completely clear, tasty, and a warm 50 degrees. The depth of this basin, however, seemed to be limitless, and in fact Herr Robertson, who climbed this volcano a decade ago, found no bottom at 125 feet when throwing out a weighted line.[17] Consequently, there is no doubt that this cavity with the two basins is the burned-out crater of Toluca, and surely the perpetually melting snow is sufficient to keep it filled.

At the crater (14,000 feet high) we abandoned our horses and climbed toward the highest peak. This was more of a creeping upward, and was so extraordinarily difficult that I despaired of achieving my objective. Moreover, although I had wrapped two handkerchiefs around my head, the thin air made itself so painfully palpable that I found myself unable to breathe deeply. For a while a singular pressure in the chest seized me, and a ringing in the ears, and although I am in no way susceptible to that form of giddiness known as vertigo, still I had to rest, completely exhausted after every three steps.[18]

Finally, after two extremely laborious hours we had reached the highest point, the Pico del Fraile, at an altitude of 14,616 feet, and a truly unbelievable emotion took hold of me in that instant. Oddly shaped piles of basalt and other volcanic stone resembling organ pipes lay about in utter confusion; here these rocks formed a sharp edge, there a table-like flat surface, while between them thousand-year-old snow clung firmly in the eternally shaded pines. Almost no vegetation is to be observed outside of a few very small grasses and—what a wonder!—small Indian paintbrushes that send up red flowers from beneath the white snow. Certainly this is the highest altitude for the Arcamphibryen (Endumsprosser *Endl.*), and for the botanist this plant is a most remarkable phenomenon.

I had another experience here. When climbing mountains in the tropics, onc is almost nevcr rewarded with a beautiful vista, since the underlying regions wrap themselves around in clouds, and from time to time pull themselves over the peak of the volcano as well. For that reason I had to scramble back down to the crater. I managed this quickly, and since it seemed that the weather would remain fairly favorable, I resolved to linger a bit longer, partly to rest somewhat from the exertion of climbing the peak and to fortify myself with a bite to eat; but also to wait for a favorable view at that moment when clouds disappeared, if only for a short time.

Luckily, my wish was granted, since the clouds suddenly parted and my enraptured sight passed over the entire high plateau of Toluca—on which I hastily counted more than twenty bodies of water—and far beyond, over the mountain range at incalculable distances. It was not a complete panorama, since one might have this only from the pinnacle,[19] but nonetheless I was richly rewarded with this highly exalting view, and I almost convinced myself that I would never see such a vista again in my life. Only one time in my travels did I have a similar view.

We collected specimens without rest, for the weather was extraordinarily favorable. On the same evening we reached the hacienda Cocustepec, where we remained until August 14 in order to put the collection in order and transport it to Toluca. But before I depart forever from this point I should include a few observations concerning the agriculture there. The fields, as I have already explained, reach up to nine thousand feet, and are sown every year in the month of October with wheat and barley, which here give a three- to fourfold harvest, and thus a bit less than in Germany, where the harvest is fivefold. Here the farmers never allow a field to lie fallow and scarcely ever use manure. Perhaps in those extreme cases where the soil's fertility is most depleted, they work in the ashes of useless straw, which they burn in the same place. Horses and mules tread upon the mature grain on an unadorned threshing floor with tiles, then using shovels the workers toss it into the air for a long time, until the breeze has purified it. In this manner eight people produce not so much grain in a whole day as a single man does in a few hours in Europe. The price of grain fluctuates between 8 and 12 pesos per carga, what in our calculation would be 4 florins, 30 kreuzer, to 6 florins per *Metze.*[20]

Twelve days after my return from this last excursion (August 27) I undertook a journey to the south side of the volcano Toluca, and first of all I set my sights on Tenancingo, which lies directly on the opposite side of the range. For this reason, of course, the traveler must cross over not only the entire plateau but also the cordillera, which encircles the former toward the south and west.

The road leads through well-cultivated fields and over San Felipe, a small hamlet, toward Calimaya and from there to Tenango, which lies on the edge of the plateau and consequently at the foot of the range. At the churches of both places one comes upon immense trees of incense juniper, the same variety that occurs at Toluca on the porphyry range of San Miguel. It is a gigantic relic of ancient times, and the trunks here and there have a circumference of eight to ten feet and a height of sixty to eighty feet.

As soon as we had passed through Tenango, a village where many respectable homes are found, we reached a good road that pushes uphill in countless turns and among beautiful forests of pines and oaks throughout. At San Pedro, a small hamlet that lies practically at the highest point along the way, and where the path drops off a few hundred feet, the vegetation undergoes a noticeable change. It bears the character of San Bartolo in Orizaba, and while the traveler scarcely sees a tree other than firs in the high plateau northward to Toluca, here so many oaks appear at once that they seem to include all known varieties. I was particularly excited over a few specimens, such as Mexican white pine, which stands isolated at San Pedro, and which harbors immense pine cones—from a foot to one and a half feet long—among its branches of fine, splendid needles.

Not only the vegetation but also the terrain bears many similarities to the eastern side of Orizaba. Just as mountain follows upon mountain and hill upon hill in the latter, so it is in the former as well, where even the barrancas compete in depth with those of the aforementioned volcano. Only one thing is lacking, and that is the general abundance of orchids and parasites. This circumstance is certainly quite remarkable, since the altitude, climate, and even the soil, which consists of red loam, are entirely similar to those of Orizaba. Perhaps the explanation lies merely in the scant moisture of the atmosphere. In any case, the seldom-visited south side of Toluca is still rich in plants and could allow many subsequent explorers profitable results.

From San Pedro we rode down toward Tenancingo in the most frightful rain, and on very poor roads to boot. I had put on my black raincoat, and the Indians therefore took me for a clergyman, in spite of my beard and my sword. Since these poor devils did not even respect their own white trousers and knelt down in the muddy road in order to implore my blessing, I could not refuse them the same, calling to my mind the saying that faith sanctifies.[21]

We reached Tenancingo toward evening . . . soaked and hungry, as might easily be expected after a ride of twelve hours. This is a town of approximately six thousand inhabitants, in a small and singularly charming valley situated at the feet of a mountain. To the town's left and right, symmetrically to the main church of the place, stand two dainty-looking chapels, from which one enjoys an extraordinarily beautiful sight. The climate is splendid in that place, and the oranges, custard apples, apples, pears, and peaches grow superbly; and in the vicinity one comes upon many avocados with first-class fruits and lovely thickets of oaks, willows, and poplar trees. The entire region has many native species, to which wild jasmine, wild roses, sage, nadderkopf, and other plants contribute not a little;[22] remarkably, however, this sort of vegetation is interrupted by clumps of a gigantic reed known as wild cane, as well as by Endorchideen and small sedums. In short, Tenancingo is a city that seemed particularly attractive, and in fact it would have been so had the inhabitants the same good-natured character of those on the eastern slope of Orizaba. They live principally by the cultivation of corn and maguey and by manufacturing cotton scarves, or *paños,* an essential item of clothing for Mexican women. These paños are two feet wide and usually four times as long, just like the *cenidores,* or bandanas, that men wind around their hips. They weave both articles by hand, with the help of a frame through which the threads are crossed in a highly simple but also quite imperfect form. For the production of a paño, particularly if it is multicolored, they spend fourteen days to three weeks. The color design requires a great deal of trouble as well; for the weaver must weave in individual white or colored thread depending on the desired pattern, and repeats this tedious and laborious process many times until all the colors have little by little fallen into place. Nevertheless, one such paño costs no more than 3 pesos, and a cenidor 4 to 8 reals.

One of the loveliest excursion from Tenancingo is to the barranca of Tequaloya, which is approximately eight hundred feet deep and resembles Orizaba in form. Jagged and seemingly unclimbable rocks tower up on both sides. At the bottom rages a rapid mountain stream, on whose lovely banks imposing oaks (here once again covered with parasites) unfold their luxurious canopy of leaves, and where the same overshadows handsome ferns in addition to other deep blue plants.[23]

The luxurious spruces and handsome shrubs were just as abundant. Among these the Mexican cherry, profusely flowering hammer bush, and blackberry bushes stand out;[24] in short, this barranca is as rewarding to the botanist for its shade plants as to the nature lover for its stately knots of forest and rock.

After I had come to know Tenancingo and its environs fairly well I returned once more to Toluca, where I stopped only long enough to put my collection in order and prepare for a new journey. Namely, I was determined to visit the nearby mining district. I set out for this point the following day, even though my friends tried to dissuade me from it, since the roads had become quite dangerous for a solitary traveler on account of banditry.

Chapter 12

On September 5 I greeted the rising sun on the road to the mining district of Zacualpan. This time I directed my steps to the west and discovered parts of the Toluca valley that I had never seen before. Here stiff agaves closed around luxurious fields of corn, wheat, and cereal. A few small hills interrupted the plateau, then once again came marshy places with standing water, on which isolated trees stood here and there.

It is never so easy to lose one's way as on an enormous plateau, and I learned this soon enough, for after a ride of two hours I came upon the sizable village of Zinacantepec, which lay a considerable distance from my road. Since I had undertaken the journey without a guide, I had informed myself as well as possible and followed the road to San José, which lay at the foot of the mountain range, and from which the road to the mines led. Because the weather was wonderful I hardly regretted the detour I had made, for the ride among the handsome fields and meadows was utterly enchanting. We now climbed up and down through the mountains, and since I believed myself to be on the right road, the loss of time did not worry me. Unexpectedly, however, a narrow mountain path turned down to the left, and since I believed that I had to follow the broader road, I traveled on, all the more confident because I came across no one who could have given me instruction. At last after an hour I met an Indian who slowly drove before him a donkey laden with wood. I asked him whether I was on the correct road to Sultepec or Zacualpan, and learned to my considerable horror that I had embarked on a wrong direction, namely, toward Temascaltepec, and had carelessly ignored the earlier mountain path. I immediately turned around once more, and after I had ridden about uselessly for four hours I finally found myself on the right road.

We soon reached the thick woods of the higher region and found ourselves enveloped by a thousand-year-old virgin forest of gigantic spruce and firs whose tips rose to a height of 150 feet and whose trunks five men could scarcely have spanned. Never have I seen something as magnificent as this ocean of trees. It was as if man had feared to touch this virgin sanctuary; for fourteen leagues there was nothing here that called humans to mind, and although the beauty of this forest is inexpressible, a certain anxiety nevertheless fills the wanderer's soul. Such an anxiety has its origin not in fear but rather in the limitless solitude that surrounds him, and in the idea that to lose his way in this untouched forest must inexorably carry the price of his own destruction. But if the traveler keeps to the correct path, he is nowhere more exposed to the risk of being helplessly murdered than here: because of the silver transport, a horde of skilled and highly dangerous bandits have their lair. Indeed, few days pass without some lonely wanderer exhaling his last breath, and there are places where a cluster of crosses marks the scene of ghastly murders. These sad testimonies to human cruelty—the deep stillness of the forest, the eerie rushing of the wind through the pine needles, and the sublimity of nature's powerful forces—made an impression on me that I will never forget.

I only succumbed to this reverie for a short time, for a mere two days earlier travelers had seen spots of blood on this path, and the utmost vigilance on our part was therefore required. We readied all weapons in order to sell our lives as dearly as possible if need be. It was not easy to prepare oneself against a sudden attack, for the winding of the road, as much as the small ravines, permitted us to see no further than a few steps ahead, and we had to entrust ourselves more to hearing than to sight.

More hours had already passed, and we had still not caught sight of a human form as we came closer to the highest and most frightening point—Cerro Gordo, approximately ten thousand feet above sea level—and with profound apprehension we began to wind our way down the mountain. Suddenly rapid hoofbeats sounded in our proximity, and we were instantly convinced that an assault would now follow, all the more as we could neither see nor venture a judgment about the approaching party owing to the thick forest. Without saying a word to my companions, I cast them a meaningful glance; we cocked our pistols, readied the sabers that hung at our sides, and awaited the supposed adversary in a highly favorable position. It did not take long before we spotted two well-mounted Mexicans coming toward us, and followed by a distinguished-looking man. They were as well armed as ourselves; they too had drawn their sabers, since the sound of our hoofbeats did not escape them either, and they rode boldly upon us. At the right moment we revealed ourselves to be peaceable travelers, and after I had exchanged a few words with the stranger, a Spaniard, we passed along, wishing each other luck.

This small adventure had come off so well that it might serve as a proof of the dangers of this road, since both the Spaniard and I were prepared for an assault. I left him unscathed as we passed through this road, but a highly curious turn of events transpired: a quarter hour after our encounter, this solitary traveler whom I encountered was assaulted by bandits, a servant killed, and he himself and the other servant so severely wounded that they barely managed to reach Toluca. I learned about this only later, and when I thought about the immense danger in which I had moved I could scarcely explain to myself my lucky escape, for almost miraculously I had eluded the bandits' ambush.

The road led on, uphill and down, among the forests and through extremely suspicious places, but the danger of this journey eventually amounted to nothing. But we came upon no inhabited place, something we desperately needed, since already at 2:00 in the afternoon the rain had begun to fall in torrents. Still, nothing in the world could persuade us to rest; it was apparent that only a rapid advance could save us from the perils of the road. For that reason we neither ate nor drank anything as we rode resolutely onward in dense rain—now over slippery footholds, now on stony paths. We had already been in the saddle for twelve hours and the water had not left us a single dry thread, when at last we glimpsed the point of a church tower among the opening pines, a sight we greeted with joy.

Now the road pushed further down into the valley, and in a little more than an hour we reached the small hamlet of Tisca, where we could spend the night safely. At 7:00 in the evening we stopped in the small establishment of a shopkeeper and collapsed exhausted on the nearby benches, worn out as much by the emotional excitement as by the prolonged ride. In addition to that came the most frightful hunger and thirst, for we had traversed twenty-three hours of road without having eaten anything, while the water covered our bodies, making the evening breeze extremely penetrating, like winter forest . . . in short, the journey from Toluca to here was one of the most difficult and dangerous I had made since my residence in Mexico.

Our host was a friendly man who, for the price of a few coins and a kind word, loaned us dry clothing, gave us something to eat and drink, and ordered us a place to stay in his store. Moreover, I was not a little joyful to learn that we were only four leagues from the next mine, in the possession of a German, and soon, lying on my hard bed which seemed as soft as eiderdown, I dreamed of the forests, of struggle and death, of my fatherland, and of the rewards of my journey. It was a lovely dream.

The sun was already climbing high over the horizon when I rode out of the hamlet Tisca and toward the mine Los Arcos. An animated guide showed us the way, which led through an extraordinarily charming valley in which luxurious cornfields flourished on all sides, and to whose right rose low but quite picturesque mountain ranges. Clear bell chimes rang out from the church of the village that lay close by, calling the devout to Sunday prayers. Everywhere people streamed out toward the market towns, and the road was as popular today as it had been lonely the day before. Delighted we rode along, since a peace entered into our souls, a peace that came from the harmony of the lovely valley with its industrious residents, and from the splendid morning with its beautiful vegetation. Now and then our guide let out a small song on his *harfita del pastor.*[1]

We rode out into this enchanting valley and had already passed a few silver works when we suddenly came upon something like a huge series of steps, I would say more than a hundred feet high, with which the valley appeared to have been hollowed out, like a terrace. From here a new scene presented itself. In the deep-lying valleys that turned to the left lay the charming tableau of the villages Almoloya and Jaltepec, and in a straight line in front of us rose the chimneys of the hacienda Los Arcos, from which mighty columns of smoke billowed forth. These chimneys belonged to the important smelter that serves a great part of the mines of Sultepec and Zacualpan.

The vegetation here became tropical once more, and was joined by the handsome evergreen, oaks, eritrea bushes, anona, lichen, and splendid orange trees that took the place of the unvaried pine forests in a gratifying way. On the mountains lying nearby one spied here and there over the protruding rock formations silver streaks—small waterfalls—that pleasantly interrupt the dark green. In short, the surroundings of Almoloya are highly charming and, because of the foundries, pleasantly animated. They offer a picture of bustling industry that recalls the homeland.

Soon we put Jaltepec behind us, and in a short time found ourselves at the hacienda and smelter Los Arcos, whose owners are the Herren Stein, reputable Germans and worthy compatriots. Herr Gustav Stein, who at the present found himself alone there, received us in his home with extraordinary hospitality. In the course of my visit he offered me every opportunity to become acquainted in detail with the entire process of silver extraction, in return for which I am greatly obliged to him.

The more noteworthy features of this process are worth mentioning. The silver ore, which is divided into rich and common ore (*metal rico y común*), comes first to the furnace house (*quemador*), where it is roasted. That is, the ore is place on a layer of wood and coal; once kindled, this is heated little by little, gradually purging all volatile materials such as sulphur, arsenic, and so forth. Or else they employ a more effective method, in which the ore is pulverized to a fine dust in a grinding mill and then roasted on a heated iron plate. The unrefined metal is then put into the blast furnaces, of which there are four in Los Arcos, and if it is lead-bearing, so much lead is produced on the side that the silver-to-lead ratio is 1 to 100. In these situations it becomes a struggle to lose as little silver as possible, since in molten form it readily joins with lead. The blast furnaces receive their air in a simple and highly practical way through a water cylinder bellows. In this device the water tumbles with immense force onto a stone, funnel-shaped cylinder, the air squeezes itself out immediately, and brings forth a strong, unbroken stream of wind. In other regards as well I found the blast furnace quite practical in construction, all the more so once an experienced German miner explained to process to me.

The oven is stoked (*se sangra el horno*) for approximately six hours, at which point the two to three hundred pounds of silver-bearing lead flows out. The so-called stone that forms out of the same is a slag that nevertheless contains something of precious metal, and is placed yet again in the ovens. The molten metal is at this point poured into round cakes, and after it has cooled goes into the purging oven, when the silver is extracted by the oxidization of lead. This process is called the dry method, in contrast to the amalgamation or wet method,[2] which I had the opportunity to see on another hacienda near Jaltepec.

According to the latter method, the metal is ground to fine powder. Next, this same is spread out on a walled terrace under the open sky, sprinkled with water, and, according to the richness of the ore, a certain quantity of quicksilver added. These two metals are then mixed in the most exact combination possible through treading by men, in other places by means of mules, and finally, a specific quantity of crushed salt is added for the formation of horn silver.[3] When this process is complete, the mass is washed in an apparatus constructed for that purpose, which is organized so that the silver, which has bonded with the quicksilver, remains behind, while the barren dust flows out with the water. The refiners now squeeze the purified metal thus produced first through linen-lined sacks and then through tanned animal skins in order to take out as much quicksilver as possible. Finally, this not yet entirely pure silver is brought under a form of bell (*capilla*), under which the quicksilver is eliminated by heat and the pure silver remains behind on the burner. Refiners consider metal extracted by amalgamation finer than that produced by the molten method. The four blast ovens in Los Arcos, when operating well, yield eight hundred to a thousand pounds of silver each month.

I stayed in Los Arcos for the length of four days, and amused myself so splendidly in the agreeable company of worthy countrymen that I began to get over the loneliness of my residence in Toluca. I did not fail to make a few botanical excursions, and although the region cannot be called extraordinarily rich, I still found a few charming flowers and plants.

On September 10 I left Los Arcos in order to visit some mines, and set out on the road over the mountain range to Zacualpan, since on the plateau the rivers were so swollen that we could not ford them. There accompanied me to this place a German miner, Herr Wilhelm Müller, who was so thoroughly troubled by malaria that he had sought a temporary change of climate.

Here stood splendid forests of firs and oaks, partially covered with exuberant parasites; trees, bushes, and plants shone with the most luxurious green of the rainy season. After a long residence in the interior of the country, I was once again journeying through tropical-looking virgin forests, and it saddened me greatly to have to leave untouched many of these splendid natural products because of the blockade, a dilemma that prevented me from taking along more than a few Sämereien and bulbs of *Cuclopatrea.*

We traveled extraordinarily slowly, in part because of the poor roads, in part because of Herr Müller's extreme weakness. Although he rested on a mattress we had taken along, he could scarcely do more than keep himself in the saddle. For that reason, around 5:00 in the afternoon, when on top of everything the rain that had earlier failed to appear now surprised us, we had to pass the night in a small Indian village called Ayatusco, where we found a not-too-hard bed on the ground. There was also a highly populated camp of certain small, leaping insects that did not allow us much rest, even less so since Herr Müller was seized by a powerful attack of fever and required our complete attention.

Fortunately, the next morning our pitiable guide at least found himself strong enough to set out with us on our journey to Zacualpan. The road moved out of the valley in which the Indian village lay and onto a mountain that was covered only sparsely with trees, but all the more with handsome meadows and flowers. In the early-morning hours many a lovely sight awaited us. The sun climbing above the horizon in the distant east illuminated a succession of beautiful mountain ranges; the pure dew, stirred by a fresh morning breeze, trembled on the leaves and flowers; the birds formed a lively choir; and we were deeply charmed by the loveliness of the joyful nature scene that surrounded us.

For two hours we followed the footpath that wound here and there, when at last we saw and soon reached Zacualpan, highest of all, lying scenically before us on the mountain. Zacualpan is a small town approximately sixty-five hundred feet above sea level, with two thousand inhabitants, whose homes, mostly built of stone, stand beside one another in attractive rows. A handsome church adorns the rather large plaza, and from it the traveler enjoys one of the loveliest sights in the world. I had already heard of it earlier, and the next morning, when I stared at it for a long time, I could scarcely believe that what I saw was reality.

Before me lay a small plateau, and stately hill country with luxurious valleys, splendid forests, and fields on all sides. To the left rose the *nevado* of Toluca, in the middle towered the two volcanoes of Puebla,[4] and to the right, in the far distance and illuminated by the morning sun, shimmered the snowfields of Orizaba. The vision of the astonished traveler then moves over the four highest mountain peaks in Mesoamerica. This vista almost borders on the unbelievable, because Orizaba lies at least 237 miles away in a straight line; one can only comprehend this spectacle when he takes into consideration the extraordinary transparency of the air in tropical lands, particularly during the rainy season.

I have never seen anything more stunning, and it was scarcely possible for me to separate myself from this magnificent sight. I returned again and again to that vantage point and stared into that sea of mountains and refreshed myself through this indescribably lofty scene. And as I lingered for hours and hours there, I believed that it must be a trick of the mind, that it must be something supernatural; but it was reality, for my companions too saw the same scene with equal enchantment. The rapture generated through this vista completely compensated for every toil and inconvenience of the journey, and one can rightly say that whoever has not seen the like has not beheld the most beautiful thing on this earth. It is a scene that indelibly impresses itself upon the traveler, and which can sweeten the bitterest hours of his life.

In the vicinity of Zacualpan are found many silver mines and amalgamation works that I inspected as much as my time permitted. On September 14 I visited the mine La Golondrina, in the possession of the Herren Stein in the hamlet Tecicapan, in order to become acquainted at closer hand with the Mexican mining industry, which is quite different from our own.

One enters this place either through a hazardous crawl forward or through perpendicular descent. In the first manner, the explorer comes upon a tunnel so narrow that he can scarcely stand upright, much less twist and turn. Now and then he has difficulty going through it on all fours, a nuisance that results from the fact that one balances himself not on a secure mass of support but rather on the thickness of the veins of ore. When the ore vein is broad, the tunnel is broad; when the vein is narrow, the tunnel is narrow and impedes the entry and exit in a highly disagreeable way. The miners utilize this irregular system not out of ignorance but for reasons of economy, because it would cost vast sums to work the barren stone days on end in order to produce a comfortable tunnel. It also follows that miners cannot use dogs, and that small boys must carry out all ore to daylight in baskets.

The second way to enter is far more dangerous than the first for those unacquainted with Mexican mines, for one enters not on a rope or a ladder but rather on a notched tree trunk that rests at an obtuse angle from one wall to another. It is almost unbelievable how quickly and safely the Mexican miners, for the most part half- or full-blooded Indians, hasten on and off this tree trunk with a ponderous basket on their heads, often without steadying themselves. It is ever so astonishing to see these people working almost naked all day long in the highly uncomfortable mines, something that testifies to the Indian's inexhaustible strength.

In Mexico, miners differ from other workers less than they do in our country; moreover, they lack the many unique customs of their European counterparts. The sole peculiarity they have is that whoever comes to a mine for the first time is tied up there for a long while by the same workers, until he has ransomed himself through a generous tip—the very same custom, incidentally, that sailors have, when a traveler ventures upon a ship's rope ladder for the first time, where he is likewise bound until he frees himself from this unpleasant situation by a gift.

In the company of Golondrina's overseer, a German named Herr Strunk, I inspected the mine in all directions and thereafter returned again to Zacualpan, where I passed five highly agreeable days.

I left Zacualpan on September 16 and struck out on the road to Toluca, through Ixtapan, both to be able to see a new region and also to avoid the great dangers with which the journey via Tisca is fraught. I previously spoke of a small plateau. The traveler rides through this without difficulty until he comes unexpectedly to a barranca that cuts from west to east and is of singular depth. It takes its name from the hamlet Manialtenango on the other side; this village lies in a straight line before the traveler but requires two hours to reach.

The steeply descending rocks were at that time covered with bluish achimenes, among which yuccas and a few *Cereae* cacti rose in their powerful, stiff forms. Further down at the bank of a small stream stood a few gigantic bald cypress of enormous height and magnificent beauty. On the other side, the extremely tortuous road wound upward among the stone masses, and as already mentioned we only reached the hamlet after two hours of steady exertion. From here we had now to ride through small meadows, now to wander through lesser valleys and barrancas or climb over low mountains, until at last at 1:00 in the afternoon we safely reached the hamlet of Ixtapan, an authentic picture of decay.

Ixtapan seems to have once been inhabited by many affluent Spaniards. However, in spite of the natural curiosities of its environs its name is now virtually unknown. Nearby, more hot mineral springs bubble up from the earth with such force that in one place the water gushes up one and a half feet and almost a man's width. This water has a temperature of 102 degrees and contains sulphurous sodium and carbonated calcium, which deposits itself in the small, countless overflows of the spring thereabout, so that in all directions it forms small stone gullies through which the clear water trickles. The odor of this same spring suggests a scant amount of hydrogen sulphide. The stony soil around Ixtapan consists of calcium deposits in turn resting on transitional layers of shale. These springs, which everywhere seem almost to be forgotten, and for the Mexican might be as healthy as Karlsbad is for us,[5] were without doubt known to the Spaniards, since a stone of the principal low wall enclosing the spring bears the year 1788.

We passed the night under the protection of the alcalde, on hard benches in the court chamber of the village. The next day we soon came to the barranca and village Tequaloya, and stayed in Tenancingo, of which small city I have already spoken in the preceding chapter.

On September 18 we finally reached Toluca safe and sound. In fourteen days we had therefore made a journey of more than sixty leagues.

Chapter 13

After I had returned from the arduous journey just described, and had seen everything in the environs of Toluca and had made use of it for my research, I faced no small dilemma as to where to direct my travels. I simply did not know where I was to turn, since the war with the North Americans still raged, and travel in the Mexican republic became more dangerous each day. Yet I still held out the hope of being able to push further on to the west, and for that reason on September 21 I hurried to the capital to put my financial affairs in order and to secure my letters of credit for Morelia.

I reached Mexico City in a diligencia without mishap, and in a short time had everything prepared for my departure. But here I was unexpectedly detained, since because of the migration of the province of Mexico's government to Toluca, the seats on the diligencia were sold out for ten days in advance, and reluctantly I had to tarry longer than I had resolved.

While at first this grated on me, conversely I managed to put the time to the greatest use, since exactly in those days the political circumstances of the republic took another turn and abruptly forced me to change my travel plans. In order to give a brief account of the conditions of that time, and the opinion I had of Mexico then, I here reproduce a copy of a letter I addressed to my friend and travel companion Fink:

> Mexico, September 28, 1846
> Dear Friend,
>
> Everything was ready for the trip to Morelia, but I suddenly changed my plans, the reason for which I will explain to you herewith. Santa Anna arrived here on September 15, and as you will note, it was the evening of the celebration of Mexican independence, which he selected—not without a sense of timing—for his entry into the capital. The reception was altogether chilly, yet there was no lack of homages from the side of his adherents and a part of the clergy. Salas offered him the presidential chair; he declined to accept it, how-

ever, and garbed himself in the pretense that he was only to rescue his fatherland with sword in hand. I set so little store by the promises of Santa Anna that I cannot grasp how he intends to use the momentary enthusiasm of the capital, all the greater as Salas had already prepared everything earlier to a masterstroke, and had summoned all Mexicans between ages sixteen and fifty, whereby the contingent of all states put forth thirty thousand men. All this, while one is at pains here to form a citizen's militia that is to protect the capital.

Meanwhile, after the Washington government's offers of peace were rejected by Mexico under the pretext that they had to await the assembly of congress on December 6 of this year, the Americans have made considerable progress. Six thousand men advanced on Monterrey, two thousand invaded New Mexico, and Governor Armijo was forced back to El Paso del Norte. The port of San Blas is blockaded and California already seized, and with it the prospect of a speedy conclusion to the war once more becomes remote. In fact, rumor now has it that General Taylor has already taken Monterrey, along with a thousand prisoners and sixteen cannon; in short, Mexico seems to be heading to its doom, or to a peace in which it will surely lose a third of its territory.[1]

All troops that Mexico had stationed in the cities for the security of property will be deployed against the enemy, and while I write this, Santa Anna has unexpectedly withdrawn to San Luis Potosí with a few infantry and cavalry units, along with some cannons. I cannot grasp what harm he believes he can inflict on the enemy there, since the latter stand far to the north. The goods and property of foreigners and natives alike now lie in the hands of the most brutal people, and in fact matters have been so bad here earlier that the streets now swarm with audacious bandits and assassins. Moreover, animosity against foreigners, which until now was still slumbering, grows more virulent with each passing day, and yesterday evening in the vicinity of the Plaza de Voladores a cry rang out: "Mueren los extrajeros e invasores!" ("Death to foreigners and invaders!"), so that a person cannot reveal the slightest sympathy for North America if one wants his life to be safe. In the most recent days already several have fallen victim in this way, and the important houses have all prepared themselves for a powerful resistance in case of an assault by the léperos. In a word, the unrest and agitation are boundless, so that I am not a little bit worried for our countrymen in Mexico.

On the other hand, they are making use of everything in order to be able to present a sword point to the enemy. All the large cities have witnessed assemblies and speeches in the plazas for the purpose of forming voluntary troops, who lack not only arms but all munition. In many places—and this is especially the case here—demagogues already have the population so whipped up that even fathers of families are inclined to take the field. Still, it may be difficult for the Mexican to vanquish the well-disciplined army of the North Americans, and although the Mexican troops might be entirely beaten, I still do not believe, given the obstinacy of the native government, that a prompt surrender is being considered, and am convinced that they will allow the enemy to march into the capital rather than negotiate peace.

You will easily gather how dangerous the situation of lone travelers such as ourselves has become. For my part, I cannot long remain in Mexico, because for me an extended residence here in the country would mean a loss of time and money without any sort of favorable result. For that reason I have resolved not to go to Morelia, but rather to Yucatán, which has now determined to remain attached to Mexico by means of a federation, but which otherwise has involved itself in none of these political upheavals, and whose ports still permit free entry and exit. As soon as I receive a place on the diligencia, you will see me in Toluca in order to be able to arrange the return trip to Veracruz.

Your sincere friend.

I was only able to carry out the return promised in that letter on October 5. In the shortest time Herr Fink was ready to head with our luggage and our animals to Orizaba, where we planned to meet up. I myself preferred to travel via Mexico City, Perote, and Jalapa, as much to save time and expense as to be able to see new regions. In any case I still had to remain a few days alone in Toluca in order to organize, pack, and store the collections, since they could not be shipped to Europe owing to the blockade.[2]

I left Toluca on October 15, in truth never to see it again, and luckily reached Mexico City a day later, when the léperos tried to rob a home in the capital, and every individual owner had to fend them off by means of his own servants. This time I paused only a very short time in Mexico City, and since I had with me but little luggage and of scant worth, I therefore hoped to reach the coast safely. The valuable items and the horses went with an enormous arriero train of forty mules, a train that was transporting hardware merchandise to Puebla, and I had believed that it reached Orizaba in complete safety. The reader may well imagine my horror when I received a letter on that very day, informing me of the deeply distressing news that I had been robbed of almost all my possessions. It happened like this. The train to which my servant had attached himself had entered into the vicinity of Venta de Córdoba without incident. But when they reached the so-called Barranca de Juanes, they were suddenly assaulted by fifteen well-armed robbers on horseback, hauled into the woods, and tied to trees. My goods and property were the first things that the bandits found on closer inspection, and out of my coffers they took, in a word, everything. I lost not only all clothing but also a body of small items of note, and what pained me most terribly, all my scientific instruments.[3] They immediately plucked out the remaining packages that were being transported, selected what seemed most suitable for their needs, and loaded them on my best horse, while the arrieros, bound, had to look on helplessly. The band of robbers had already moved on with their splendid plunder when my lad managed to bite through the ropes that bound him and hurried to Córdoba to seek help. In that place he found a few men who were willing to pursue the bandits, but the search went poorly for them. As luck would have it, they found nothing other than my valuable mule, which the thieves had abandoned. My excellent riding horse, together with saddle and all other effects, were lost forever. With the trifles that remained my lad set out on the journey as directed. However, this unhappy twist of fate had so impoverished me that I had nothing to show beyond my diary and the clothes I wore.

It was a terrible blow, and only my credit in Mexico and Veracruz helped me out of this bleak predicament. Utterly furious as a result of these events, I felt all the more urgency to depart from a country that could protect gangs of thieves and bandits but not honest men. In the firm belief that I would lose the little I still had, I left Mexico City on October 18, 1846, after I had taken a heartfelt farewell from my countrymen, who had shown me so much attention and friendship. Only a minor detail prevented my gloomy misgivings from being fulfilled and saved us from robbers—the fact that we drove out of Mexico City at half past five, instead of four in the morning. For as we approached the ominous Barranca de Juanes we came upon a courier from Veracruz, who called out an “en buena hora” (“Welcome”) from afar and told us that bandits had awaited us for a long time, but finally out of boredom they had robbed several travelers of their horses and then retreated back into the woods. Our fortunate arrival in Puebla (a city I have already described, along with the road leading to the same) soon corroborated the facts of the matter.

I remained in Puebla no longer than one night, and the next morning I was already traveling on with the diligencia. We now pursued a lonesome road of thirty leagues across the high plateau, soon reached Amozoc, Acajete, and approached the dreaded Pinal, a small pine forest that is notorious throughout the republic for its scenes of robbery and murder. But we soon put this dangerous place behind us and now came to the region that goes under the name Ojo de Agua, and where particularly in this time of year (the autumn) one enjoys the most intriguing natural phenomenon of *fata morgana.* For a long time we saw ourselves surrounded by water there, something which seemed so real that we could scarcely persuade ourselves to consider this apparent mass of water a mirage, and we amused ourselves for over an hour with the marvelous spectacle.

At noon we passed the village Tepeyahualco, and toward evening came safe and sound to Perote, a place that lies at the end of the immense high plain, and where we quartered for the night. Perote is a small city that takes its name from a volcano lying close by, and enjoys a certain importance on account of a military school and stout fortress that dominate a considerable part of the main street. In this place many political prisoners, among them Europeans, have languished for years. The lodging in Perote is a rather good and enjoyable one.[4]

The next morning we abandoned this small town rather early, for we still had to pass a dangerous place, the so-called Barranca Seca.[5] But so far we had proceeded with good luck, so we engaged some well-armed men to accompany us, and in this way we managed to reach the state of Veracruz, which until now had no ill reputation for banditry. With the break of day we found ourselves in the village of Las Vigas, where the road became so bad that midway we toppled over in a deep, muddy hole, and we had to pass more than an hour setting ourselves right again. Luckily, no one was injured, and this unfortunate incident brought out more amusement than horror and grief.

After Las Vigas very shortly began the so-called *Mal Pais,*[6] which consists of immense lava masses that have piled up and clustered themselves in the most singular fashion. A lovely road leads through this place, and the traveler has many opportunities to marvel at the seemingly artistic shapes of this volcanic scene, which in places gave way to small grottoes, in other places to pointed and wonderfully jagged cones. Here the vegetation is quite poor, and only a few firs prosper with difficulty; nevertheless, the trip through Mal Pais is quite romantic and far less tedious than I had imagined.

The incline leading to the highest point is not very steep, and all the less noticeable as the driver negotiated his way quite skillfully over the mountain pass. When we had reached the highest point, the road immediately led down the mountain and the landscapes became even more enchanting. To the right loomed more and more the volcano Perote (12,934 feet high); oaks mingle with the firs, while lively flowers are prominent among the dark green colors.

In the village San Miguel we changed mules for the last time, and two hours later, at 9:00 in the morning, we reached the city of Xalapa, in a manner of speaking the center point of the Mexican paradise. Xalapa lies 4,175 feet above sea level in one of the most splendid areas of a small plateau; it has many charming houses and approximately fifteen thousand inhabitants. Here the Franciscans own an opulent cloister, and the lovely church has much costly adornments, along with beautiful paintings by old Spanish masters.

The vegetation in the environs greatly resembles that of Mirador, from which it lies scarcely fifteen leagues in a straight line. The extraordinarily attractive and healthy climate, the cleanliness of the well-paved streets, tidy homes, gardens, and stores, the good hotels and coffeehouses make this city a pleasant resort of wealthy Veracruzanos during the time of yellow fever, a place where at every moment they awaited the bombardment of Veracruz in a highly comfortable refuge.

It is difficult to describe adequately the beauty of this region, and the view from the hill Macultepec is truly stunning. Nestled within the mountain range, Orizaba and Perote stand in all their splendor and appear to be but a brief distance apart. A fertile hill country rings the city itself, and this country yields the fruits of all climates; small Indian homes are nestled here and there, and their quaint thatch roofs emerge from the dark green of the trees. In short, there may be no other place in Mexico where everything unites to the favor of the industrious inhabitants, and the first-class guest houses arranged in European style offer proof that foreigners are no rarity here. Although I only stayed in San Miguel several days, the time was too short to fully witness all the beauty of Xalapa. But I have no doubt that it is the most thoroughly agreeable place in the republic, and offers everything that the traveler—and the settler, for that matter—can desire.

On October 23 I set out on my way in the diligencia, and now the road led us over a vast stone mass, now through small forests of mimosas or through low-lying areas where it had to be paved. We continually plummeted downhill at a dangerous velocity, since the North American coachmen who drive these vehicles are less concerned with the safety of the passengers than with arriving punctually at the station. At approximately 2:00 in the afternoon we reached the ranchería El Plan del Río, and thereby found ourselves in a place whose huge ravine subsequently became so ominous for the Mexicans.[7] To the right stood the town of Cerro Gordo, to the left more hills. At midway the road crosses over a small river, so that the totality translates into an austere pass that can be easily defended but is ever so difficult to seize.

From here the traveler passes through many picturesque estates of perfectly tropical character, until at last he arrives at the small village of Puente Nacional (formerly Puente del Rey), which is the second important pass on the main road to Mexico. Moreover, here the dense mountains crowd up to the bank of a branch of the river from Antigua, over which a splendid bridge of the same name leads. They tower so imposingly over the place that I could scarcely believe that any sort of invading force could pass through this point if it were to any degree well defended.

In Puente I found my mozo waiting for me with sad countenance, for we had not seen one another since the last time he was set upon by robbers. He had nevertheless arrived here punctually in order to complete the last part of the journey in Mexico with me. Early the next morning we left Puente and departed from the main road in order to reach Zacuapan as soon as possible through a shortcut that runs along a thicket of mimosas. But Zacuapan lay twelve leagues away, and since the heat was withering this journey demanded no trifling effort, as much on our part as on the part of the horses. I felt the hot sun of the tierra caliente all the more, since I had already accustomed myself somewhat to the higher regions, and the refreshing fruit of the orange tree almost never seemed to me as sweet as at that moment when I luckily managed to buy a few from an Indian who came upon us.

By 3:00 in the afternoon I found myself again in the circle of esteemed friends. Dr. Eichhorn of the coffee plantation Mocca, Herr Fink, Herr Baetke with his wife and daughter—in short, all had gathered to greet me in Zacuapan and to offer me the same hospitality they had so generously extended before. I would scarcely have enjoyed myself more if I had set foot on my homeland as in the moment when I found myself again in Zacuapan, where a number of upright and sympathetic friends had gathered as only a lonesome traveler could wish. This spiritual and physical recovery did not last long, however, because I had firmly resolved to leave Mexico, so I hastened to carry out my plan.

Once more I greeted Mirador and Huatusco in order to pack my surviving things; once more I hailed the lovely mountains and valleys where I had spent such a hopeful and happy time; once more I saw the house I had built, the trees I had planted, the running brook in which I had bathed, and the abundant meadows I had so often roamed. Everything here was so wonderful to me, such diverse memories attached themselves to all, and I tore myself away from that region with such a heavy heart that from every hill I continued to look back on it through eyes moist with tears, and speechless could only embrace the friends who accompanied me.

I left Zacuapan on October 29. A dark and eventful future lay before me, and as I retraced the path I had taken a year earlier my trusty lad rode with me in silent company; deeply lost in thought, I forgot about the heat, the hunger and thirst, and the difficulties and dangers, and rode all day until I had reached Paso de Ovejas. Here I again climbed on my horse and hurried onward. Once again pale moonlight illuminated the road, just like a year before; once again the hoofbeats of the horse resonated far away into the stillness of the night, and again we stood before the grotesque figures of the nopales wrapped in half-darkness until the morning sun climbed up behind the mighty Orizaba,[8] and before me lay the desolate coastland, the bare walls of Veracruz, and the raging sea.[9] I entered the city with understandable melancholy, spiritually exhausted by the memories of the recent days, and physically spent by the uninterrupted journey of twenty-four leagues. But the next day I discovered that no ship departed Veracruz for Yucatán, and in fact I thought I would have to take my way through Havana, when I came to learn that a ship was to set sail for Alvarado, one that was consigned to the Prussian consul in Veracruz, Herr d'Olaire, who had the kindness to inform me of this vessel's impending departure for Campeche.

Since the day of departure was not yet determined, I had to undertake the journey there as soon as possible, and was ready to leave Veracruz on November 2. In arranging my financial affairs I had suffered considerable losses as a result of transferring credit to Campeche, and I closed my account with the commercial house of Drusina and Company, so that there remained nothing else for me to do but gather my luggage and depart. My lad Pancho, who had accompanied me the entire year and served me faithfully, only bid me farewell at the last moment, and I have to confess that the extraordinary devotion of this Mexican—a devotion he showed with tear-moistened eyes and his assurance that he would go with me to the death—moved me not a little. But my scanty resources did not allow me to pay the costly passage for a servant, and indeed I left Veracruz on the afternoon of November 2, utterly alone.

The road led along the seacoast for almost the entire distance, and passed over the deepest sand, on which the sun beat down frightfully. After two hours I reached Boca del Río, the mouth of the rather considerable river of Medellín, where we dismounted and had to pull the horses along in canoes, while the night was rapidly falling. By the time we found ourselves on the other side, the moon had already climbed into full splendor out of the clouds, and with its wonderful luster illuminated the bare sand dunes of the coast and the waves of the sea rolling in onto the strand. Only when we had moved on a distance from there, in search of a shortcut to the promontory of Antonio Lizardi, did we again came upon grass-grown spaces, and into a small woods where, at least as nearly as I could observe by moonlight, a splendid tropical vegetation proliferated. Hundreds of exposed roots dangled from ancient wild fig trees and formed whole columns in clusters, while bushes and running plants covered the soil; even orchids grew here, and in particular we often saw *Schomburgkia tibicinis.*

At midnight we found ourselves in Rancho de las Salinas, where we lingered only long enough to outfit the horses, in order to be able to take advantage of the evening cool. For that reason we soon saddled up once more and hurried along the ocean strand. The noise of the waves rolling onto the sand resounded monotonously, a multitude of sea crabs ran around at night on the beach, so that the horses trampled a few of them, and only the constantly glowing cigars, together with thoughts about the past and the future, kept away sleep and exhaustion. As the sun rose I was only two more leagues from Alvarado, and arrived at the same at 7:00 on the morning of November 3, after I had put a road of eighteen leagues behind me in fourteen hours.

Alvarado is a small and charming village that lies on a natural harbor into which pours a river of the same name. The harbor would be among the safest and most handsome were the entry not inaccessible to large ships owing to the sandbar at the mouth. Marshy lands surround these waters, on which a small steamboat moves up and down between Alvarado and the island community of Tlacotalpan. In the latter case, this small population acquired the name of an illustrious *villa,* because it gallantly fought off two assaults of the North Americans, and now everyone was working with great enthusiasm to fortify the entry from the sea in every possible way, particularly since the last news of the war confirmed the enemy seizure of Tabasco and of five ships lying in that harbor.

In Alvarado I spent five days awaiting the schooner's departure. It could not set out because of an unfavorable north wind, and during this time we were severely tormented by the frightful heat (95–100 degrees) and the millions of mosquitoes.[10] The environs of the village, much of which is submerged during the rainy season, offered a rich hunt, but except for a few cornfields there was nothing that suggested agriculture. The entirety is flat, hot coastland, such as I so often saw later.

Second Part

Travels in Yucatán, Tabasco, and Chiapas

Those things which mark the character of a landscape: the outline of the mountains, which circumscribe the horizon in the hazy distance; the darkness of the woods; the forest stream, which hurtles raging among overhanging crags: everything stands in old and mysterious communion with the cheerful lives of men.

—Alexander von Humboldt, *Aspects of Nature*

The rivers, with their countless tributaries, are the sole roads of the nation.

—Alexander von Humboldt, *Aspects of Nature*

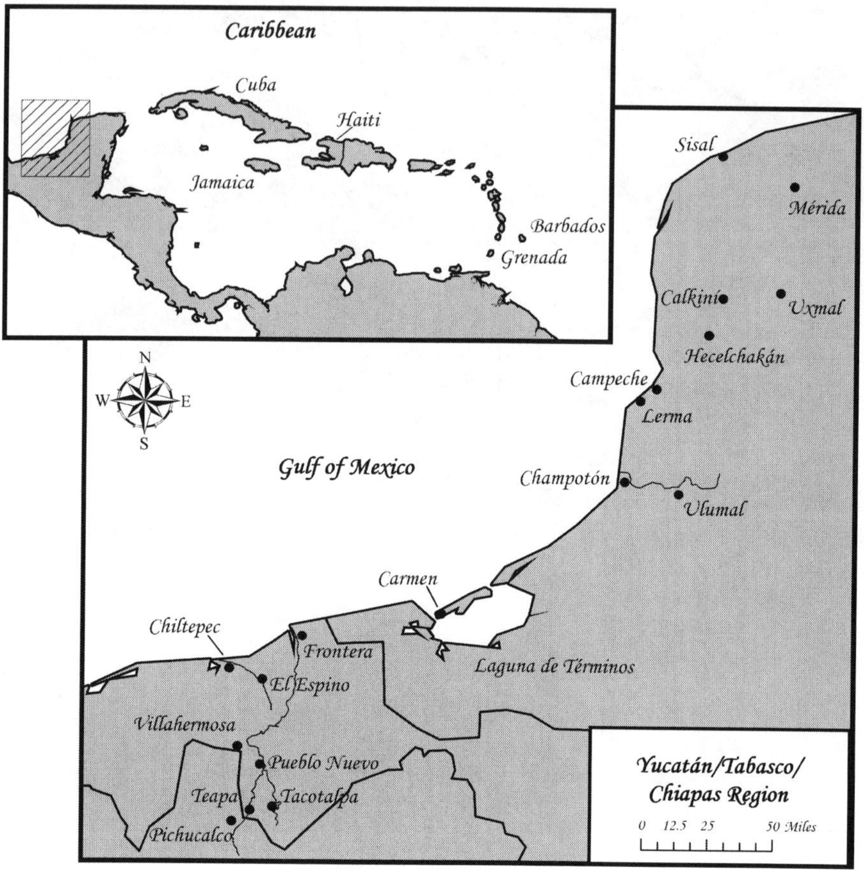

Southeast Mexico and the Caribbean

Chapter 14

After we had already waited several days for a favorable wind, as I have said, we finally had to have a steamship tow us out of the harbor. It was not advisable to remain any longer in Alvarado, for we risked exposing ourselves to seizure by the Americans. We feared their new attack at every instant, and as much as possible tried to protect ourselves. Furthermore, after we had luckily managed to set to sea, the greatest caution was necessary to conceal ourselves from the American squadron, which lay anchored twenty warships strong at Antonio Lizardi. If our schooner had breached the blockade there, it would have been sighted and trapped. We put out from there in the evening, in order to make for the open sea at night, so that we could move our ship beyond the enemy's horizon.

Our schooner, the *Rafaela,* was a seaworthy vessel of 115 tons, and swiftly set a northeastern course. We traveled the entire first night in order to move as far as possible from the land, since the Prussian flag under which we sailed would not have been safe from the Yankees. The next morning we were already sufficiently distant to be able to stop, although we could still see the volcano Tuxtla, and we now hoped to navigate for the southeast, weather permitting. But an opposing wind beat down upon us, until we sailed out over the 21st latitude north, where it first became remotely possible to set a course to Campeche.

With a good wind one can reach this city in four days; on the third day, however, we still reckoned ourselves to be on the 20th latitude. I began to grow dreadfully bored, for the schooner, which was otherwise so nicely built, provided little room to walk around; and I still did without the incalculable pleasure of reading, since my luggage, through the negligence of the arrieros, had come too late to Alvarado.

Close upon the southeast wind followed a calm that tormented us for an entire day, and afterward a light breeze from east-northeast. In fact, this would have been propitious had we been able to use it properly, but we had to beware of the shallows of Cabezo, which consist of a mere thread of water, and which we could not see in the night. Instead we were forced to head east-southeast to southeast in order to avoid the danger of running aground. The next day we finally sailed in the proper direction, and the following night we came so close to the land that we would soon have reached our goal, had not the weak wind once more returned, and had the Gulf Stream with ensuing calm not forced us almost an entire degree to the west. On the eighth day at evening we once more neared the land at Mount Cacamalson; however, we had to move away from it once again, since the wind was not sufficiently favorable to travel along the coast.

On November 13 we finally caught sight of the stone Morros of Paypotón,[1] and consequently had not moved further from Campeche. Even so, we would not have reached it that day had a good land breeze not sprung up, one that drove us with extraordinary speed toward our destination. We had run up so many sails that the masts bent and the ship, leaning strongly to one side, cut through the ever choppier sea like an arrow. No steamship could have measured up to us, and still it was 8:00 in the evening before we laid anchor. This we did at a harbor mouth, because vessels must take great care when finding themselves in the shoals before Campeche. The sea is so shallow in the small inlet that lighter vessels must weigh anchor two to three nautical miles away from the land. There we could expect the visit of the sanitary commission, which awaited us at any event; we could not go ashore before that, and once more we entertained ourselves over excellent canned sea crabs,[2] English pale ale, some good cigars, and chatting away the evening with the captain in a pleasant fashion, until the time of leisure drew to a close.

At last I stood on the deck. Campeche lay scenically before me in a soft morning light, offering an astonishing picture. A stout ring of walls washed its feet in the sea ripples,[3] while beautiful buildings surrounded by innumerable coconut palms connected to the left and right of these walls to form the suburbs. Overgrown birds stand in the background and greet the traveler with joyful anticipation. In short, the first glimpse of the city left nothing to be desired.

The sanitation boat arrived with the doctor and the commander of the security guard. They demanded the necessary papers, and took along the captain and two passengers who were Yucatecans. Since I was a foreigner, they left me for quite a while, until I could obtain permission to go ashore and could be vouched for. This last item was not difficult for me, since I was supplied with sufficient letters of recommendation. After two hours I was taken ashore, presented before the port captain and the *jefe político*,[4] and questioned about my reason for being here, and over news from Mexico, whereupon I

"After Mérida, Campeche is the most important city in Yucatán, and lies, in strictest sense of the term, on the sea; it has handsome, well-laid-out streets with one- and two-story houses." Although automobiles have made their entry, the streets and architecture of inner Campeche remain very much as Heller would have seen them. (Photo by Terry Rugeley)

received permission to remain ashore. My arrival from Mexico caused such a sensation that I was invited to an audience with the highest political authority, the governor. Here too they questioned me once more over the innumerable fine points of Mexico's political condition, and when I had given the particulars as best I could they discharged me with a great many expressions of courtesy, whereupon I went off to inspect the city more closely.

After Mérida, Campeche is the most important city in Yucatán, and lies, in strictest sense of the term, on the sea; it has handsome, well-laid-out streets with one- and two-story houses that, like the entire city, stand on sturdy coral rock. The inhabitants number 15,357 and profitably distinguish themselves from all others as much for culture as for industry. Here reigns a level of activity I had found nowhere else in all of Mexico. Among the upper classes the traveler encounters an elegance in society, culture, and civility fully rivaling that of the European. Many gentlemen of the commercial class speak two or three languages, ladies devote themselves to music, and well-to-do men of leisure occupy themselves with the culture of their fatherland's literature and history.

Campeche has several lovely churches, among which a number are particularly noteworthy: the ancient cathedral,[5] which was erected in the year 1540 and is named after María Concepción; the cloister of St. Francis; and further off a college for judicial and philosophical studies, a school established by a Frenchman, a hospital, and still other beneficent establishments. To the assortment of available diversions belongs the so-called Lonja, or trading house, access to which the well-to-do inhabitant gains through a subscription, and where he finds a reading salon next to parlors for gaming and billiards.

The dress of the lower classes (that of the upper class is altogether European) distinguishes itself quite remarkably from the Mexican. The men cherish wearing their wide white trousers, and over them a linen shirt that is particularly hard to iron. At their side they frequently fasten the machetes which are customary here—shorter than those of Mexico, and possessing a clublike form.[6] A hat of palm straw overshadows the dark, coppery-brown beardless countenance. The women of Campeche, famous for their beauty, wear nothing wider than a single skirt (*fustán*) that reaches to the ankles, and over it a long chemise (*huipil*), whose border is mostly adorned with charming embroidered flowers. Their long, thick hair is braided in a plait whose end is tucked into the waist or else dangles loosely. High combs, at times fashioned out of gold and quite costly, sit firmly atop the head and serve to secure the white or brightly colored cloth that these women expertly toss over themselves in so charming a fashion. Over the breast hangs a long, golden chain on whose end is fashioned a cross or gold medallion; the faces of these latter bear a saint or the Mother of God, and it is indispensable that they shimmer in the middle of the street. The footwear, if such is required at all, amounts to costly silk shoes, the Turkish-like slippers with curled toes, or leather sandals. The small feet of most Yucatecan women are admirable, and at times scarcely measure six inches in length.[7]

The environs of Campeche are only slightly mountainous, and outside of the many coconut groves offer little that is picturesque. There are many beautiful properties with gardens and fruit orchards, particularly noteworthy for cultivation of camotes, marañones, ciruelas, mangoes, mameys, zapotes, corn plums, melons, and vegetables.[8] They carry the name *quintas,* and they serve partly as residences, partly as profitable estates. Coconuts are greatly valued here; locals frequently take their agreeable and tasty milk as a midday refreshment. Especially in the mornings, men and women go to the gardens to drink coconut milk, which keeps them in excellent health. I must confess that I very soon came to prefer this over the singularly poor cistern water of the city, water that accumulates from one rainy season to the next.

Just as the environs of Campeche have little to offer a party of travelers, so too the entire countryside is extremely poor, something more or less true even for the most beautiful area. Yucatán is a flat peninsula which in itself bears the character of having been thrown up by volcanic upheaval; it has almost no mountains, its soils mostly consist of limestone and coral; and it is extraordinarily hot and dry here, both because of its location and because of its rocky nature. Except for the rainy season, this is a rather barren land, for it lacks adequate rivers and good soil. Five-sixths of the inhabitants are pure Indian of a single tongue. They speak the Maya language and, as I subsequently had opportunity to observe, might be the true descendants of the Toltecs. In the present day they live quite peacefully, and for the most part in great poverty; but at the time of the Spaniards' first arrival in the year 1517 they were so warlike that the discoverers nowhere suffered so bloody a reception as here.[9]

On the coast a great part of the population lives solely from fishing, which is endlessly profitable. In particular they serve young shark, called *cazón,* a universal food and so popular that it is only seldom lacking on the table of the well-to-do. In the interior of the country they frequently cultivate corn, rice, and coconut palms, and with these products work the only commerce the countryside offers, along with stock ranching. Above all they send cattle hides to Havana, to which industry are added the products of palm leaves and the agave twine. Recently the trade with this twine (henequen, or sisal hemp) has gone on the upswing, since Yucatecans found it quite durable and cheap as ship rigging. In addition they ply a brisk trade in hanging mats, straw hats, honey, and wax, all of which are produced in Campeche. They export much dried fish, coconuts, and smaller items, especially citron and other tropical fruits, to the different provinces of Mexico and North America. Nevertheless, agriculture in Yucatán is quite limited and with greater diligence might yield still more products suitable for export. For example, there is tobacco—of high quality and agreeable aroma—but at the present it is consumed only in the country itself.

The Indians of Yucatán keep themselves considerably purer in their speech, uses, and customs than any other Indian tribe in Mexico. Only within the environs of the cities do they understand the Spanish language; further into the interior Maya is spoken exclusively. Usually they go with upper bodies naked, the women not excepted, and only when they come to the city do they tend to cover their breast with a type of small blouse. On the whole, however, they are friendly, and like all Indians mistrustful, taciturn, and laconic, and have no desire to come into contact with white men. They reside in their villages in patriarchal style, and select as chief an esteemed Indian who holds the title cacique, who as supreme judge leads the community. The innocence of these folk is quite remarkable; it is so great that often one comes across both sexes without distinction bathing nude, and in no way do the Indians allow the arrival of a stranger to interrupt this naked affair. Although one may think that great licentiousness reigns among the Indians, it seems that on the contrary the laws of nature are nowhere more stringently observed as with them. The traveler frequently encounters noble and especially well-shaped forms among the women, whose face carries at all times the stamp of sweet temper upon it.

The climate of Yucatán is extremely arid (68–102 degrees) and in general is considered healthy, although this could merely be because foreigners seldom come here, and for that reason have been unable to disparage it so easily. There is little doubt, however, that on the coast in particular yellow fever is found, and during the rainy season malaria and also bilious fever frequently make their appearance and pose great danger. At times the heat here is extraordinarily great, and in the dry season the land often seems withered for miles and miles.

Yucatán is a state belonging through federation to Mexico, but it possesses vastly more freedom than any other. For example, the seaport has unique privileges; moreover, while tobacco is a state monopoly in Mexico, it is free here and is processed in Campeche in the method of Havana. In addition, Yucatán has little in common with Mexico, and has already fought many difficult battles with the same.[10] Presently it maintains neutrality in the republic's affairs, and in fact one could almost predict that it will separate itself from the motherland at the first opportunity. The government usually resides in Mérida, but now, as this land as well was dismembered through discords by the time of my arrival, one governor is to be found in Mérida and a second in Campeche, each selected by his own party as leader of the land.[11] I will soon touch upon the reason for this peculiar discord, which for Yucatán has had tragic consequences, for it exerted such a prejudicial influence upon my journey.

Yucatán had enjoyed a profitable tranquillity for a few years when Santa Anna returned to Mexico; consequently, when he once more established the Constitution of 1821,[12] he demanded aid for the war with North America, to provide money as well as troops. Yucatán is a poor land that needs its money and its own people only too dearly, and through this act would have violated neutrality and opened itself to a blockade of the ports, a blockade that would have brought economic prostration. It was in Campeche that the peninsulars found their first patriots, who on October 25 of this year declared themselves against the 1821 constitution and championed that of 1841, which guaranteed neutrality. Mérida, where to the contrary they considered themselves adherents of Santa Anna, was incited by the same and was moved to remain loyal to the first constitution; whereupon the inhabitants of Campeche, who in the year 1840 had fought bravely and victoriously for the Constitution of 1841, felt themselves so offended that they resolved to compel Mérida to their position by force of arms. In consequence of this the National Guard and the few military units were put on a war footing, a provisional government set up, the troops immediately sent into the field, and a destructive civil war launched.

In this state of affairs I came to Yucatán, contrary to all my expectations, on November 14. Every tie with the interior of the peninsula was severed, and I was forced to await the conclusion of the matter in Campeche. For eight days I stayed in a wretched fonda, since I was not in a position to afford a suitable residence, until Herr Gutiérrez Estrada, one of the most influential, cultured, and wealthy men of the city, and to whom I was recommended, furnished me with a room in the Lonja. It provided me the basic necessities, and I immediately moved into my new and agreeable quarters. I cannot sufficiently extol nor too thankfully acknowledge the politeness and kindness this estimable man showed me during my entire sojourn in Yucatán.

After I had settled into my small household as well as possible, my first priority was to inquire about the Europeans present. There I was delighted to meet Herr Adler, doctor of medicine, who, although born in Rige,[13] had received his upbringing in Prussia, and was now at so great a distance from the fatherland that I could easily consider him a compatriot.[14] He had already lived for quite a long time in America, and had happily practiced his art in Laguna[15] and for a short period in Campeche.

The tremendous value of meeting a fellow countryman overseas soon required us to draw nearer. We held our midday meals together, so that we spent many pleasant hours in one another's company, and at least for the time being I could expand my excursions to the environs of the city. Outside the fortress walls lie the beautiful suburbs of San Román, Guadalupe, San Francisco, Santa Lucía, and Hermita, upon which the quintas and coconut groves bordered. A small range of hills extends from the southwest toward the city, but the vegetation, which had seemed so charming to me upon my arrival, soon proved itself to be of the poorest quality. It bore the character of the hot coastline and consists of mimosa undergrowth, some cinnamon, willow-leafed gentia, and a few running vines, which at the moment hung about almost withered on the branches. It was quite a sad scene for the natural scientist who was assigned to live here for a long time. Only the cultivated fruit trees to some extent brightened the landscape, but otherwise a pale, lifeless tone lay over it, something that made no good impression.

An excursion to the remote seaside village of Lerma only further confirmed my impression of this poverty, as did a visit to the hills known by the name of *eminencia,* from which one at least savors a beautiful vista of the city and the sea. Still, I looked forward to a greater abundance during the rainy season, for three months had already passed without a drop of water falling, and to me it seemed impossible that something could sprout in the white-hot chalk rock. On the other hand, and in contrast to the poverty of the land, the sea offered a vast richness, and because of the many shoals with fish and conch, perhaps no coast of America is so extraordinarily well provided as that of Yucatán. From the greatest shark to the smallest sea needle, from the largest of sea mollusks to the tiniest tubeworm, from sea turtles, starfish, coral and mollusks, the waters here are overabundantly populated. The fish market in Campeche ranks among the most interesting sites, and I lacked the means to make use of these collections of animals, since my mission limited me to the plant kingdom, and I could only devote so much attention to the conches.

However, and despite all efforts, my attempts to enrich my collection in the domains fate assigned to me met with precious little reward. No orchids were to be found, no palms, nothing more than unimportant seeds and a beautiful bulbous plant known as the sea daffodil, which I brought home in triumph. The place was even lacking in insects, and it seldom occurred to me to seize one or two of the little creatures. Only the mosquitoes remained present in limitless number.

Fourteen days had passed, and since the hostile parties in the countryside had settled their quarrel, I thought of making a journey into the interior. However, men experienced in politics advised me against it, assuring me that this dubious tranquillity would not last for long. In fact, the hostilities renewed themselves once more in December, and the Campechanos moved in earnest on the Meridanos.[16] Every day one awaited the clash, and the civil war resumed with devastating bitterness.

Following these tragic events my captivity in Campeche grew longer, and since, as I have already mentioned, I could make only modest progress, I dedicated myself to filling the time profitably with the study of medicine, to which end Dr. Adler offered me all manner of theory and practice. Tropical fever frequently made its appearance in that season, and under the direction of my friend I had the opportunity to study it in its most horrifying form, an experience that proved incalculably useful for me later on.

On the other hand, my circle of acquaintances in Campeche increased; among them the French consul, Mr. Villévèque, and two clergymen, the brothers Padres Camacho, were especially valuable. The former received me in his home regularly and with great camaraderie, and not infrequently invited me to be his guest; likewise, the latter was very friendly and highly knowledgeable in the history of their country, and possessed a small private collection of antiquities and objects of natural history that caught my interest in a high degree. To be certain, I could obtain nothing from them, since they had made it a rule not to give away even the most trifling item, but they were highly informative and made no secret of their place of discovery. The antiquities, which they had arranged in their home, were of incalculable value, and in some cases belonged to the oldest epochs of Indian civilization. I often regretted that this great treasure had to remain so hidden, and perhaps someday will be lost to the entire world.[17]

Although at times I was not lacking in diversions in that place, I was nonetheless tormented by uncertainty over my situation and greatly depressed that support from Europe was not forthcoming. I lacked the wherewithal to develop a daily routine. By now the North Americans had occupied Laguna[18] and forced the Mexican magistrate to leave, thus closing off my access to Tabasco. The coast and most ports of the Mexican republic were blockaded. Here in the countryside civil war had broken out, and I remained without prospects and without the means to forsake this unfortunate land once and for all.

I tried in vain to cheer myself up, and in vain were the encouraging moments working with Dr. Adler. My situation was and remained horrible. Soon came the profound effects that all this had wrought on my spirit as well as my body. Symptoms of fever made their appearance, and before the year's end I soon lay alone on the sickbed. Every ray of hope, every spark of joy, was extinguished for me, and an infinite sadness filled my heart. This time, however, my friend Dr. Adler stood helpfully by my side with his knowledge. In a few days he had me out of danger of being a victim of yellow fever, which had already stretched out its frightening arms toward my life.

When I found myself well again, Christmas was upon us, without anything in the political equation having changed in my favor. A solemn mood ruled on this holiday in the city, and it seized me as well, even though it was still hard for me to imagine a Christmas without snow covering the fields and trees. Here one finds no trace of the beautiful customs of our country; only the midnight mass, the so-called matins, was held. I tarried in the beautifully lit church and in that place found devoutly assembled the greater part of the inhabitants, who made a picturesque gathering beside the glow of the innumerable candles. It seemed altogether a scene from home, and I do not know how it happened, but the vision warmed my heart. After my return from the evening service a peculiar calm came over my soul, and for more than an hour there I wholly reveled in the sweet memories of my childhood and my homeland, until their presence gradually faded from before my eyes.[19]

Chapter 15

The new year was upon us, and both the political situation and my own state had improved but little. The civil war gripped Yucatán, destroying all around it, and ties with the Mexican interior remained severed. On the other hand, to be sure, Laguna de Términos, although under North American occupation, curiously enough remained open to foreigners, and would have afforded me a way out if I had not been compelled to wait here in Campeche for a new stipend from Europe.

Under these circumstances the New Year's Eve leading into 1847 could bring me but scant joy, since it reminded me so much of the festivities of my homeland. It was the lack of poetry among these people, who but scarcely commemorate such a day; it was the want of persons with whom one could joyfully greet the arrival of the New Year. I do not know how it happened that I sat alone in my room and sadly and silently fell into deep reflection.

In one corner lay heaped the collected objects, plants, seashells, animal and bird pelts. In the other my rifle rested beside large and small chests, in one of which I had carefully enclosed an American boa and faithfully tended him, although he had by no means reconciled himself to captivity. At the window stood jars with tiny tortoises (*Emys picta*), scorpions, and other live animals I had collected. Finally, a bed filled up the remaining room, along with a table, in front of which I sat, swarmed by buzzing mosquitoes, beside a melancholy burning light. Before me lay the letters of Victor Jacquemont,[1] which I read with enthusiasm, and had just finished the last one, which he had dictated in Bombay on his deathbed, and which is so full of lovely and moving passages, when I leapt up unsettled for a breath of fresh air. Perhaps never in my life had I been able to understand this talented and sensitive traveler more than now, when I felt so lonely and forgotten, like someone in his final hour. I stared up for a long time at the dark blue and glittering sky, where thousands of beautiful stars seemed to shimmer with twofold light. There was the deepest quiet thereabout, and no breeze wafted by. The longer I marveled at the magnificence of this wonderful night, the more my spirits rose.

"My boa constrictor seemed not to want to be still. He struggled frightfully in his cramped box, which seemed dangerous to me considering his extraordinary length of twelve feet." Heller might have stretched both the snake and the truth, but large if harmless boas do exist in the Tabasco and Campeche region. (Photo courtesy of the Latin American Library, University of Texas at Austin)

When I returned to my room it was past midnight. A glance convinced me that all was in order; the only problem was that my boa constrictor seemed not to want to be still. He struggled frightfully in his cramped box, which seemed dangerous to me considering his extraordinary length of twelve feet. Still, I inspected the wood clasp nailed on top, found it firm, and went to bed reassured. I had slept for perhaps an hour when suddenly an uproar awoke me. I sprang up, lit the lamp, and beheld the snake with half its body protruding over the chest. With its terrible efforts it had forced itself through the boards, so I beat it furiously. Swiftly I pounced on it, seized it with both hands around the neck, and tried to force it back into its chest. It seemed to me as if I were struggling with a giant, for I could not budge it a hair's breadth out of place, and it stood upright in front of me like an inflexible column, more and more forcing its body through. Now its final moment had come. I now had to kill this snake, which I had fed for so long with eggs and chicks and had so often petted, since if it had escaped from its captivity it most certainly would have given me a hug that would have crushed my bones. Immediately an ominous noose fell over its neck, and to my immense regret the traitor had to atone for its treachery with its life. I was worn out and distracted by this late-night struggle, and a soft sleep came over me, which slipped away with the first glimmerings of dawn.

For the next ten days I frequently visited the small fishing village of Lerma, where the sea is deeper and marine life much richer than in Campeche. The inhabitants, 1,173 in number, are mostly fishermen, and lavishly supply the Campeche market, in return for which they obtain the necessary articles for their households, since outside of fishing they neither farm nor otherwise work a trade. I liked to tarry here; the surrounding woods offered a splendid hunt for doves, turkeys, and wild hens.

On January 21 I undertook a journey to Champotón, which had been described to me as a particularly lovely place, and where, because of the river, I could expect richer vegetation than I had yet found. In fact, I would have liked to make this excursion earlier, but no opportunity had presented itself to forward to Europe the body of specimens I had collected until now, when Dr. Adler promised to return to North America, and to take with him my lovely treasures mentioned above.

Here these small crafts bear the name *canoas* and, depending on their size, carry from six to sixty tons, although the largest rarely exceed twenty-five tons in capacity. Then there are, broadly speaking, small vessels like our European riverboats, which, propelled by two great foresails, cut through the waves of the often choppy sea with great security. Their navigators never read compasses or use other nautical instruments, because they never let the coast out of sight, and they know its promontories, bays, and hills with the greatest exactitude. Often huge lone trees on the mainland serve them as markers of distance of certain hard-to-find points.

At 3:00 I embarked from San Román, a suburb of Campeche, in the company of a German, Herr V. Napp, who not long ago had come from Europe, and whose destination was Laguna. The ship's cabin was entirely filled, so we sought out a comfortable seat for ourselves on the rooftop (one could hardly call it a deck), happily sat down together, smoked our cigars, chatted about Europe, and I in particular asked a thousand questions, which my trustworthy Rhinelander was pleased to answer and in so doing made it a genuine holiday for me.

Meanwhile, the sun beat down upon the shadeless vessel with such furious insistence that my German friend found himself scarcely able to endure the heat, and complained not a little about the extraordinary temperature. Just before evening a refreshing breeze wafted from seaward. The evening fell in this way, and I stretched myself out lengthwise on a crate, where I, accustomed to that sort of bed, soon fell asleep. My fellow traveler made his bed with much trouble between the crates and barrels under the roof. It did not last long, however, for huge raindrops woke me from my gentle slumber. I glanced around: terrible thunderclouds hung in the eastern sky, a sharp and unfavorable sea breeze lashed the water, the sail was hauled in, and the night grew so dark that we could scarcely make out the coast. The rain became more violent and I fled to my friend, whereupon the crew covered up the entire canoe with a waterproof tarp, and we lay firmly buried between crates. The disagreeable odor, the heat in consequence of the lack of fresh air, and the limited space, which scarcely permitted one to stretch an arm, even less a leg, made our situation altogether disagreeable. Still, my good humor rarely abandoned me in such instances, and I found some distraction in the way my fellow sufferer fell out of his bed, since through the rolling of the vessel he had no way to support himself, while I, leaning upon the windward side, could calmly watch his comical struggle with the discomforts of coastal travel. Finally, however, the heat became so intolerable that despite all danger we stuck our heads out from our prison under the tarp in order to take in some fresh air, and discovered to our considerable delight that it had stopped raining. Immediately we crawled out, sitting amid the dampness and leaning against a small mast, instead of suffocating in the dry area.

Toward midnight the sky cleared a bit, but the wind was still so unfavorable that we moved further from our goal rather than nearing it. The wind only turned favorable at 2 A.M. The day dawned, and to our great sorrow we saw that after fifteen hours of sea travel we had come no further than six leagues. But by luck the wind remained favorable enough for us to reach Champotón by noon.

Champotón, or Potonchán,[2] as the Indians called it before the conquest, is now a small village of sixteen hundred inhabitants on the left bank of the Champotón River as it empties into the Gulf of Mexico, but in other times it was without doubt an important point. Francisco Hernández de Córdova, who in 1517 tried to conquer Yucatán for Spain, was ambushed there by thirty thousand Indians and suffered such a rout that he counted fifty-seven dead and twelve wounded and only with difficulty managed to reach his ship with the rest of his men.

Today this village is of scant importance, and has suffered so much, especially on account of Yucatán's war with Mexico in 1840,[3] that many houses lie in ruins and most of the wealthy families have migrated. Only a few stone houses on the riverbank are fully intact; many consist of wood poles with palm thatch and testify to the profoundest poverty. Champotón maintains only a minor commerce with the peninsula's interior. This commerce consists of lumber and dyewood, in corn, rice, and fish, and even this scarcely extends to all of Yucatán. A road that was to stretch from here to Bacalar, and which would contribute as much to this village as to the country generally, and to the greatest advantage, has been mapped out but never completed. By connecting the Gulf of Honduras with the Gulf of Mexico by a long line of scarcely twenty-four hours, it would necessarily have amounted to the cultivation of the interior lands and to the promotion of commerce. For these reasons it would be best for them to set about this project once again, and to complete it as soon as possible.

Opposite the village, divided by a river nearly eighty paces wide, lies the hacienda El Paraíso, which I happened upon while in search of accommodations and where I tarried for some days while in the region. For me it was a rare pleasure to see once more a river of exceptional size: how silently and with what majesty it flows out and merges with the raging sea! Furthermore, the vegetation here was fresher, more luxuriant, and more invigorating than at other points along the coast, although the heat is just as severe and at times perhaps even fiercer than in Campeche. The climate was regarded as an unhealthy one, a fact easily explained by the humidity, something that, sadly, almost always turns out to be the case in the flat, well-watered regions of the tropics.

The region from Champotón to the interior is very sparsely populated. Even along the river, which might have afforded so great an advantage to colonization, the traveler finds virtually no place where he can pass the night. Small ranchos lie scattered two to three leagues apart and seldom consist of more than a few palm-thatched huts.

Ulumal,[4] five leagues up the river from Champotón, is the sole hacienda with masonry residences. Everything else is pure, impenetrable tropical forest in which only here and there the inhabitants make use of the wetlands (called *alcachés*)[5] that are situated along the river, and which are perfectly suited for rice paddies. Corn, which thrives everywhere in these parts, is cultivated in the vicinity of the ranchos. Only recently the owner of Ulumal experimented with sugarcane, and, as I myself was persuaded, to great success. I could not sufficiently express my astonishment over the unpardonable neglect in agriculture and husbandry, which with scant effort would produce endless bounty. Except for the scattered ranchos, the riverbank offers no favorable landing place, since trees and bushes ally with underbrush to form a dense mass that extends far into the river, and many dangerous alligators take shelter under their branches.

Before the Spanish conquest, however, Yucatán was not only populated but in fact densely so, and especially in this region. Even now along the jour-

"Except for the scattered ranchos, the riverbank offers no favorable landing place, since trees and bushes ally with underbrush to form a dense mass that extends far into the river, and many dangerous alligators take shelter under their branches." The banks of the Champotón River still resemble the topography—and the isolation—Heller described. (Photo by Terry Rugeley)

ney one finds a huge number of man-made stone cones of pyramidal form, which are sometimes thirty to forty feet high and tower over the trees. However, I do not believe that these cones conform to the Mexican teocallis or divine temples, since their number is too great and their height and circumference too small. Rather, they might have served as tombs or perhaps as places of refuge during the frequent flooding of the river. They reveal none of the adornments commonly used in the teocallis.

Here the locals refer to them as *cuyos,* and their significant number, which points to a very robust population, establishes beyond doubt that other ancient structures are to be found in the vicinity, which either lie enmeshed in woods that have grown up subsequently or else were destroyed earlier by the Spanish. Doubtless when locals reclaim the land through cultivation here they will also discover ancient palatial buildings of the Indians, like those ruins of Palenque, Uxmal, and other locations. In the neighborhood of the spot, three cuyos are conspicuous; their extraordinary circumference suggests that earlier they might well have been true pyramids, all the more, as they assure me, because from time beyond memory all building material was fetched from there and all Champotón was built from the stones of these cuyos, which by the large piles of stones that still exist point to an unusually large size. Now their form can scarcely be recognized.

In addition to these remains of an earlier culture I was unable to find something extraordinary around Champotón, and I began to turn my attention to the area's plant life. For the time being I endeavored to make use of the environs of Paraíso, and wandering here and there soon made my way eight or nine miles into the woods. Everywhere I found that beautiful tropical vegetation which I have often described and which time and again filled me with new joy. An eastward excursion was especially rewarding; in the course of this ramble I stumbled upon a tumbled-down hacienda named Niop, and an hour further on came to a primeval forest that exhibited a luxuriance seldom seen earlier in Mexico. Orchids and other parasitic plants adorned the mighty trunks of mimosas, turpentine trees, and palms; here too liana girded thousandfold the branches, and only solitary sunbeams broke through the half darkness of the evergreen canopy of leaves. I lived anew in this handsome vegetation and a spirit of activity seized me, one that made me forget all previous hardships. The clouds that for a long time had lain over my brow disappeared, my former cheerfulness returned, and when evening came I rested satisfied and was every day more edified in Paraíso, whose owner, Don José María Lanz, was at pains to show me every attention.

On January 26 I made preparations to travel upriver. To this end I packed some roasted meat, some particularly thick corn tortillas, a freshly filled bottle of rum, a hammock, and the appropriate weapons. The journey was to be made in a *cayuco,* that is, a vessel consisting of a hollowed-out tree trunk; this craft was so unsafe, however, that only a highly skilled individual could trust himself in it, since even the slightest movement to the side can capsize him. Nevertheless, I wanted to risk traveling in such, since despite the fact that one must sit almost immobile, the vessel can be launched quickly and easily. On top of this, I had already undertaken many small journeys over the river completely alone in such cayucos, and was altogether skillful in steering them. However, when it came to the departure, and four more travelers climbed in beside me, it soon appeared that this six-foot-long and one-and-a-half-foot-wide cayuco would not be able to hold us, and that at the first opportunity we would tumble into the water. I immediately selected a larger vessel, and we were soon traveling swiftly upriver, in which endeavor the surging ocean tide helped us not a little.

In countless turns the river wound among mangrove trees that lined the banks, and this uniform vegetation lasted as far as the seawater was able to penetrate and wash its roots. Approximately one league from Champotón the so-called *manglares* ended, and an exuberance of beautiful trees and bushes increasingly emerged.

At nightfall a great number of seabirds alighted on the trees, and sitting quietly with their white plumage among the leaves under resplendent moonshine, they appeared like flowers that bedeck the vegetation along the riverbank. Only occasionally were they alerted through our gentle oar strokes; if that happened, however, they rose up with a ruckus and withdrew shrieking over our heads, and moreover placing all the inhabitants of the forest in alarm. Immediately the banks offered the most distinct diversity, and since it was already late at night and the moon shone like the light of day, the different woodland creatures offered enchanting and beautiful scenes and magically illuminated landscapes, scenes I could not possibly have discerned were it not for the moonlight. Toward midnight, however, the sky suddenly darkened and a fierce thunderstorm loomed on the southern horizon. Huge raindrops began to fall, and unprotected we now feared to be exposed to this same fury, when by a most fortunate stroke it turned to the west and spared us. Two hours after midnight we reached Xantel, a small wood-cutting rancho, where I proposed to hold up for the night.

A few shelters of palm leaves over wooden poles had been set up here. The workers, pure Indians of Maya tongue, had strung up their hammocks under the same, and protected from the dew rested very comfortably, while by the melancholy glow of a flickering fire a few old women were already busy preparing tortillas and pozole for the morning meal.[6] Since the weak fire illuminated only isolated persons and parts of the rancho, it was to me an unforgettable and highly curious evening that we passed.

There was little more place for our hammocks under the shelter, and I had to hang my flimsy bed between two trees under the open sky. There I was exposed to the consistent drops from the damp leaf canopy and to the furious bites of angry mosquito swarms, until by early morning I had scarcely been able to close an eye, and thoroughly drenched in dew I rejoiced to greet the rising sun.

When it was broad day, my first item of business was to survey the plant life in my environs. To my overwhelming joy, I discovered a mass of beautiful orchids on the first trees standing nearby. An *Epidendrum stamfordianum* orchid was situated on an old zapote tree clasped tight with hundreds of panich flowers in sumptuous blossoms, wild vanilla, myrtles, and mimosas that sent out an almost stunning fragrance, and I could scarcely wait to penetrate deeper into the rain forest. I soon found myself with some Indians en route, and cutting a path with my machete I wandered for an entire day in the forest among the splendid vegetation. Two hours before sunset some Indians and I returned overloaded with specimens to Xantel. Since I could not expose myself for long to the evening camp in this damp forest without running the danger of contracting a throat fever, I hurried on to Ulumal in order to have a look at the hacienda, which lay here like an oasis in the desert. We arrived there in half an hour and found, as I have already mentioned, some decidedly poor properties next to corn and rice fields, and also some sugarcane, with which the owner had obtained highly favorable results. Otherwise, however, everything was so wild, so desolate and overgrown all around, that it seemed to me entirely like an outpost on the edge of the civilized world. I tarried in Xantel only a short time and had scarcely arrived when a furious downpour began to fall, and I forced myself under the palm hut of some Indians there in search of refuge. These Indians sat at the fire and consumed their tortillas or roasted tortoise shells and freshly captured iguanas (large lizards), to which I invited myself and found them singularly delicious to the last bite. However, when I wanted to hang my hammock under the same shelter, I met with no small difficulty, since the narrow room was hung crisscross with the same, and finally I had to stretch out my hammock in the gable of the shelter above the fire. Climbing up into my hammock was difficult, and when I lay there I realized to my considerable horror that all the smoke concentrated itself here overhead and threatened to suffocate me. I was only able to close my eyes without danger after they extinguished the fire upon my insistent requests.

Before daybreak on January 28 I found myself once again in my canoe beginning the return journey. It was still so dark that I could barely steer the boat; once again we passed by the picturesque ruins along the banks, until the sun rose with the usual splendor and put the seabirds to flight from their resting places. It beautifully illuminated the immense cluster of trees, and in solitary places we glimpsed a misshapen alligator sunning himself, awaiting his prey; upon our approach these creatures threw themselves clumsily into the water.

The sea was at low tide, and the river flowed out so rapidly that great banks of oyster shells appeared. It was highly dangerous to pass beside them, for they left our vessel only a very slender channel and in some cases formed small cataracts. We ran aground twice but finally reached the deeper water, and at midday we arrived safe and sound at Champotón. Soon after that I abandoned this village with the treasures I had collected, and on February 2 at 7 A.M. set out on a highly enjoyable sea voyage of twelve hours to Campeche.

Having arrived here, it seemed to me that everything had now worked out in my favor: the civil war was over, communications with the interior had been reestablished, and my former room, until now always empty, was filled with collections of natural history specimens. However, the conclusion of the war was not a joyful event to report. The Campechanos had attacked Mérida from two sides (by sea through Sisal, and by land through Umán) and had cut off supplies, and the capital prepared itself for a desperate resistance. At that point, however, gloomy news came from the interior, for more than a thousand Indians had risen up against the white population and had threatened all the settlements with total annihilation. It was high time that the sister republic declared independence, if it did not wish to fall victim to the incensed Indians, since these latter had already seized more villages and had slaughtered all who were white.[7] Mérida surrendered itself on January 22 to the power of Campeche and began to work feverishly there to resist the common enemy.

This Caste War was just beginning, and one could already see that the Indians were determined to face annihilation rather than let themselves be defeated. Their multitude quickly swelled to eight thousand men and carried out the most frightful cruelties. Toward the middle of February the Yucatecans managed to bring some halt to their rampages, and the inhabitants were awaiting a good end to this new war as soon as possible. Until now they had lived with depressed spirits, so they gave themselves over with almost unbridled joy to the diversions of Shrove Tuesday. Bands of giddy masqueraders wandered in the streets of Campeche. Everywhere was music, dance, and gaiety. Here Negroes danced their frantic African tango, there Yucatecans their fandango. Here was an earsplitting serenade, there a spirited *contradanza.* In short, a boundless gaiety had seized and numbed everything.

The great world, among which many a person from Europe and the United States was to be seen, came together here and transformed a section of street into a dance hall, where for three days they held masked balls with enthusiasm and extravagance.

Chapter 16

For a long time now I had gone without news from Europe. Given my already doubtful situation, this isolation exerted a thoroughly evil influence over me, since I could not easily leave Campeche once and for all before receiving new instructions for my journey. All my hopes now rested on the English postal steamer, which was to have landed in Veracruz in mid-February, and I passionately longed for the day when a new road for my labors would open, when suddenly the city was profoundly convulsed by news of the terrible shipwreck of that same vessel. Additional reports soon appeared, and among them was the following account of Mr. John Davis, which I reproduce in faithful translation.

> Shipwreck of the postal steamer *Tweed.*
>
> The following report concerns an investigation held in the market and harbor of Santa María de Sisal on February 14, 1847. Following a northern storm which raged on the twelfth of this month, the Spanish brig *Emilio* arrived here in port, bearing with it the post officer of the English vessel *Tweed.* He and nine other men from the said vessel had set out on the sea in a boat after they had suffered a shipwreck out on the Alacranes. Immediately the port captain asked the name, nationality, occupation, their port of embarkation, the ship, the name of its captain, the duration of the journey, the day and time of the shipwreck, and whether it had passengers; the location and the date when they came upon the brig *Emilio;* and in which direction and what distance from the port. He answered as follows.
>
> His name was John Davis, was born in England, and was supercargo of the ship that came from Havana, set sail bound for Veracruz and Tampico, and bore the name *Tweed.* Its captain was Mr. Parsons, and three days had passed since they left port until reaching the Alacranes. It was at approximately 3 A.M. on the twelfth of this month when they ran aground because of a furious storms. They had on

board fifty-five passengers and seventy-five crewmen, as he believes, and approximately sixty from the shipwreck made it to land. The remaining people found themselves on said sandbar, and as was his duty he determined to set out in order to see who could help them. He suffered a great deal while he sailed out with the boat of said steamer in terrible weather, since this boat turned out to be in such a horrible condition that they had to bind it together with ropes in order to be able to go on. The remaining five boats which had set out were entirely dashed to pieces. It was approximately half past six today when the Spanish brig *Emilio* found them twelve nautical miles from this port. Their cargo consisted of 1,170 casks of mercury and other wares. He declared this to be the truth, which he verified and signed.

At this point the account ends, which he undersigns with me for the sake of truth on the above mentioned date.

José María Covian, John Davis, Mérida, February 15, 1847.

Thus all my hopes for a speedy reassignment were once again dashed, and my position was hardly less tragic than that of the people rescued from the shipwreck. Some of these poor souls were now found in Sisal, others in Mérida. On the last day of February a few of the castaways arrived in Campeche, among them a German as well, Herr F. Probst, who had at least made it alive but, like the other survivors, racked with injuries. To the degree that my scant resources permitted, I tried to provide accommodations in Campeche for this amiable countryman, who, it goes without saying, was in no comfortable position. We soon got to know each other, all the more since he had been in Mexico earlier, and knew many of my friends there. He gave me a description of the shipwreck, which captivated me not so much because of its horrors as for its vivid portrayal. I felt it deep in my heart, and it fascinated as though I had participated in his tragic fate.

I pictured that moment during the dark night of howling storm and fiercely churning sea, when the ship was thrown with full violence on the reefs. Colossal volumes of water began to surge in violently, and the ship began to list and sink. One no longer heard the voice of the captain, but rather confused screams of men trying to save themselves, and cries of the women, children, and dying, cries that resounded through the ship as its timber broke into pieces, and two boats filled with men were dashed to pieces by the waves. Death in its most terrible form stood before the eyes of all those still alive: it had to be horrible—it had to be heart-rending! In such moments one truly believes that Nature has no compassion for her most noble creatures, and in this sense I could understand how one who still possessed his presence of mind might rather hasten his own end than try to save himself.

So it fared with my countryman, who, catapulted into the waves, fell between two beams that threatened to pulverize him. But luckily he managed to escape them and by swimming for a long time rescued himself from the waves. But at length perceiving his situation to be hopeless, he decided to kill himself. With a thought about God, his mother, his wife and children, he pressed his arms to his chest and sank down. Providence determined otherwise, however, for when he opened his eyes, there he lay on a rock upon which the waves had tossed him, senseless!

Some eighty people died in this pitiable manner, among them all the women and children, two Germans, and many other well-to-do individuals; approximately fifty, including the captain, had saved themselves on the reef. There they languished for four long days between the sky and the ocean, suffering hunger and thirst, until the ship *Emilio* rescued them from their wretched situation. The greater part of the rescued men returned with the *Emilio* to Havana, and only eight resolved to continue their journey to Mexico via Campeche, where they fitted out a small schooner in order to travel to Veracruz.

At the same time, six schooners left Campeche for the Alacranes in order to possibly salvage something of the mercury cargo (which alone had a value of 24,000 florins), along with anything else that one found washed up by the sea and by rights lost. Soon, however, a few of the ships returned after abandoning their search as fruitless.

How great was my surprise, then, when one morning the employee of a local merchant handed me a half-washed-out letter that he had found floating alone in the waters at Alacranes and had fished out, and which bore my address. It was my letter, the one I had passionately awaited, the only one of the thousands that were rescued which was still entirely legible! I did not believe my own eyes, since it seemed to me something more than mere chance. It was like nothing I had ever heard of, almost wonderful—it seemed to me a sign from heaven not to lose courage in my sad situation. The contents of the letter were scarcely encouraging, but for me this document was to forever serve as a memento of my journey, and so often afterwards, whenever I am again feeling defeated, then I take out my miraculously rescued letter, and with a glance my courage grows and gives me hope for a better future.

I have said that nothing about my situation had changed for the moment; but luckily for me a French natural researcher arrived here, a Mr. Morelet,[1] who not long before had come from Europe via Havana, and who intended to travel to Guatemala by way of Chiapas. I passed many agreeable days and hours with him in excursions and in conversations over the affairs of our profession. Unfortunately, he departed for Laguna on March 17, while on the same day the castaways set sail for Veracruz, so that I was once more all alone and limited to my monotonous life in Campeche.

I tried to occupy my time by frequent rambles in the nearby woods and along the seaside, and above all by statistical and geographical research in the city. In the course of all these projects the French consul, Herr Laisné de Villévègue, who regularly assisted me in the friendliest and most courteous manner, lent me an energetic hand with his collected observations and experiences. One product of this time was a draft of a map of Yucatán, to which end I made particular use of Ceballos's sea charts and Juan José de León's handwritten letter, together with all the detailed drawings then available in Campeche from the collection of the highly respected Carvajal family.

Meanwhile, minor friction had started once more between Mérida and Campeche, while the schooner that had brought the castaways happily to Veracruz returned from there with the news that approximately twelve thousand North American troops encircled the city, and that every day the Veracruzanos awaited an assault by land and sea. This assault began on March 27, whereupon Veracruz gathered itself into the famous fortress of San Juan de Ulúa on the twenty-ninth of the same month. From this moment on, General Scott had gained a firm footing on Mexican soil.

Because of these events, all subsequent communications with Yucatán were now blockaded, since up to now the Americans had not recognized their neutrality. I looked toward the outcome of this unwholesome war with depressed spirits. All life seemed to have gone out of Campeche, until finally Holy Week with its festivities moved the population into action, something that has a beneficent influence over the spirit.

On the morning of April 2, 1847, the city already swarmed with people who had streamed hither from all surrounding villages and plantations in order to be present in the afternoon for the grand procession for the burial of Christ. The hour everyone longed for—5:00—finally struck; the regular troops of Campeche, consisting of a division of artillery and a division of infantry with uniforms suitable to the climate, stood ceremoniously in formation with their musical bands in the plaza; while all other space was lined with spectators who awaited the departure from the church with religious awe. More crosses led the procession, accompanied by the dignitaries of the city. A coffin followed them, adorned and illuminated in the most tasteful fashion,[2] carried by men who were dressed in black, like monks; they had bound their waists several times over with cords, and seemed more like carnival masqueraders than servants of such a solemn event. They are called *pipirongos,* and their origins derive from the *auto-da-fé,* where they functioned as executioners. Yucatán excepted, they are now everywhere forsaken, although their duty is not as sad as formerly. Images of saints carved by these pipirongos followed the coffin; an immense number of men and women accompanied these images, along with a huge number of Indians, who in turn were succeeded by the infantry and artillery with two cannons that brought up the rear. This imposing procession took more than two hours to pass through the principal streets of Campeche, so that night had already fallen when they arrived once more at the church and the festivities ended for the day.

Here the people observe the ceremonies of the Resurrection at 1 A.M. in the church. These rituals were consummated the following morning, whereupon the visitors hastened back to their villages, and Campeche was as empty and barren as it had been before.

Chapter 17

While the lone stragglers of the festival left the stores and rum taverns to wander off through the streets of the city in wild abandon, I threw myself into preparations for a journey to the interior of the country. In particular, it was my intention to visit the famous ruins of Yucatán, an intention that was reinforced when educated men of Campeche expressed a desire to accompany me. In addition to myself, it was the two kindly and informative Carvajal brothers, the secretary of the French consulate, Mr. Durand, and a Spanish portrait painter who made up a small travel party.

Since Yucatán, as I have already mentioned earlier, is a very level land and much of it can be traveled by coach, we consequently hired a type of carriage in order to travel as quickly as possible, at least as far as the roads were passable. This device was created out of two old wheels; it had a quite singular appearance and was called the *Carlota.*

On Sunday at 4:30, on the morning of April 4, 1847, we traveled with a clatter out to the gates of Campeche and soon reached the bumpy and dusty highway that led to Mérida, the capital. Soon the sun rose in the east behind the small hill range, and with its warming rays it not only danced among the small mimosa trees that grew everywhere along the roadside, but also animated the spirits of our small company. Everyone wanted to do his part to help forget about the tortuous journey of the carriage, but in spite of all the storytelling and laughter we could hardly avoid banging one another's heads, something which in our cheerful spirits only increased the fun. Thus we rolled on, scarcely noticing the length of the journey, passing through trees that were almost leafless in this season. It was all quite tiresome, but we moved rapidly, for we had harnessed a team of five horses, and by 7 A.M. we had already reached Hampolol, a small village that had grown up behind an older community of the same name, and which lay four leagues from Campeche.

We got out at a lone and moreover quite miserable store, and there we drank some chocolate with a bit of bread; they offered eggs and water there, so our breakfast was soon ready. Meanwhile, we had a look at the church, an ancient building where mass was said only seldom, and which is scarcely distinguished by anything beyond its profound poverty. Beyond a few houses of stone construction, this village offers nothing worth seeing, but rather presents a picture of gradual decline—which, since Yucatán considers itself politically independent, is a sad and unfortunately all too frequent feature throughout the land. We returned to the store; but half an hour from the village, close to the road, a lovely spring with good drinking water is found, so we preferred to go on foot and let the *Carlota* remain behind.

Beyond the village the terrain drops some thirty to fifty feet in elevation, and consequently the rainy season turns this place into an impassable swamp. For this reason the Spanish raised over it a bridge, or rather a stone dam, or *calzada,* which has three arches in the middle for the flow of water but is otherwise of extremely solid walls and measures close to a thousand paces in length. Not far behind the same one comes upon a ranchería and to the right a splendid hacienda, in front of which lie a spring and a natural pond. The water, as clear and good as I had ever found in the mountains of Mexico, gushed forcefully from between abundant shrubbery, trees, and stones. In the pool, blue dotleaf waterlily bordered with logwood and beautiful ficus trees, around which wind blue begonias and lovely sandpaper vines. A flock of songbirds and waterfowl enliven this exciting spot still more.

After we inspected this spot (sumptuous for so arid a land as Yucatán) and had thoroughly refreshed ourselves, we continued on our journey. In spite of the heat and the dust, which almost suffocated us, we resumed our earlier and spirited efforts to entertain ourselves, until at noon we reached Tenabo, five leagues from Hampolol, a village somewhat more important than the latter.

Yucatán possesses the *casas reales,* now called *casas nacionales,* buildings that usually serve as quarters for those passing through and at the same time as a jail. These remain in good repair, a fact which sadly is not the case in Mexico. In the peninsula they still operate according to an old Spanish ordinance, whereby one always finds a multitude of Indians, called *tupiles,*[1] who are obligated to serve the traveler at no cost. Accordingly, our first step was to present ourselves to the alcalde of the village so that he would give orders to make us a place. Since the hall of the casa nacional was not cleaned, he offered us the guardroom, and just as quickly we hung our hammocks there, for we wanted to escape the burning heat of midday and recover from the bruising shocks of the *Carlota* while swinging in the breeze in those hammocks.[2] A frugal meal calmed our hunger; the food consisted of a pot of pigeons, beans, and tortillas, prepared in the Mexico style; despite the lack of water, some fresh coconuts slaked our thirst.

Only at 4 P.M. did the heat let up somewhat and we resumed our journey. We had scarcely reached the outskirts of the village when a hot smoke came toward us from a burning cornfield. These fires (*quemas* or *quemazones*) are especially frequent in the dry months of March and April, and increase the heat and lack of fresh air to a significant degree. Indeed, they are often the most unpleasant and dangerous things the traveler can come across, since he is compelled to go midway through the fire burning on both sides of the way, or to wait for days until the road is passable. One frequently comes upon these in the dry season, because the Indians set fire not only to the harvested fields but also to the freshly fallen woods of the clearing, in order to give a bit more fertility to the stony soil by means of the ash, the manure of the land. This, combined with the daily rains which increase after the planting, is sufficient to produce outstanding corn harvests, even more essential for Yucatán than for any other part of Mesoamerica.

The fire before us stretched to the first Indian huts of the village, and since they are constructed only of wooden poles and palm thatch, one had already been seared by the flames. The almost naked Indians worked amid these embers with astonishing speed and busily doused the still undamaged houses, so that the fire could not sweep forward. The women, clothed only to the waist, stared vacantly, illuminated by the fire in a picturesque manner, while amid the sea of flames the naked children danced around the huts like tiny Lucifers. But we were visibly moved by this moment, which so suddenly had placed a barrier to our journey.

Luckily, the conflagration moved away, fanned by a sea breeze, and we resolved to travel on. We hurried at a gallop over the path bordered by glowing fire, and luckily reached the other side, with our entire bodies half toasted with heat, and nearly choking because of the thick, asphyxiating pangs. From that point, and after a brief recovery refreshed by the evening breeze, we briskly pursued our journey.

At 8 P.M. we reached the market of Hecelchakán, a large and beautiful village of 4,912 inhabitants, with a lovely church, school, and an ayuntamiento, which astonished us all the more by its size, its stately buildings and churches, since from all the maps one otherwise expects an almost unpopulated land. In fact, these villages, in spite of their current deterioration, are still larger and more attractive than many towns of Cuba or the Mexican republic. Hecelchakán even has lantern-lit streets, like the two capitals.[3]

We proceeded to rest ourselves here as well behind the casa nacional a few hours, since we had determined to continue our journey at night because of the ferocious heat. Sadly, Herr Rafael Carvajal became so ill that he returned to Campeche with the postal carriage coming from Mérida, explaining that because of his fragile health he was unable to endure the strain of the journey. We regretted his loss to the utmost, since he had the best knowledge of the land and the ruins, and moreover was skilled in the Maya language, which except in the villages along the highway is spoken exclusively throughout the countryside. We therefore had reason to fear the difficulty of coming to an understanding with the Indians.

But it was now beyond remedy. We spent a few hours half-asleep until 11 P.M., by which time the moon had risen with its usual splendor and our night journey could begin. A few fires still flickered in the market where the Indians were preparing their evening tortillas, but there under the dark blue firmament, which the brightest glow of the moon could not diminish, a deep, stately quiet reigned all around.

Our coach rolled noisily out of the village; in the vehicle we soon grew silent one after another, for sleep demanded its tribute. In this way we passed Pocboc, a small village with 911 inhabitants, and at daybreak we reached Dzitbalché, a large town with some 3,406 inhabitants, of whom more than two thousand are pure Indian. But since we were only one league from Calkiní, the *Carlota*'s destination, we traveled on without stopping and arrived there at 7:00 in the morning.

Calkiní is an important town on the highway to Mérida. It has 2,822 inhabitants, an ayuntamiento, church, school, and a Franciscan monastery that is half in ruins and is inhabited by only a solitary monk. The design of this monastery is striking, for although the interior and the towers, or *campanarios,* allow no doubt as to their purpose, so too they could also be taken as belonging to a small fortress, since they are encircled by stout walls furnished with rifle holes, while the flat roof is entirely adapted like a fortress bastion, whereupon its defenders might post cannons. They tell me that in the last war with the Mexicans this was frequently done, and that in consequence such cloisters frequently become the scenes of important conflicts between opposing troops. Here the alcalde of the village secured for us not only more tupiles but also horses for the continuation of the journey, and at 4:00 in the afternoon we were already following the road to Bécal, in the direction of Uxmal.

In an hour and a half we reached Bécal, a terribly run-down village with 1,446 Indian inhabitants and a clergyman, to whom we directed our steps, since the priest (*cura* or *padre*) was an old friend of the Carvajal brothers.[4] This venerable priest had lived forty years among his Indians, and since a visit such as ours constituted the greatest rarity, he tried in all possible ways, through reception and hospitality, to publicly show us his delight. Since we were thinking of traveling again today at the first rising of the moon, we accepted his invitation to dine with him that evening and exhausted ourselves in mutual questions and answers about the situation in Mexico, in Yucatán, and so forth. Sadly, on this occasion the priest verified for us the news of the evil disposition of the Indians and assured us that to his profound regret he anticipated a full-blown uprising against the whites; indeed, all was still quiet in his community, but each day rumors made the discontent more and more apparent. At the same time, he recommended that we take the greatest care and provided us with an Indian guide who enjoyed his full confidence.

It was midnight when we saddled up and rode out again. The road curved to the left, and we followed our adroit guide over sticks and stones in the true sense of the words. Now through thick bushes, now through small savannas, the road meandered through an empty and uninhabited region; no house, no rancho was to be seen, and only from time to time a startled deer or the whistling of a lonesome nightbird gave some sign of life, since even the noisy cicada had gone silent.

We rode on for five hours in the still of the night; when the morning dawned we were able to proceed at a brisk trot, and finally at 6 A.M. we reached the hacienda Uxmal, our journey's destination, twenty-eight leagues from Campeche. Profoundly exhausted by the sleepless night and the stressful journey, we wanted nothing more than to rest for a few hours; but we were far away from the cooling sea breezes, and surrounded by the burning fields the heat was so extraordinarily ferocious that in spite of everything we could scarcely endure one hour in the hammocks. Over the course of the entire day the temperature never dropped below 97 degrees even in the deepest shade, and we thought we would surely perish from the absence of refreshing drink.

The hacienda Uxmal (perhaps originating from *ox* and *mal,* which in Maya means "three passageways"), although scarcely large, is an outwardly attractive property that is constantly beautified and improved by its owner, Don Simón Peón, a well-informed and pleasant man. In construction it resembles all other haciendas of Yucatán. Various walled plazas that connect to the house are furnished with corridors and flat roofs; these serve to close in the cattle and provide drinking water. One or two large ficus trees overshadow these plazas, behind which the water is directed through conduits from the *noria,* or pump wheel, and from this same place the Indians in the evening get the water supply for their households in tapered jars. A small chapel that stands in the main building also provides for public worship, for in general Herr Peón aspires to do all possible to secure decency and order among the ninety Indian families of the estate. In this moment of clandestine unrest this seemed all the more important, since these same Indians were not free from the suspicion of being in league with the eastern inhabitants and had once already murdered a white mayordomo.[5] Still, all seemed quiet here, and we could anticipate a frugal meal, in order to be able to inspect the famous ruins.

The mayordomo, who was highly recommended by Herr Peón and had already accompanied Herr Stephens in his travels, came with us as well as a guide through the ruins of the American Egypt. Already in the distance we glimpsed the pyramids projecting upward over the now almost leafless woods. A number of great buildings towered over the bramble and aroused our curiosity concerning the highest, until we had arrived at that very spot and stared in mute wonder at the works of Indian diligence. We forced our way through dense undergrowth of mimosa and sedum and stared for half an hour before the front of the so-called House of the Magician, the pyramid of Uxmal. It is this, a massive stone building 105 feet high, whose basis is 225 feet long and 135 feet wide, but it by no means forms a rectangle, as is the case with the pyramids of the Old World and those of Mexico, but rather is rounded on both sides, approximating an oval form.

On the east side ninety fully preserved steps, each a foot high and half a foot deep, lead up to the very top. However, since the angle of incline on this side amounts to seventy degrees and on the other side eighty, it is dizzying to climb and not entirely without risk, all the more so as solitary places had suffered terribly during the tumultuous interval of three hundred years. In spite of that, the entire structure is a truly well-preserved building; yet the prolific trees and bushes on it contribute powerfully to its destruction, and perhaps in fifty years only little more of it may be seen.[6] The platform is 70 feet long and 20 feet wide. On the same stands a structure that is 20 feet high, 60 feet long, and 12 feet wide and consists of three vaulted rooms, which are magnificently erected out of cut stones. The exterior decorations have suffered significantly; however, in isolated places one still recognizes the extraordinary diligence with which it was fashioned.

On the uppermost platform three doors open to the east, one to the west. This latter leads to two rooms under a small ledge. The entryway is so adorned with sculpture that upon seeing it I felt myself instinctively reminded of Hindu sculpture, without being able to make a definite comparison to the same.

The House of the Magician could without doubt have served the same function as the teocallis in Mexico, that is, as a temple and a place of sacrifice, and doubtless at the same time as the residence of a high priest, who, as history teaches, generally played the role of great prophet, from which their name as well may have had its origins.[7]

"We forced our way through dense undergrowth of mimosa and sedum and stared for half an hour before the front of the so-called House of the Magician, the pyramid of Uxmal." (Photo courtesy of the Latin American Library, University of Texas at Austin)

Approximately forty yards to the west of the pyramid are found the ruins of the so-called Nunnery (Casa de las Monjas), one of the grandest and most luxurious structures. It stands on three terraces which together are 18 feet high, forming a rectangle that measures nearly 300 feet on the southern and northern sides and nearly 200 hundred feet on both ends. The main portal, opposite the House of the Governor, consists in a stone arch converging at a sharp angle, as in Gothic design, and constructed exactly like all the arches of the still-standing rooms. Ten of these are found on both sides of the gateway, one beside another, not joined to the interior through doors; nor do they seem to bear any particular decoration beyond their smoothly fashioned stones. Stout vaults without windows, they closely resemble the cells of an old cloister. In many I noticed two stone rings that might have served to fasten hammocks; other than that, there was nothing that might have suggested their purpose. The posts of the doors leading to the courtyard are of zapote wood, and for their tremendous age still remain in remarkably good condition.

Facing this front, a still-magnificent building rises up on a lone terrace of 20 feet, the north front 260 feet long, 34 feet wide, and 25 feet high, a broad stairs leads up to the same, to which on each side two smaller buildings attach themselves. Twelve doors lead two at a time to a room lying behind them, which are exactly the same design as those described earlier. The building to the left is 170 feet long, 34 feet wide, and 25 feet high, has seven doors which open into fourteen rooms, and distinguishes itself on the outside through the decoration with two massive serpents that wind their tortured way among the smaller motifs. Although these serpents are already quite deteriorated, the visitor recognizes quite clearly the head of one and the tail of the other on a preserved section, which Catherwood's accomplished pencil has faithfully captured in the previously mentioned work. The most fully preserved part of the entire building is ultimately the right, or eastern, side. It is a mere 150 feet long and only has entrances that lead to fourteen rooms, of which one surpasses the adjoining quarters four times over in size. The other rooms are uniform in size and have more the look of a family residence than of a cell. The decorations of this wing belong to the most admirable sort, as much for reasons of flavor as for symmetry and execution; and with a glimpse of it the traveler is in truth seized by that hushed and solemn respect which must silently be rendered to the vanished people who once constructed such grand and magnificent things!

In total the Casa de las Monjas has eighty-two rooms in these four buildings, rooms that without doubt must once have functioned as quarters for the servants of the Indian priests. Facing the so-called Nunnery, to the south lies the greatest of the Uxmal ruins, the Casa del Gobernador, or House of the Governor, 42 feet in height over the earth's surface. It is built on three huge terraces, of which the first is 3 feet high, 15 feet wide, and 575 feet long; the second 20 feet high, 250 feet wide, and 545 feet long; and the third 19 feet high, 13 feet wide, and 360 feet long. The main front is directed toward the east and measures 320 feet long, 40 feet wide, and 26 feet high. Eleven doors of the front side and on both sides lead to twenty rooms of the same design as in the Nunnery. The largest of them, located in the middle of the building, is 55 feet long, 11 feet wide, and 22 feet high; the rest in symmetrical arrangement, considerably smaller than the two middle rooms, are only 23 feet long and 11 feet wide, and each stands only two by two with each other in union. No light illuminates these rooms other than that which falls within through the doors, and thus a musty and dank air prevents one from lingering there at the present time.

This building has no plaza, and because of the high foundation it presides over all other ruins, with which it was undoubtedly connected. On the northwestern corner of the two terraces rises a lone building 94 feet long and 34 feet wide, the Casa de las Tortugas, or "House of the Turtles," so called because of the four cornices with turtles cut from stone. Already quite deteriorated, it shows in the four still-intact parts a splendor and simplicity of decoration that satisfies artistic standards and is scarcely surpassed by that of the other buildings. Sadly, with all its splendor it will very soon come to be only an unsightly pile of rubble.

The buildings of the Casa de las Palomas, or "House of the Doves," stand in no less pitiable a state. They take their name from the ruined wall built of nine pyramids fashioned in stone, each of which is furnished with a multitude of small openings. This wall runs lengthwise over the middle of the weak roof, so that it calls to mind pyramidal dove houses. Mr. Stephens gives the length of the building as 240 feet. All the rooms of this structure have already collapsed, and only the plaza and a teocalli can clearly be recognized, so that little worth seeing remains except for the strangely constructed wall just mentioned.

Finally, I will mention a collapsed building, the so-called Casa de la Vieja, or "House of the Old Woman," to the easternmost side of the ruin. It takes its name from a mutilated statue of a woman that one finds there. And there is the *picote* in front of the Ruins of the Governor, which concludes my short description of the ruins of Uxmal. The picote, or great rock, is a stone block three feet long and two feet high representing two lions joined at the middle; perhaps an idol of the ancient Indians, Mr. Stephens found it there covered with earth and had to dig it up in order to make a sketch of it, and it looks as though the Indians, before they abandoned the place, buried all idols that they could not take with them, in order to protect them from sacrilege. In any case, it is strange that in all the ruins of Uxmal one finds no more effigies, and since in reality Waldeck, Friedrichstal, Stephens, and Norman[8] were there before me and had taken away relatively little, then in so extensive a ruin there must be more to be found, even if they lie buried God knows where under the ground and must be left to a chance discovery.[9]

Entirely satisfied by what we had seen during our last excursion to the ruins, we returned the following day to the hacienda Uxmal. As we arrived a lame Indian limped to meet us at the gate; he carried on his back the drum common to all the dances of the Indians. This is a three-foot-long hollow tree trunk, both sides of which are covered with an animal skin. Using a small rod, the Indians strike up unchanging and repetitious drumbeats; this provides the harmony of their characteristic music, which puts them in a state of enthusiasm, while the traveler is likely to fall into despair over this perpetually melancholy monotony. Since we not only wanted to hear this music but to see the dance as well, we therefore gathered with a number of Indians in the corridor of the hacienda in order to be able to watch the dances in comfort. The Indians crouched down low in a circular dance; they performed such comic leaps to the rhythm of the drum, and with such serious expressions, that we could not help but laugh. The whole affair was as original, as altogether indigenous, as anything I had ever seen before. We were in a state of general amusement when a skyrocket, which rose at a rather great distance and was immediately answered from some Indian huts of Uxmal, put an end to our fun. Such rockets are in reality signals with which far-removed villages often communicate, and since the mayordomo as well could not make out from which hut the answer had come, he suspected that someone had signaled some nasty business to Uxmal, in order to advise the Indians there of it. Since he did not know the meaning of this signal, he advised us to travel once more by night. Given the ever-widening Indian rebellion, the fierce hatred toward the whites, and the great honesty of the mayordomo, we had little reason to think these anxieties groundless. Our small group therefore decided to set out and journey on, all the more so since already in the area further excesses had taken place, and earlier at Uxmal a white mayordomo had been murdered. Unfortunately, we could only round up three horses, in consequence of which a *koché* had to be built for the four of us, in order that they could carry us away quickly.

The koché is a type of sedan found only in Yucatán. It consists of two long poles that are bound fast together with crosspieces in a six-foot square. In this square a hammock is hung tight, and over that a covering of velvet canopy is fastened. With the passenger lying within, four Indians take this sedan on their shoulders and hurry along with unbelievable speed behind horses moving at a trot. The traveler lies back comfortably in this manner for six to ten leagues, and pays no more than a medio real per man per league.[10]

These preparations delayed our departure until 3:00 in the morning, when, led by six reliable Indians who preceded the koché, we set off and took a path through the forest to Dzitbalché. The ruins, somberly illuminated in the light of the half-moon, and by which the road passed, looked down augustly upon the small caravan, which spent its hasty steps in the darkness of the woods.

When the day broke we glanced over the wilderness and saw nothing other than an inferior vegetation consisting merely in mimosas and a few euphorbia, which scarcely boasted a green leaf and had very few flowers. No arid steppes occasionally interrupt the underbrush, which is densely inhabited by deer and pumas.

In the entire distance of fifty-seven miles there are only a few places where some water—clearly bad but still potable—is found, so that under a heat of more than 122 degrees[11] we had to suffer unspeakable thirst, and in a short time our reserves, which we kept in tattered gourd flasks, became partly exhausted, partly undrinkable. However, the tortures of the journey increased still more when at midday we neared a forest fire, which spread so furiously that we in fact heard the roar from a quarter league away, and the heat had reached the highest degree that men can endure in that situation.

Only the greatest exertions on the part of the Indians and our horses rescued us from the area of this appalling fire, which raced toward us with unbelievable swiftness, threatening annihilation. Luckily, we escaped and came at midday to Dzitbalché, but the exertions of the journey had exhausted all of us, the Indians not excepted,[12] and we literally collapsed at the first house. After a few refreshing drinks had given us breath and speech once more, we looked for an inn where we might rent a room.

The following day we set out on our journey to Campeche, on the road from which we had come, and on the evening of April 10 arrived safe and sound.

Chapter 18

In Campeche I once more resumed my former life. Either because of complications from my last journey or because the pressing heat of the season, a nausea overcame me, one that gnawed feverishly at my body and contributed not a little to worsening my condition. But I tried to cope with my sorrow through daily journeys, however limited, and so one day came to a small village an hour from Campeche where the atmosphere was far more lively.

This village was Sambulá. It was destroyed in 1840 by the Mexicans,[1] who had their camp there, and now has only a few houses with 160 inhabitants and a church with a miracle-working San Antonio, who exerts a powerful attraction upon the female world of Campeche. It is often said that this saint has the power to bring fortunate marriages and to find good husbands. Whatever the case may be, this much is certain: that every Tuesday a gaggle of women and girls make a pilgrimage to San Antonio in Sambulá, to which point, naturally, the male world follows after and thus makes use of the small village to rendezvous. The people come there on foot and by carriage, enjoy themselves in country fashion, crown themselves with flowers, and return loaded with fruit, singing and rejoicing. I determined to have a look at the pilgrimage to Sambulá; and in fact, I was just the right man to support San Antonio, and would eagerly have reduced the number of his devotees.[2] Moreover, Campeche is so poor in places of entertainment that this weekly festival has already become a necessity for half the residents, who have no diversion outside of cockfighting, which is held in a small amphitheater. For that reason the Campechanos eagerly seize every opportunity to amuse themselves. I enjoyed visiting such small festivities everywhere possible, and I readily confess that I enjoyed seeing this procession. I had become partly integrated into Campeche life.

In the meantime more ships had arrived here from Veracruz and brought sad news from the scene of battle. The defeat of the Mexican army on February 23 at Buena Vista had scarcely left the minds of grieved Mexicans when now came the additional news that Generals Scott and Worth had landed with twelve thousand Americans on Isla de Sacrificios, opposite from Veracruz. The bombardment of the city's fortifications began by land and by sea on March 19; on the twenty-seventh the groundwork for a settlement was signed, and on the twenty-ninth the city and the fortress San Juan de Ulúa surrendered, along with four thousand men, who in the face of the enemy laid down all their arms. The Americans immediately set up a government in that same place, opened the port to their business, and formally proclaimed themselves masters of Veracruz. Soon after these events the Americans prepared to launch their march to the capital.

On April 16 the army set off and a bloody epoch of this war had begun. The terrain described in chapter 13 produced more than an almost insuperable *defilée;*[3] the Mexicans forgot about the loss of Puente Nacional in order to concentrate on the second encounter of Cerro Gordo, at Plan del Río.[4] Santa Anna and Ampudia[5] had taken an intimidating position with all troops on standing orders; however, the boldness of the American corps under Twigg, Worth, and Shields had already won an advantage on the seventeenth, and on the eighteenth began by storming the hill, forcing their way by fighting man-to-man, a massacre that usually happens only with the pirating of ships. Soon the mountain slopes were strewn with death, and it was only the lack of good officers and munitions that brought such a heavy loss to the Mexicans, who defended themselves heroically. The battle came to an end, and the Americans had won a complete victory. They had taken an enormous number of prisoners, among them the best officers of the Mexican army. The North Americans captured twenty artillery and 22,000 pesos from the luggage of Santa Anna, and thereby opened a path to Mexico.

Already on April 20 the victors of Cerro Gordo took possession of Jalapa, soon thereafter captured the fortress Perote, and in a short time marched for Puebla, where for a long time the resistance of many volunteers halted their progress. Santa Anna and Ampudia had escaped from the above-mentioned battle, and because of this the former in particular was accounted a traitor to the fatherland. In spite of that, he tried to salvage his honor by concentrating a new force at the capital. But this project failed, owing to his lack of personal valor and his highly perfidious character; moreover, he subsequently and quite inexplicably failed to take advantage of those moments most favorable for a victory. Thus stood matters at the end of July, when the Americans began to move forward again.

Yucatán hid itself by quietly requesting neutrality from the North Americans. But dismay over the apparent disintegration of Mexico was so great that it was uncertain what the conquerors could expect following their subjugation of the country, which still lacked the means to build a self-sufficient state. However, with the sanguine hopes that are innate to the Mexican, the agitated heads soon calmed down, and thereafter the citizens busied themselves exclusively with their private affairs.

Things had quieted down considerably in the countryside here, and for that reason I decided to make a journey to the capital city of Mérida. Even though I was quite reduced in means and would have to seek an advance for it, nevertheless I did not want to die of boredom in Campeche, so I had to undertake a new journey at any cost. I set out from Campeche in a diligencia on May 22, 1847, at 5 A.M. The diligencias in Yucatán are equipped just as in Mexico, but they lack good draft horses and mules as well as good inns. The length of the journey fluctuates between two and eight days, depending on the condition of the road. Since the rain had still not begun at the time of my departure, we counted on a rapid progress and in reality toward evening had already reached the first village that I had not yet seen, one named Halachó, which lies a few miles beyond Calkiní on the main highway. Halachó has a beautiful church and walled houses that compare favorably with most villages on the Camino Real. Here we changed the horses, and since the night was so very clear, we continued without delay.

At 8:00 the next morning we reached Mérida, our journey's destination. Mérida lies at 20°58′40″ north latitude and 83°23′30″ west longitude from Cádiz, twenty-four feet above sea level, has twenty-five thousand inhabitants, was founded with wide and orderly streets on a stone plain in the year 1542, and is surrounded by suburbs known as *barrios*. It is the seat of government and the bishopric of Yucatán. Although not large, the houses of the city are still nicely constructed of stone and with flat roofs. The most peculiar buildings are as follows.

The Cathedral, built from 1,598 square-cut stones, stands on the side of the plaza opposite the Audiencia. It is a glorious edifice, decorated inside with twelve Doric columns. Its length comes to 291 feet, its width to 110 feet. Although quite impoverished, there still exist very many decorations of silver. The exterior is simple; the two steeples are not very high and in terms of splendor rate far behind the cathedrals of Mexico and Puebla. Along with this church Mérida has a dozen others, among which that of San Juan de Dios is remarkable, because the hospital is connected with the same, just as the Cathedral adjoins a college and a seminary.

The buildings that surround the 18,265-square-foot *plaza mayor* all distinguish themselves through their antiquity. This is especially true of the house of the first Spanish governor,[6] which is decorated with grotesque figures representing the defeat of the Indians, and which now finds itself in the possession of Simón Peón, who until now has been able to protect it from the destructive tendencies of the Liberals.

The Convent of San Francisco, also known as its Citadel, lies in the southern part of the city on a small hill. Presently a ruin, it was built by Franciscan monks on the site of an idol's temple and is surrounded by a strong stone wall, which even now retains its integrity and makes a good fortification, and which encircles three ruined churches and a few other destroyed buildings. Along with the convent of San Francisco of Campeche, it is one of the oldest constructions of Yucatán's modern age. Everything about them points to the fact that however well the first monks of this land preached, they also knew how to defend themselves against the warlike Indian tribes of Yucatán at the time of the conquest, and necessarily had to be able to enclose themselves together within a protected space.

The peninsula's previous government (under Barbachano)[7] had allowed a few buildings of the cloister to be renovated in order to serve as jails and barracks. Finally, the nuns' cloister, likewise an extremely old building, still stands in good condition and with forty pious sisters, and exhibits remarkable size and strength.

The residents of Mérida have an advantageously favorable character, and I can only acknowledge their kindness. They are known for confidence, openness, free movement in society and in household circles, and love of song and piano. The daughters of Mérida are among the most beautiful women I have found in Mexico, all the more as their open, uninhibited behavior greatly increases their attractiveness. In all, their character has many similarities with that of the women of South America: namely, they are passionate, daring in their undertakings, and charming at the same time. In Mérida there is no lack of places for relaxation and refreshment of the inhabitants. Cafés, icehouses, billiards, shops with European luxury items, gardens, and promenades are available and are considered necessities; only the theater has stood unused for a long time, as in Campeche. The people of Mérida are more accustomed than the Campechanos to every form of entertainment, and for that reason have a far greater inclination for carriage rides. Every household owns a volante, the same form of double-suspension carriage as in Havana. Although somewhat old-fashioned, these are nevertheless comfortable and at times fitted out with great luxury. After dinner at 5:00 or 6:00 the Meridanos drive up and down in the streets and enjoy the fresh evening air. The ladies, who at noon spend their time at home, sit in their second-story quarters, at the windows made in Spanish style with wrought iron. They smoke their cigars and share provocative greetings with their fans, which they know how to handle with extraordinary grace, through which they receive the friendly reciprocation of the passerby.

As a commercial city, Mérida, along with its port of Sisal, is of less importance, and the number of export articles quite limited. Corn, rice, wax, honey, deer- and oxhides, together with henequen, are the most important commodities. Henequen, also called *sosquil,* is the fiber that is obtained from the leaf of a furcraea agave,[8] and it is found both in the wild as well as commonly cultivated in Yucatán. This fiber, which North Americans know as sisal hemp, is scraped out of the green leaves of this plant with a piece of wood, cleaned, and pressed into a bale, or processed as hand-turned rope and exported. Because of its great strength, in North America it is processed into ship rigging and sacks, which are respected for their durability. Until now no one has produced a functioning machine for the extraction of this fiber; once introduced, however, this will make henequen an extremely important item.[9] The process of macerating the leaves does not work well, for it causes the leaves to darken or at least lose their beautiful shining silver color.

Mérida has almost no industry. There are, however, two book printers with four newspapers: one daily, one three times weekly, one every eight days, and one monthly. This latter is the *Registro yucateco,* a review dedicated to the promotion of belles lettres and the edifying sciences.[10]

As I have already explained, I came to Mérida on a Sunday morning and proceeded to the *posada*[11] of Doña Micaela Lavalla, the only proprietor of some form of hotel where for 1 peso a day the traveler receives room and board and is truly well served.

That very same day presented me with a favorable opportunity to attend a fiesta to be celebrated in the suburb of San Sebastián in honor of the santo. The windows and doors on the left and right were hung with curtains and richly decorated; in front of the houses of the best streets stood rows of chairs set up for those who did not participate in the procession to join in the festive atmosphere. A multitude of people surged up and down, from time to time making room for a light volante, which with ostentatious luxury rolled along in stately fashion.[12] It was toward evening when, surprised by the great number of beautiful volantes and still more beautiful ladies who sat in them, I drew near to the great plaza in front of the church. From afar it seemed to be covered in snow. Hundreds of Indian men and women, as well as mestizos and Negroes of both sexes, had assembled in that same place to attend the procession, which had just now left the church and was circling around the same under a passageway constructed of branches. The snow-white clothing of both sexes revealed a cleanliness that borders on the unbelievable, and which could have no equal in any tropical land. On the men, with their white shirts, just like the women with the beautiful *huipil* and *fustán* previously described, not the smallest stain was to be found. On Sunday the popular classes, whether or not they have money, and in disregard of social rank, appear in identical dress and with great neatness. Moreover, they keep their bodies extraordinarily clean, and even the poorest take a bath at least once a week.[13] Most frequently they use the so-called *baño de pájaro* (birdbath), which consists of a sprinkling of fresh water, just as they never sit down without having washed their hands and feet. In Mexico I had never encountered this fastidiousness that characterizes the Yucatecans and was therefore pleasantly surprised to discover the same. The celebration lasted until evening; the people let loose racket upon racket, drank rum in abundance, joked and caroused, while the coaches of the city rushed on and dispersed toward different points according to their purpose.

An equally dazzling festivity was that of Corpus Christi,[14] which had been celebrated the evening before with music and promenades. Noteworthy were the offerings of the Indians, which they would hang next to and above the altar, and which consist of fruits of all manner, chickens, eggs, and sometimes even of turtles, snakes, lizards, and conches.[15] I received new and clearer evidence of the Indians' confused ideas in matters of religion from my conversation with one who placed a sacrificial wax candle to St. George. When questioned why he did it, he answered with true naïveté that he had a sick horse at home, and since he imagined that St. George would not much comprehend the matter, he turned to his horse, which in any event would surely understand a horse's nature.

Regarding these people who until now did without all enlightenment and education (I refer to the converted Indians of the Americas), it is obvious that they wholeheartedly respect the ceremonial dimension of our religion and completely fail to grasp its spiritual meaning. Like all uncultivated peoples, they believe deeply in heaven, hell and its eternal physical torture, and the protective power of innumerable saints.

The festivity lasted until late at night, and many only returned to their villages the following day.

In the course of my residence I made a few excursions to different haciendas in the environs of Mérida, something that guaranteed me many cheerful moments. The vegetation is the poorest in the world, as one cannot expect anything else from this rocky soil. Still, these small estates are extremely agreeable. Fruit trees of all sort, such as caimitos, mangoes, guayabanas, oranges, bananas, coconuts, and so forth, are planted and tended with great care. In this regard the quinta of the current bishop of Yucatán[16] in particular distinguishes itself. But its fame is at the moment nothing compared to that of Chucausín, which is in turn related to a powder mill where they produce truly beautiful and high-quality gunpowder with North American machinery.

Another three weeks had passed, and since I had still received no news from Europe regarding the continuation of my journey, I therefore had to return once more to Campeche in order to at least secure necessary means of support through my friends there. On June 14, 1847, with 1 peso in my pocket, I set out on my return journey.

The first villages—Umán, Chocholá, and Kopomá—offered little that was remarkable unless one cares to mention the occasionally luxurious churches. At least in the last village, however, the traveler also encounters one of the so-called *cenotes,* or natural wells of fresh water. The cenotes are nothing more than grottoes of significant depth that often contain stone basins filled with good water. The most outstanding in terms of its depth is that of Bolonchén Ticul; endlessly long steps lead down to the spring itself and must be illuminated with pinewood chips when fetching water.[17] Still, the frequent occurrence of cenotes in Yucatán is such a unique and peculiar phenomenon that it tempts one to determine their origins.

In its totality Yucatán is an altogether flat, stony land without rivers, so that in the rainy season the water remains standing in the depressions and at times converts great savannas into veritable seas for three or more months. It could be that the water of the cenote is filtered rainwater that accumulates among the crags. Against this, however, speaks the continually high water level itself, in which one should necessarily observe some variation during the eight-month dry season. But strangely enough this is never the case. Rather, I am inclined to believe in a subterranean influx to Yucatán originating in the mountains of Chiapas, something that is not improbable, for it is proven that Yucatán has many underground rivers that come to the surface here and there. One such is without doubt the spring of Hampolol, described in the previous chapter. On the other hand, trustworthy men assure me that on the north coast they have come upon an enormous number of freshwater springs in the sea, not far from the shore (called Bocas de Conil), springs that erupt with such force that the Indians journey out in their boats in order to bail up drinking water for themselves.[18] However, with the total absence of mountains in that region, the notion of underground bodies of water is the only possibility. Surely it comes to that place from a great distance, descending from the mountains of Chiapas and in some places bubbling up out of its subterranean currents in deep grottoes, while in other places in seemingly level terrain, and flows on again from the same villages far under the earth. Thus the rainwater in reality plays only a very small role in this phenomenon, and no better explanation for it can in fact be supposed. Earlier I have mentioned a pair of underground rivers in Mexico, and this strange trick of nature repeats itself beneath the rugged soil of Yucatán.

After Kopomá comes the handsome village of Maxcanú, and from there the remaining towns that I have already described at the beginning. Since the road was very bad, we reached Campeche only on June 16,[19] and in consequence of my depleted resources, which reduced me almost to starvation, I arrived at my quarters so famished that for the first moment I forgot everything else and, not to be stopped, fell upon the stores I found.

The time of trials was not yet over, however, since upon returning I found no letters of salvation, and I now began to sink into a melancholy that I could not shake off despite all efforts, and which gnawed at my interior like a devouring worm. I was and would remain abandoned to my fate, helpless and hopeless, and a discouraging fate it was, too!

Chapter 19

On the morning of July 1, 1847, I saddled my horse in order to see the hacienda Chivic and the Campeche timber forces of the vicinity. It was a beautiful summer morning, the kind that one frequently enjoys in tropical countries during the rainy season. Everything had rejuvenated itself once more with the dawn. Seemingly withered trees and bushes flourished again with the splendid green of their leaves, cinnamon, mimosas, and incas. Clinging begonias were decked with aromatic flowers from which industrious bees and other insects gathered honey,[1] while the cicadas greeted the morning with their buzzing song. Innumerable birds, among them the delightful hummingbird with his brilliant plumage, lured the sun from its hiding place in order to enliven the scenery once more. Soon everything seemed to breathe only cheer—from the serpent hidden among cold rocks, from the tiny and annoying mosquito that drones in circles around the traveler, from the worm wriggling blindly in the dust, to the vulture soaring high above in the blue ether! And in this moment, what man would not have felt joy? Even if his inner self still wanted to be sad, even if he were at first inclined to remain paralyzed, untrusting, and friendless—soon he will have to rejoice with all that surrounds him, laughing and forgetting the past and the future. He will seize the glorious moment of the present in order to chase away the gloomy clouds that darken his brain.

It was a beautiful spring morning, comparable to the month of May in our land. The air was so refreshing and restorative that it seemed as if I were riding in my homeland among the orchards bedecked with a million snow-white blooms, on whose splendor I so often reveled, and on which I reflected more than usual. Ah! It is something beautiful, when one wanders alone among sweet-smelling woods and wildflowers, and everything appears to stir and shift in the most profound harmony. Nothing is capable of disturbing the magnificent impression when, as the saying goes, alone and unobserved one converses with splendors of nature and feels one's heart grow ever warmer. In such moments we become reconciled to the hand of destiny, which clutches us tightly like iron and so often forces us to drain the cup filled with the bitter drops of life.

For a long time I had not felt as much joy as on that day, and I trotted cheerfully through the delightful woods until I reached the hamlet of Chiná, two leagues from Campeche. This is a tiny town of nine hundred inhabitants; in the year 1840 they were eyewitnesses to a bloody clash that took place between Yucatecans and Mexicans.[2] Now the church and many buildings lie in ruins, just as in the Mexican republic where all was destroyed during and after the struggle for independence.

A few hours later we found ourselves at the hacienda Chivic, five leagues from Campeche. It is this small, attractive estate surrounded by Campeche wood,[3] where in addition to logging, locals farm corn and raise cattle. Aside from the *tintales,* or dyewood forests, the vegetation here is better than on the coast, since now and then the traveler discovers a few pseudo-parasites on the high mimosa and turpentine trees, and there is no lack of euphorbia, zapotes, and mulberry, while the ground is covered with small heliotropes, sedum, cinnamon, and sage.

However, the forests of dyewood trees take up the greatest part. This tree distinguishes itself by its cracked trunk and its complete absence of undergrowth. It is an altogether peculiar phenomenon that the dyewood tree allows no other plants to grow up alongside it, and even on ships transporting plants it is highly dangerous, all the more so since the analysis of the wood shows that it is not only astringent but in fact highly poisonous in nature. Since the moist forest breathed out a vapor smelling strongly of tanning acid and wood vinegar, it occurs to me that perhaps these vapors contribute to the suffocation found lurking in the ships' rooms. But strangely enough, this quality is found with other American wood types without their exerting such a harmful influence on nearby organisms. In spite of the immense quantity they log each year from this forest, an unlimited number of young saplings dot the soil there and grow in profusion. Moreover, the peninsula has vast campeche wood forests on the north and east sides, which are still not at all touched and appear to hold inexhaustible riches.

Tabasco, however, produces the best dyewood at present. This is known by the name laguna wood, so called from the point of embarkation on the island of Carmen, on the coast of Tabasco. The wood will be sold by quintales (100 Spanish pounds) for 30 kreuzers to 2 florins, 30 kreuzers, according to the greater or lesser demand of Europe at the moment, and at times yields unbelievable profit for the owner of the forest. Consequently, this branch of industry divides the Indians on such haciendas into fieldworkers and woodcutters, of whom the latter stand higher in rank and are better paid, because a certain skill is required for the felling and hewing of trees. Despite this fact, both classes live in the poorest manner, since their annual salary amounts to not more than 20–40 Spanish pesos, for which they receive twelve or more cargas of corn.[4] The tiny huts, the naked children running around everywhere, the ragged clothing of the adults: all this sufficiently indicates their poverty, and yet everyone has a clean suit for Sunday, even if he also goes around all week before in rags.

The waiting owner of Chivic troubled himself to show us all attention, and for our entertainment arranged a dance among the Indians of his hacienda.[5] Three flasks of rum, two candles, two guitars, and a tambourine were all they needed for it. As soon as the strings jangled and the tambourine rattled, the monotonous dance began, accompanied by the muffled ring of the Indians singing. Sometimes the guitars fell silent and the *tambora* alone kept the beat. At other times the passionate music of the strings seized them and the ground shook from the stomps of the enthusiastic dancers, so that the whole did not fail to make a deep and indescribable impression. The dance seemed so monotonous, something so charming lay in the rising and falling of the stimulating tones, that it made one want to express joy, sadness, good cheer, and rage. Enviable people, I cried out, how little you need in order to satisfy your needs! A straw hat, some corn and water, a sip of brandy, a Sunday suit, and how lucky you are!

In our excursions into the environs we came to the haciendas Bocmun and Yaxché in the vicinity of the pueblo Seiba cabecera, which has 650 inhabitants and marks the limit of cultivated land. From here southward are endless woods and savannas, which were used partly as pasture for the cattle herds. Otherwise, however, it had now lain unpopulated in a complete state of nature for a century, awaiting industrious hands in order to bring forth its fruits in abundance!

On July 6 I returned again to Campeche only to fall ill once more to an attack of fever, a condition my sturdy constitution luckily overcame. In other regards as well nothing turned out in my favor, since meanwhile in Yucatán the dreaded Indian rebellion had broken out. The tribe of the Huits in the eastern part of the country,[6] six to eight thousand in number, had fallen over the communities lying close by and had begun to murder all who were white or of mixed blood, leaving only a few women alive in order to drag them away with their wild hordes.

At the very beginning sixty victims fell in one village, while in others the numbers of horrible crimes grew day by day. This news broadcast terror and horror over all the land. The government, still on weak footing, stood helpless before a war of extermination of the whites. Soon, however, another spirit ruled the Campechanos; the citizens armed themselves in a show of force against the Indians, arrests were carried out, and the strongest and strictest guidelines were established to work against this Caste War. Luckier than their counterparts elsewhere, they detected the plot and learned with shudders that on September 15 the signal would go out for the Indians to murder all the whites.[7] Immediately they imprisoned the headmen and after a short trial shot them. Among them were found also two caciques, who had issued the following proclamation to the whites and to the comrades of their tribe:

> We poor Indians testify to what evil the Spanish do. Many harms they do us, and indeed, the same to our children and poor women. Much harm happens to us without reason of a crime: so certainly that when the Indians rise up, so it will be because the whites have given cause for it, because the whites said that now they do not adhere to Jesus Christ. They have burned all the cornfields, and so they must account for their crimes against the Indians. At the time we endured their attacks, but since they have already begun this conflict, it will last twelve years.[8] And they always harmed us, but we will make them suffer; since we are creatures of God and will have to say, whether God gave them the right to kill all of us and we had no desire, since Juan Vázquez began,[9] who deceived us. And after he had deceived us, he began to kill us again, and that's why if we were to die at the hands of the Spanish, patience. The Spaniards think that the matter will end thus: never, since so it stands written in the book of Chilam Balam.[10] Thus also allows us our Lord Jesus Christ here on earth and for that reason, if the Spanish would calm themselves, we would calm ourselves as well. That is the last thing that we Indians say. There is only one single God in his revered Unity: may he and the angels be beloved.—Manuel Ay, D. Hyacenth Canek, Rancho San Francisco on 3 September 1847.[11]

Although lacking proper continuity of thought, this letter nevertheless shows sufficiently the views of both ringleaders, who were immediately executed, along with sixteen other avowed guilty caciques who followed thereafter, and it proves how well the Indians until today know to assess their injured rights. It also gives a clear proof of how the whites have continually practiced their bloody handiwork of oppression and how they have brought upon themselves the frightful consequences of this pitiable disaster. Certainly, in the course of a month the energetic guidelines quieted the Indians somewhat, and only in the east did the troops of the government pursue an isolated rabble that fell back toward the unpopulated area between Valladolid and Bacalar. Regardless, however, Yucatán still hangs in the danger of being the scene of a dreadful war, one whose end is not foreseen.

Meanwhile, things were chaotic in Mexico. On August 7–9 the North American army departed from Puebla in order to make for the capital. On the seventeenth of this month the vanguard, under General Worth, stood before Mexico. On the nineteenth and twentieth the Mexican strongholds at Contreras and Churubusco were taken, and after a desperate struggle old Tenochtitlán fell into the hands of the Americans. To be certain, enemy troops were still marching into the city, and they opened peace negotiations; but these came to nothing, and consequently hostilities began again on September 8. Immediately on the thirteenth the Americans encircled the final stronghold of Chapultepec, stormed it on the fourteenth with twelve hundred volunteers, and took possession of this last sanctuary of the Mexican army with eight hundred men captured under General Bravo. From here they forced their way along the aqueduct at two gates in the city abandoned by Santa Anna, and the starry banner of the United States soon fluttered over the plaza of the conquered Mexicans.

With this conquest the war was over. Partly dismembered, partly annihilated, the Mexican army had no more power, the country was subjugated, and now began the peace negotiations, which were first ratified in May 1848 and in consequence of which Mexico handed over more than a third of its land to North America. Upper California, New Mexico, and all land north of the Río Bravo del Norte were lost. Santa Anna fled to Jamaica, and the formerly glorious New Spain was left to its hopeless fate, out of which it will never again be able to raise itself![12]

Apart from this sad news, September 5 was for me a joyful day after so many cloudy, dissipated weeks, since the long-desired letter from Europe finally arrived here by way of a schooner from Veracruz. Sadly, only a small sum of money could be transferred to me beforehand, since the remainder of my travel account credit was only to be accessible in Havana. Since I therefore still had no tidy sum of money for necessities in order to be able to raise a continuation of the journey, I therefore had to persevere in Campeche a while longer, until this last barrier was surmounted as well. This circumstance prolonged my stay for almost two months, and consequently I had the opportunity to make my preparations for further travels with all leisure, a fact which allowed the additional advantage that in the meantime the rainy season came to an end.

My prolonged residence in Yucatán made me a spectator not only of the fiesta of San Román, a barrio of Campeche, but also of new unrest in the country, an unrest that tore through and devastated the interior. However, we will first talk about the festivities in San Román. This famous fiesta takes place on September 14, and under better circumstances thousands of people would have attended, thus making it one of the largest popular celebrations in Yucatán. The event it commemorates concerns a statue of the crucified Christ that the people of the sea revere as an important patron. Moreover, from very olden times different accounts have been attached to this wonderful likeness of Our Lord of San Román, and of these accounts the following is the most famous.

A rich Campechano promised to have a crucifix made for the church of this barrio if God would restore him to health. He traveled from this point to Havana and had the luck to recover. Mindful of his vow, he searched everywhere for a skilled master who was to craft the image for him, something that seemed unattainable in that time when art did not prosper in the West Indies. There a youth presented himself; he promised to produce the image in a short time, and completed it artfully.[13] This youth must have been an angel, for in those days no man would have been able to complete so wonderful a work in so short a time and so masterful a fashion. Moreover, as soon as he had finished his work, the youth vanished without a trace.

At that point the ship bound for Campeche was to take along the Christ; but since the rich man demanded a single room reserved for himself alone, the captain therefore refused, and the crucifix was sent in another small craft, which went from Havana to Campeche in exactly forty hours, the briefest journey in living memory. But the first ship was lost, never to be seen again. From this came sailors' great reverence toward this cross, which supposedly has worked many wonders with storms and the dangers over the sea as well as on the land.

This fiesta lasts approximately nine days, but it goes on longer, since bullfights, dances, and games encourage so much diverse merriment that locals prefer to extend for a few more days. The whole world gathers there in the evening, when countless vendors of sweets offer their sugary confections, while the lottery and card games attract young and old, rich and poor, to all sorts of pleasure. Everything around the church is lively, while in its interior a luxurious illumination assures a pleasant scene, and the organ tones rising from its chambers strangely mingle with the gossip of the people. The fiesta was an entirely cheerful one and amounted to Campeche's resurrection and a new zest for life, for no one suspected that on the same day (September 14) Mexico had become the spoils of North America!

Shortly after the fiesta, the fire of discord erupted once more between Campeche and Mérida, since Mérida on October 6 had declared in favor of Mexico, while in Campeche, Don Santiago Méndez, acting as constitutional governor, took an oath in favor of neutrality. In the capital a triumvirate formed with the purpose of seizing the reins of government and making common cause with Mexico. Méndez, who was determined to maintain his right as elected governor and advocate of neutrality, sent all the troops of the assembled National Guard to Mérida and had the city occupied, whereupon the triumvirate had to dissolve itself. Don José Dolores Cetina, one of the leading insurgents from the eastern part of the peninsula, fled under the pretext of deploying his force of men against the Huits, who had begun to commit new atrocities. At the bottom, however, he seemed to entertain the intention of joining with these same Huits in order to strike a blow against the government in Campeche at the first opportunity. It was very sad to see how eagerly the National Guard of Campeche, among whom were found many fathers of families and hardworking day laborers, marched out to battle against their own brothers, an altogether dark omen for a nation still convulsed in the dreadful Caste War.

After the capture of Mérida all was indeed still once more. Despite all his energy, however, Méndez failed to restore the nation to peace and harmony, and so his downfall became certain. This new unrest exposed Campeche and all its troops to greater mayhem, to such an extent that Méndez himself had all the foreigners, above all the Spaniards, form a battalion to uphold the peace and security of the city. No one was exempted from it, and I myself had to deign to do patrol duty at night. Even when my turn came up, we did not take too seriously this service in the company of good friends. We often made boat trips along the coast as well, with which opportunity we cheerfully hoisted our nation's flag on our small masthead. Soon the French flag went up, then the Spanish, then the Austrian and Mexican in the seagoing vessels of Campeche, and on hotter days we enjoyed ourselves immensely. However, a strong breeze rose up, so that often we had some trouble getting back to dry land, all the more so since the few of us were all the sailors there were.

Thus the time passed until October 30 arrived, at which point I had been instructed to continue my journey to Veracruz. I would gladly have abandoned the land of Mexico forever, and a Colombian boat which by chance had landed here thereby offered me the opportunity to do so. But my limited means did not permit such an undertaking. Nothing could be done, and I therefore resolved to go to Tabasco, where I had every reason to expect a rich vegetation as well as a most frightful climate. On top of this I had to steel myself to go tranquilly toward the manifold dangers. My friends in Campeche counseled me against this plan in the most heated terms; but the notion of the terrible climate, of the plague of mosquitoes, of the unrest and war, even the distinct possibility of my own death could not weaken my resolve, since I had already decided a long time ago. Soon all was prepared for the journey, and this same was set for November 3.

From the day of this decision onward I no longer ate at my fonda but rather found myself every day at the table of a different family that invited me in order to bid me farewell. In particular the French consul, Herr Laisné, took charge of me and showered me with displays of friendship I will never forget. However, a breakfast invitation I had received on Monday gave me the clearest proof that I had acquired many friends in Campeche. This same was signed by three prominent individuals who had assembled the respectable young men of the city in order to bid me good-bye. We exchanged toasts, and they presented me with a written farewell. I cherish the memory of that most beautiful day. I went away deeply moved by this company which in those days held me, the foreigner, in such high regard—a regard I never again encountered, even in my homeland amid countrymen.

Since I had already attempted an overland journey to Tabasco and was unsuccessful, I chose a smuggler for my journey there, a man of whom I will speak in the following chapter.

Chapter 20

I have already mentioned that Yucatán's ties with Tabasco were rather restricted, but communication between their ports had now been severed altogether. That is, the North Americans, who as a preliminary measure had burned all the ships in the port of Tabasco on October 24 and 25, 1846, returned once more on June 15 of this year[1] and took the city of Villahermosa after a completely unsuccessful defense attempt on the part of the Mexicans.[2] But there the unhealthy climate among the tropics brought about a huge number of fatalities, so on July 22 they withdrew to Frontera at the mouth of the Grijalva (or Tabasco) River, in a manner of speaking the port of the capital city, to secure every access point for themselves. Initially, some communication between the Palizada River and the Río Seco toward Laguna and Campeche still remained possible; soon, however, the North Americans detected this hidden route and blockaded both points with complete thoroughness.

Since I had intended to take this route, which now had been rendered almost impossible, I therefore thought my project would have to be abandoned, all the more since no overland road existed from Campeche to Tabasco, either. In spite of that fact, an opportunity soon presented itself, since the forceful blockade shortly produced a brisk commerce of smuggling. In spite of the watchfulness of the enemy, more small boats learned to sneak into the Río Seco, which flows into the sea seven leagues west of the Grijalva, from whose banks the capital lies only two leagues distant, and from which it can easily be reached. This opportunity was extremely dangerous, but I decided that no other options remained for me than to entrust myself to a tiny smuggling vessel.

On November 3, 1847, I embarked on the *pongo*—for thus one here calls the small sea vessels of twenty to forth tons—of the name *San Luis.* I was accompanied by all my friends, who still doubted the favorable outcome of my undertaking and showered me with sympathy from the onset. At 9:00 I found myself on board the smuggler. The pongo *San Luis* was a vessel of thirty-two tons, forty years at sea, but in spite of everything still strong and firm. Two undersized slanting masts bore a flying jib, jib sail, forestaysail, staysail, and mainsail, ample fitting to be able to get away from the faster sailing vessels if necessary. The hold was loaded up to the deck, and on that same deck were secured such a multitude of objects that we sailed with the ship's gunwale almost in the water, and the waves in fact washed over the deck in calm weather in the harbor. No one could think of comfort, for no consideration was given for passengers; they appeared so seldom that they had to consider it a huge favor if permitted to travel along at all.

The captain, a Catalan named Don Juan Sánchez, was a young, fearless-looking man, pleasant and engaging, of stately physique, dark hair, and beard. His crew consisted of six sailors and a cabin boy. Before we put to sea, he explained to them the danger of being captured and invited them to serve truly and faithfully, which they all swore to do. After this they speedily hoisted the anchor and unfurled the sails, and in the shortest time a strong northwest breeze carried us onto the high seas. The sea surged furiously as we pushed along, and seemed to be on the verge of swallowing our tiny ship. Wave upon wave broke over the deck, so that the beams ran with water and not even the tiniest part remained dry, while the northwest wind blew with ferocity and drove us onward with arrowlike speed.

Although I am not subject to seasickness, I still did not think about sleep, since I had to sit on a crate in order to keep my feet dry. However, the sea began to alarm us. The captain stationed himself at the helm, and since we would not have endured the blow of the waves from the side, he turned the pongo in such a way that we were blown before the winds and the waves ran with us, whereby we were able to counter the strongest waves. But the captain too shared the general anxiety and sometimes knocked out a curse, of which I could clearly understand the words "Este mar nos come," "This sea devours us."

The night passed by in slow steps, and next morning we found ourselves in sight of land, somewhere near Puerto Real, a proof of how extraordinarily rapidly we had sailed. The stately sunrise in the east illuminated in a thousandfold play of colors the waves of the raging sea, waves seemingly churned up by the earth itself. I stared almost indifferently into the dark mass of water, since I had already reached that point where the traveler, having given up on himself, begins to play a game of chance with his life, so to speak. Moreover, all dangers of a terrible climate awaited me in Tabasco, dangers I could scarcely calculate. For that reason I never traveled with greater imperturbability upon rough seas than on this occasion, when I was threatened from all sides.

We kept a sharp watch from all sides in order to ensure that no threatening sail was in sight. At first all was free, but soon a two-master appeared heading toward us from the southwest, but which appeared not to have seen us. We recognized it as American, although we could make out neither its flag nor its intention, and we readied all preparations in order to effect a possible escape. We immediately tied all letters and documents to a stone so that we would be able to sink them speedily in case of emergency. The captain, who had double commissions,[3] took out his papers for Alvarado, to which point Yucatecan ships were permitted to go, and in which my passport was also made out, in order to be able to force his way through the snare and conceal his true objective. However, our pongo was so small that we could not easily be noticed at so far a distance. For that reason we set all sails, and striking another direction we were soon out of the range of the two-master, and could now count ourselves fortunate for getting away.

The entire day we had favorable wind, although with seas higher than might be expected, and by sundown we had reached 19°50′ north latitude. The following evening we headed toward the southwest in order to hail the bars of San Pedro and San Pablo the next morning. However, an error in the calculation caused us to arrive before the Tabasco shore at daybreak, and as quickly as possible we set out again in order not to be detected by the American blockade.

When sufficiently far from shore we again headed southwestward for the bar of Chiltepec, where the Río Seco, which we had thought of ascending, empties into the gulf. For the longest time we ran alongside the land, but without catching sight of the river, which flowed out diagonally toward the northwest. Yet we could tell that we were approaching the bar by the altered breaking of the waves.

Now approached that most dangerous moment when we would have to pass over the shallow bar. The breaking of salt- and freshwater coming together became ever stronger, more agitated, and more frightening, and we believed we would sink under the waves before we had reached the bar itself. All at once we were in the breakers. All spaces were closed, and from the mast the captain commanded the small crew, calling for them to sound out the water's depth

The words "Derriva un poco, orza, orza todo, arriba velas, casa foques!"[4] quickly followed one another, while the sailor doing the soundings called out coolly between them, "Braza y media, braza y cuarta, braza larga, una braza, braza escasa!"[5] With these words he filled us all with horror—already the vessel had struck the sandbar fearfully on one occasion, and the captain cried out with hesitating voice, "Derriva, derriva! Ya estamos perdidos!" ("To windward, to windward! Now we're done for!"). I threw aside my coat, stationed myself with the sailors at the mainsail line, and helped retract it, while a mountainous wave rolled near and seemed to want to shatter us with one blow. It tumbled down dreadfully upon us. A frightening thrust followed, and when we opened our eyes we lay safely over the bar, in the gentle waters of the river. The wave had not only pushed us onto the sandbank but actually washed us clean over it and into the river. Once there, all danger was over. We had eluded capture by the Americans and death by shipwreck, and as we sailed quietly upstream the captain hugged us heartily, full of joy over this wonderful escape. The reader will not find this especially strange for rugged seamen, if he considers that they love their ship like true children . . . indeed, more than they love their own lives. To the left lay a pongo wrecked five days earlier; on the bare, sandy beach to the right stood some thatch-and-pole houses constituting the rancho Chiltepec.

It was 2:00 in the afternoon on November 5 when we reached land. There on the pongo no shade at all was to be found. The sun burned down with scorching intensity, and it so tore at my face and hands that I suffered terribly. But the comforting shade of the straw hut, whose friendly proprietor, Ramón Segura,[6] an old Spaniard who was full of hospitality and trustworthiness, refreshed and invigorated us. Wearied to be sure from the short but profoundly trouble-filled sea voyage, I availed myself of the pleasure of the hammock that hung ready at my disposal in order to rest up.

Meanwhile, the woman of the house prepared a simple meal of beef. Countless better meals could be imagined, but I assured them that they had prepared me a feast and that I wished for no finer food during my travels. Everything here pointed to a highly patriarchal way of life. Tata ("Father") Ramón was the chief of all the residents of Chiltepec, approximately forty in number, including children, grandchildren, and great-grandchildren. These industrious folk work hard at processing the harvested Tabasco pepper, or else apply themselves to other business. Never in Mexico had I come upon such hardworking and upright folk as here. Fruit trees were planted around the houses; there were coconuts, mangoes, plums, bananas, and others, under which the children and domestic animals stroll about in the sand. In the background lay a small lagoon with wild fig trees and mangroves, and a splendid landscape of life and abundance prospered in this small rancho. I also came upon the captain of the foundered pongo, who likewise could not sufficiently praise the love and friendliness of these upright people.

Since our pongo would need at least eight days to reach the capital San Juan Bautista de Tabasco, someone advised me rather to take a *cayuco,* with which I could cover the distance of twenty leagues in two days.[7] Along with it Don Ramón lent me two of his sons, who got the canoe ready to travel. They made a small shade on top of it, in order to be sheltered from the sun, and brought food supplies consisting of cold roasted venison, corn bread, and pozole,[8] since nothing else would be available during the entire journey.

After my things were transferred from the pongo to the canoe, and when night began to fall, I prepared a small place under mosquito netting where I could spend the night. Without this measure the residents themselves could never sleep peacefully. In fact, while descriptions of the mosquitoes of Tabasco had once seemed to me exaggerations, I found these devils so malicious that all which is said about them can be confirmed as absolute truth. Swarms of millions descended upon the men, and the same insects did not spare animals with thick coats of fur; dogs were covered by these tiny, tormenting gnats. Neither smoke nor anything else was enough to drive them away, and I had to take refuge at once under the mosquito net in order to have a moment of rest before these intrusive guests. To do so the traveler tucks the edges of the net securely under his bedding, thereby closing off all entryways; in this way, at least, he can spend a night without waking up, even when the mosquitoes persist in their chorus of a thousand-voice lullaby. But if exposed to their furious bites, the traveler often suffers severe fever and other evils of tragic consequence, and that is why the inhabitants would rather travel without shirts than without netting.

I slept peacefully under my net, and all the more so since I had scarcely shut an eye the previous nights. Only out of necessity of having to set out early on my journey did I get up again at 11 P.M. in order to put out in the canoe, which scarcely accommodated myself, the two oarsmen, and my luggage. With a cordial handshake I said good-bye to Ramón and his wife. Beyond payment for their sons they would accept no compensation for the services provided, assuring me that they were delighted to have entertained a European once more after twenty years.

A clear night compensated to some degree for the absence of moonlight and eased the labor of the two strong young lads, who sank their oars so steadily into the water that we seemed to glide silently over the river. The darkness prevented me from making out objects on the bank, since the river in the vicinity of the mouth was fully three hundred feet wide. We quietly cut through those stately waters, and the gentle rolling of the canoe invited me once more to catch up on lost sleep . . . soon enough my eyelids fell shut.

The day broke, and the luxuriant bank shimmered in a most beautiful light. A cool morning breeze refreshed the air and played in the delicate reeds. Stout vines clung to the branches of the trees, as if they wished to lend still more strength to these giant trunks, and bound whole areas to impenetrable thickets. Grasses six to twenty feet high waved their heads to and fro, gently stirred by wind and water, and seemed intent on denying the magnificent butterflies a resting place on their supple, flowering fronds. Moreover, lovely willows were not wanting, a fact that astonished me not a little in this region bearing the consummate character of tropical vegetation. But no orchids were to be seen, even though parasitic plants occurred everywhere in greater or lesser number.

With every bend in the river new and exciting regions appeared, so that the traveler might well have imagined himself in a man-made park. Here arched a dense canopy of leaves under which we glided along the river; there towered a palm with its wide crown. Here a thousand-year-old tree exhibited its brittle trunk; there wound coiling vines covered with blooms far off over the branches which filled the air with pleasant aromas. However, no landing place presented itself anywhere, since the Río Seco, like all other rivers of Tabasco, is swollen to overflowing through the autumn rain in this season, so that they convert an area of at least three hundred square leagues of land into a lake. The trees and bushes conceal the limits of the main current, whose level is significantly higher than the land, and which therefore inundates everything around. Of the few houses on the Río Seco only a roof was to be seen. The poor rancheros had lost a terribly great deal this year—as much in the corn harvest as in drowned livestock—and had to flee to higher ground.

By nightfall we had completed half the journey. We needed to avoid the huge twists in the river so as not to lose our way; this meant that the next morning we would have to leave the main current in order to travel through flooded fields and pastures and within woods shut off from daylight, and we therefore were forced to spend the night in this place. The mosquitoes, however, approached in such numbers that neither I nor the lads could have endured spending the night without netting, which one cannot extend over the canoe. For that reason we tried to reach a small rancho, the Espino; because it lies on rather high ground, we could surmise that it stood above the water level. We found it, but no land remained dry other than that which one mere house occupied, a structure approximately four square fathoms in all.[9] Here lived an Indian, more women and children half or fully naked, and some pigs and chickens, all huddled together in this small room in the simplicity and innocence of paradise. Along with a sort of turtle, which they roast intestines and all, a bit of corn satisfied their most essential needs. The children, however, were covered in mosquito bites and presented a pitiable sight. My God, I exclaimed, is it possible that people could live here for longer than a day! Indeed they can, but only people like this family of Indians, who live among

"No land remained dry other than that which one mere house occupied, a structure approximately four square fathoms in all. Here lived an Indian, more women and children half or fully naked . . . all huddled together in this small room in the simplicity and innocence of paradise." (Photo courtesy of the Latin American Library, University of Texas at Austin)

themselves like the blessed cattle, propagate in the same fashion, and have no needs they cannot satisfy on this tiny piece of earth.

In truth, the reader would have had to witness the scene to form an idea of it and to believe it! Here, then, we were to spend the night, and my predicament was not small, since I did not know which of the two evils was greater, and whether I should let myself be tortured on the river by mosquitoes or pass the night with these folks. I chose the latter. Scarcely had I time enough to clean out a place under the *tapestle,*[10] since the mosquitoes already pursued me in such a way that I had to close my mouth and nose in order not to inhale them and thereby suffocate. I quickly crawled under the mosquito net, and had scarcely freed myself from their murderous attacks, when I soon suffered yet more powerful bites that originated from a multitude of angry ants that had hidden their annoying brood in the reeds, and who in no small degree vented their anger on the uninvited guest. Still, they could not force me to abandon this place, since I could more easily endure their attacks, if not parry them as well, than those of the terribly annoying mosquitoes. These circumstances, the asphyxiating fumes of the *comején*[11] which someone had kindled in order to impede the mosquitoes somewhat, the frightful heat, the oppressive humidity, and my uncomfortable position on the uneven straw: all made my confinement under the netting so excruciating that in spite of complete exhaustion and humble resignation in the iron will of relentless necessity, I did not close an eye the whole night, and thanked the Creator with all my heart when morning dawned, and I had fortunately put that most terrible night behind me for good.

Soon I found myself in my canoe once more, and as I already said, we now abandoned the river in order to travel cross-country over fields and through woods that harbored no living creatures outside of marsh- and waterbirds and small insects.[12] The lakes, which vanish entirely in the months of April and May, furnished a singular picture at the present moment. Water stretches as far as the horizon, and upon it seem to swim clumps of trees, as well as meadows made of the tips of high grasses: in short, a luxurious and almost magical vegetation unrooted in firm soil covered the unbounded waters of the overflown rivers.[13]

Indefatigable, the Segura boys forced the oars and skillfully wound their way through the labyrinth of swirling water. At 1:00 that afternoon we reached the rancho Paso Real, which already offered somewhat more of dry land; still and all, it could only be called a small island. At 2:00 we again found ourselves on the Río Seco, which at that time was connected with the Río Tabasco by means of a natural channel, and through which we reached the capital in two hours on November 7 in the afternoon, happy but not a little exhausted.

San Juan Bautista, formerly known as Villahermosa, lies on the left bank of the Río Tabasco, or Grijalva.[14] It sits partially on a small elevation surrounded by luxurious and fertile landed estates. But 250 smaller houses built of wood and thatch lie in ruins since the last North American attack, and offer a dismal tableau of devastation. The side toward the river is more agreeable; it is rather picturesque and has a few good houses to show. Along the river is a cabin on the other side, and countless canoes and cayucos arrive at that point with the fruits of the land. A great deal of animated life reigns on the banks of the river, especially in the morning. The streets of the city are uneven and hilly, rather irregular, and filthy to the utmost degree. The houses are tastelessly constructed, in part from stone, in part from wood, and without exception are unsuitable to the moist climate. The inhabitants total no more than six thousand; the greater part of them live from commerce with the interior, the import and export of cacao, coffee, rice, corn, tobacco, dyewood, and so forth. Remarkably, almost all nations are represented here by one or two individuals, of whom in particular a German, an English, a Spanish, and a French commercial house[15] occupy an especially important position, and the entire importation of European articles of commerce lies almost exclusively in their hands.

Atmospheric observations show 64 degrees as the lowest and 97 degrees as the average highest temperatures, together with the tremendous humidity and moisture of the air in a land that was still almost completely covered with forests. Tabasco was thus surrounded by a climate that belonged to the most malignant of the whole republic. Malaria, miasmatic poisons that often kill within forty-eight hours, scurvy, gastritis, intestinal infections, and a slow-wasting disease are extraordinarily common and have carried off countless foreigners there, a matter that hinders both colonization and closer exploration. A short time before, a Danish naturalist had succumbed to the climate in the first fourteen days. I visited his grave. Among the luxuriously fertile plains, hills, and valleys prowls the most appalling enemy of mankind: death in every form. The entire native population, one in a true sense Mexican and quite different from that of Yucatán, has a pale appearance which because of the often filthy clothing stands out all the more and seldom fails to make an unpleasant impression on the traveler. The cleanliness of the Yucatecan is sorely missed here.

Tabasco is the residence of a governor and a general, the commander in chief of the state, and the Belgian and Spanish consulates. It has two churches, more minor schools, and an *aduana marítima,* or maritime customhouse. That was the city in which I now found myself. They brought me to the *aduana* and to the port captain, where I had to show my passport, and after that let me move on unopposed. In spite of more letters of recommendation I addressed myself to the house of Lobach & Company, since I had the pleasure to have traveled with Herr August Lobach on the same steamboat to America and for that reason already knew him somewhat. More than two years had passed since that time, and yet this friendly man again recognized me all the same and hospitably took me with him.

Since no excursions whatsoever could be made from the city owing to flooding, I was restricted to one very small room that merely allowed me to prepare a few sketches of Tabasco and to write in my diary. Moreover, I was not inclined to collect anything here in this month, but rather preferred to set out again on my journey as soon as possible. Fate had it, however, that utterly worn out with the Yucatecan revolution, I had to arrive here precisely when the troops mutinied against their commander, Don Domingo Echegaray, and on November 14 named their ringleader, a certain Don Miguel Bruno, to be chief. This latter, a character known for his political intrigues, belonged to those contemptible individuals who at the expense of their own self-interest work jointly to "put their beautiful fatherland right" . . . in order to line their own pockets and to be able to live off the fat of the land.

The Americans had twice taken the city with insignificant losses. At the time, however, there appeared none of those heroes who defend the property of the nation with their own blood. Rather, the heroes of this land always appeared when the enemy had already gone, and availed themselves of what still remained by means of the most shameful and dishonorable scheming.[16]

Chapter 21

On November 20, 1847, at 3:00 in the morning, I stood on the banks of the Grijalva in order to embark once more in a small, uncomfortable riverboat. Although far larger than the canoe in which I had come from Chiltepec, it could nevertheless be called tiny in comparison the river. I had spent the evening before my departure quite enjoyably in the company of Herren Lobach, Cabot, and Schepeler and had bid them a friendly farewell and offered my warmest thanks for their hospitality. I headed toward Teapa, on the border of the states of Tabasco and Chiapas.

The canoe, which one calls a pongo, just like the small ocean vessel, was three and a half yards long and in the back was furnished with a wooden roof against the sun and rain. On the open three-quarter foredeck over the crossboards on each side lay a beam, which serves for the *batadores* so that by standing on the same they can push their poles against the ground or against the trees and run toward the stern in order to move the vessel. I will explain myself more clearly. The pongos are not really propelled by oars, which would require four to six men when moving upstream, but rather with poles equipped with wooden forks at one end. In this way, two men fully suffice to cross eight to ten leagues per day. One calls them batadores, from *botar*, or "to throw out or cast out," since they are constantly throwing out the poles to hook onto and pull forward from the underbrush or whatever firmer opportunity presents itself. In that way they endlessly follow the innumerable bends in the river. If they come upon no firm reference point on the bank, then the canoe will easily return to the middle of the river and be driven along by the current. They will pursue this course only until they again come to the bank and can once more pull the boat forward. The loss of time with such a retrogressive operation often runs to more than an hour. When the man has his pole well placed, he runs from the fore end of the canoe to the rudder and forces the pongo forward exactly as far as the length of the vessel. The speed of the journey depends purely and simply on the adroitness and tenacity of the batador; but for all that it remains far behind a cayuco, which in any case is more comfortable and preferred for a journey on the torrential streams of Tabasco.

On the pongo I met two other travelers—Don Agustín Vilaseca and a Spaniard—who were on merchants' business to Teapa. Although for this reason the limited room thus became ever narrower, I still had the respected Don Agustín as a cultured and courteous fellow traveler. He helped me tremendously through his extended acquaintances and in Teapa introduced me to many influential persons.

At 4 A.M. we set out. The frequent rain of the past day made the weather cloudy and cool, while the Tabasco River was greatly swollen, and its width must have run to a good three hundred feet. Slowly we advanced in the manner described above, tormented by swarms of mosquitoes, and with the three of us cowering under the deck in order to shelter ourselves from the dew, which here falls in immense quantities.

Upstream from San Juan Bautista the banks of the Tabasco River are more densely inhabited than they are from the capital to the coast, since the former part is no longer exposed to flooding and moreover is boundlessly fertile. A cluster of haciendas and ranchos, which are here indiscriminately called *sitios,* follow upon one another, while excellent soil and climate permit the cultivation of sugar, corn, and rice, and further upstream the planting of cacao. Far more cultivated still than the banks of the Tabasco are those of the Teapa River. It flows into the Tabasco approximately one mile above the capital. The point of its discharge is called Las Cruces, and is an authentic headquarters for alligators, which abound here in such numbers that the explorer recognizes their presence from afar by their peculiar musty odor. On the whole the caimans or alligators in the rivers of Tabasco are quite abundant, often reach a length of twelve feet, and in rapacity stand only slightly behind the Nile crocodile. Travelers cannot risk bathing in the river, since indeed the most tragic consequences have occurred. Thus not long ago a boy in the capital lost an arm, and his father could only tear him away from the caiman after a desperate struggle. These animals have no important enemy as, for example, the crocodile has in the ichneumon.[1] Still, some consider a turtle from the genus *Kinixys* as its predator, and maintain that when the caiman devours this turtle, it swallows the animal alive into the bowels; the turtle subsequently eats its way through the abdomen with its sharp beak and thus kills these dangerous animals. At times the alligators are utterly unafraid to snap at humans who travel in small canoes, but they do little harm, for they are easy to frighten off. I shot at a few of them, but without success, for they are vulnerable to bullets only through the eye or on the abdomen, which lies deep in the water.

The Indians kill them in a peculiar manner. From wood the Tabascan natives fashion a wedge sharpened on both sides and baited with meat, and hold it out in front of the alligator, which snaps after it with such power that the animal forces it through the tongue and the roof of his mouth. Before he is able to open his jaws again, he is quickly pulled to the bank by means of a rope fastened to the wood, and then killed. The alligators live only in muddy water or swamps and are never found in stony mountain streams.

When the day broke we were already traveling up the Teapa River. Sitio followed upon sitio, and the stately banks revealed a bustling life and joyful activity in many plantations; among them, the cacao haciendas become ever larger the further upriver one goes. Here cacao thrives without that artificial irrigation which makes the cultivation of this plant so costly (although the harvest more certain) on the *costa firme.* It grows well under the shade of the so-called mother tree in the extremely moist soil and forms the main industry of the inhabitants of Tabasco.

The yearly harvest, which by the way does not suffice for the needs of the republic, amounts to from 50,000 to 70,000 *cargas* (at 60 pounds), that is, 30,000 to 40,000 *quintales,* or hundredweights, worth from 700,000 to 1,400,000 pesos or 2,893,333 florins. The cacao tree flowers and bears fruit the entire year, but so meagerly that even with a good harvest one calculates an average of not more than ten fruits (*mazorcas*) from the tree, of which one hundred normally go into a carga.

The main harvest time falls in the months of March, April, and October, and the calculation of yearly output sketched above suggests that the number of bearing trees in the entire state runs from 800,000 to a million. To that must be added many immature trees, which together with the previous come to a total of 1,600,000 to 2,000,000 and occupy a space of at least 4,800,000 square fathoms! Outside of cacao they dedicate little attention to other cultivation, since nature here produces endlessly without the assistance of man.

Sugarcane reaches a height of two to three yards, corn produces three- to fivefold, coffee and tobacco grow in abundance. The latter is especially good in the region of Huimanguillo and Chontalpa and is fully the equal of the Havana variety; in fact, during the days of the Spanish empire Tabasco supplied tobacco to the court of Madrid. At the present time this crop is produced exclusively for domestic consumption.

There can be nothing more picturesque than these sitios on the riverbanks. These inviting locales are set amid luxurious vegetation and shaded by cultivated royal palms, coconuts, and orange and mango trees covered with fruit. We frequently paused at these small spots, at times to buy some produce, at times to take some chocolate or to cook the food we had taken along, and at other moments to examine this or that detail more closely. The inhabitants of the neat thatch huts always received us with friendliness, and very politely, and seldom did they accept money, a fact I attribute to the infrequent visits by strangers.

At noon we reached the first great sitio, La Sylva, five leagues from the capital, and my astonishment over this lovely estate was no small bit heightened when I came ashore and saw the tidiness, order, and sound administration of the whole place. A handsome house built of stone stood with colonnades atop a small peninsula, its main front turned toward the river, surrounded by a vegetable garden adorned with flowers. A few enormous zapote trees threw deep shade upon the house and provided a pleasant freshness. Approximately three hundred paces behind the main building stood a straight line of uniformly sized thatch huts for the workers of the plantation; in the middle, a small and simply decorated chapel; and to the right, the cacao house and the rum distillery, or *alambique*. In short, everything was planned in the best order, afforded a pleasant sight, and demonstrated the masterful administration of the owner, Herr Duque de Estrada.

Further upriver from La Sylva the traveler comes upon still more large and handsome sitios, which yield a revenue of 15,000–20,000 pesos; but I never encountered a plantation that appealed to me like the one mentioned above. It brought together in a single place everything useful, beautiful, and practical, and to so great a degree that I cannot give enough praise and recognition to its owner. We lingered here a short time, and yet that day we went no further than Pueblo Nuevo, since a torrential rain had caught us unawares, and the river, in the process of rising, became ever more ferocious.

Pueblo Nuevo is a small village with approximately forty thatch huts on the left side of the Teapa's bank. It lies six leagues from the capital and is noteworthy mainly as a way station of land and sea travel. We spent the night with the alcalde of the town—these officials normally being in the habit of tending to the traveler's needs—and set forth on our journey the next morning at 4 A.M. by the light of the moon.

The journey on the river was no less charming than that of the previous day. Every bend in the stream yielded a new and picturesque landscape, and rather than rancho following upon rancho as we had seen earlier, here haciendas stood one after the other in succession, their cacao plantings often lining the riverbank for miles. Suddenly, however, the forest opened, and in the distance we instantly recognized the picturesque mountains of Chiapas, which rose as a majestic cluster in the background, surrounded by blue haze. I cannot describe the joy I experienced, since I had not seen mountains in more than a year. I hailed them like old friends, drank tó them, and cried out "Welcome!" and rejoiced with satisfaction in the hope that I would soon be able to wander among them. What a difference habit makes! Many persons feel constrained by such regions; they would prefer to live always by the seaside. But others feel themselves woebegone when they have no mountains or valleys, rocks and ravines, mountain streams and waterfalls, and cannot breathe in the rich mountain air. I belong to the latter. Where there is a mountain, there I feel myself more fortunate, even happier, more adept and with greater endurance than in the flatlands, which for me have been disagreeable since my childhood.

After a very hot day we found ourselves a friendly lodging and a bed for the night at the hacienda of José María, fourteen leagues from the capital. The owner, an old man with silvery white hair, took the trouble to entertain us as well as possible, and showed us much attention in a particularly forthright and reasonable fashion. Sadly, I could not much enjoy his company, since I felt rather sick and had to delve into my medicine chest. Feverish chills and a painful temperature ran through me, making me fear that the climate and the hardships of the journey had worked their pernicious influence. But this time my strong constitution, together with a few counter-irritants, overcame this sickness as it began, and the next morning I found myself entirely well again.

The following day at 11 A.M. we finally reached the tiny village of Eremita, where the Teapa River ceases to be navigable, and luckily had completed the uncomfortable and in part torment-filled journey in two and a half days. Like most small villages, Eremita consists mainly of thatch huts, but has a stone church where every year on December 8 the inhabitants celebrate a famous religious festival. Since the pongos are loaded and unloaded here, Eremita enjoys a certain liveliness absent in the other communities.

Teapa lies only two leagues from here, and we set out on our journey on rented horses. The road passed through cacao plantations and had almost been stripped away by the last rain. We often sank to the knees, so that the animals went forward only with the utmost effort, and in the process we became thoroughly covered with mud. On the whole the roads of Tabasco surpassed all others I had seen thus far in terms of filth. Only in the summer months did they become somewhat more passable.

We reached our destination two hours later. In order to travel from Campeche to Teapa (105 leagues) I had needed nineteen days and spent nearly 100 pesos. Teapa is a scenic market town twenty-two leagues from the capital, and lies at the foot of the Chiapas range, on the right bank of the river of the same name, surrounded by rough mountains covered with virgin forests. The highest of these mountains is Ixtapangajoya (approximately 3,000 feet).

Nearby, a small valley offers a charming scene, if one descends to it on a road that winds through sumptuous estates.

An attractive bridge traverses the brook toward the main street, which stretches to a plaza and a small church lying on a knoll. For the most part the town consists of good houses built from stone, of which almost a third contain merchants' freight and lend to the whole a liveliness that is certainly more apparent than real. The gabled and tile-covered roofs, the likes of which I had not seen for a long time, from afar gave the market a European appearance, and I felt no small satisfaction in seeing once more this style I knew so well, however unimportant a detail it may seem to others. Teapa has only a few streets, running along well-kept houses, yet it is surrounded by a conglomeration of straw huts which on one side make up the suburb Tecomahaco, a place that has faithfully retained its name, along with other characteristics, since the time before the conquest.

Considering the many haciendas lying nearby, one reckons for all of Teapa six thousand inhabitants, who as in Mexico divide into whites, Indians, and mestizos. No foreigners were to be found outside of myself and a French physician, Dr. Léfèvre. The character of the inhabitants of that region is good-natured, although their morality and upbringing are of an inferior sort. Only a few *hacendados* (hacienda owners) have a splattering of education, one that assumes a graceful exterior through a barrage of flowery Spanish, but which in reality is quite superficial. Commerce is limited to the cacao of Tabasco and San Cristóbal (Ciudad Real), which finds its way to all parts of the republic. Rice, sugar, coffee, tobacco, and rum are produced, but along with many imported articles are consumed strictly within the country. To this place the Indians of Chiapas bring bread, flour, cheese, and European fruits and vegetables, which one produces with great success in the highlands of that state. Here bread and flour are especially rare and expensive; for that reason the inhabitants depend exclusively on corn tortillas, and the visitor considers himself lucky to get hold of a stale piece of white bread once a week.

Teapa has only one industry, and that is the manufacture of waterproof boots of *hule* (the gum resin of the rubber tree), which a common and magnificent tree produces in mass quantities. The hule is something quite like Indian rubber and in the future might become Tabasco's export item, although for now one knows but very little about it in the outside world.

The climate of the Teapa district is the best in the entire state. Although Teapa lies in the tierra caliente and only thirteen hundred miles above the equator, nevertheless the air is pleasantly cooled through the body of virgin forest and the nearby mountain range of Chiapas, while the quick-running waters do not easily produce miasmatic fumes. Indeed, in the months of December and January, and especially at night, the evening chill sometimes becomes so acute that the temperature falls to 55 degrees, and often a temperature change of 23 to 27 degrees is noticeable.

Epidemic diseases do not occur at all here, but malaria is common. It has its origins in the damp chill of the rainy winter months. Oddly enough, a form of herpes appears on the banks of the Grijalva and its tributaries, one that afflicts and extraordinarily deforms the countless Indians and even the whites themselves. When it leaves behind reddish and bluish spots, one calls this skin disease *tiña,* and then it is sometimes curable, according to the declaration of various doctors, either through silver nitrate or through mercury ointment. If it leaves entirely white spots, then it is called *porcelana,* and is incurable.

The illness first develops at puberty, never earlier, and does not always appear to pass from parent to child. In all likelihood it is an external contagion, but the point cannot be definitely proven. For that reason whites seem to be much less susceptible than Indians, and among blacks I have never seen this illness. It begins with a painful rash, which when rubbed, as I have said, leaves behind red, bluish, and white blemishes. Thus afflicted, Indians often appear clownlike, and I have seen some who had red faces, bluish arms, and snow-white legs, on account of which one calls them *pintos* or *tiñosos.*[2] It is remarkable that these colors penetrate some quarter-inch into the skin, and that those afflicted never complain about pain or any other inconvenience.

To put it succinctly, Teapa's vegetation is one of the most exuberant in the world, since the entire and immense body of clouds, impregnated with water vapor, discharge themselves copiously at the foot of the Chiapan mountain range. The falling body of water is extraordinarily large and surpasses its counterpart in the region of Jalapa and Orizaba in the state of Veracruz. It rains almost nine months of the year, and in winter it often happens that the sun will not shine for as long as eight days. An inexhaustible fertility is the consequence, and the forests of Teapa are the most luxurious a tropical exuberance can offer.

The explorer only enters those forests with difficulty. Machete in hand, he hacks a path through countless liana and aerial roots hanging down everywhere, and thus finds himself in an authentic sea of plants. A fear involuntarily seizes him in the first instant of penetrating into this virgin forest. The gigantic trees rise up,[3] with their long limbs branching continually in the blue ether, a softly swaying and impenetrable canopy of leaves. Liana[4] gird a thousandfold their trunks and branches and intertwine to become a web through which the explorer passes only with difficulty. Insistent parasites[5] fill up the remaining empty spaces in the tree trunks' cracks, and insistent undergrowth covers the soil everywhere and completely hides it from view. And in the selfsame tangle, a fauna too inhabits the shade of this seldom-explored forest. In every crack one discovers anthills, wasp nests, and beehives dripping with honey; in the airy branches are the artfully built nests of birds, beetles in high trees and under the soil; among the flowers labors a diminutive army of insects, while on the ground brilliant and dangerous varieties of serpents lie hidden under the leaves.

Countless birds fill the air with song, interrupting the sublime stillness of the forest. Charmed, the explorer listens to the notes of the *zinzontli* (*Turdus polyglotta*), the master of the American songbirds, and the woodpecker hacking the bark industriously and with great force in order to extract a worm for himself. The ape, comical in form, mischievously slings fruit and dead branches at the explorer, and mingles his cry with that of the parrot, feathered with many colors. Here as well one finds the jaguar and cougar, which are in fact so common and audacious that they often approach the dwellings of men, and inflict no small harm among the household animals. Alligators inhabit the slower-moving waters; delicate fish swim in pools where the streams fall crashing over rocks in that high region; and the wary tapir wanders through here, stepping cautiously. Thus nature reveals such power and splendor here that the traveler almost wants to believe himself completely free of the presence of man. The human being truly seems to occupy a subordinate role here, when in astonishment he admires this dominion of nature everywhere! It was a region where one could live anew. And not only do these forests surpass everything in beauty; they also contain inexhaustible wealth in the form of yellow wood sorrel, sarsaparilla, cacao, achiote, Tabasco pepper, and aromatic herbs, and offer mankind an overabundance of incalculable riches.

I immediately resolved to remain a longer time here. However, it happened to be difficult for me to find a residence suitable for my activities. For eight days I had to stay with Herr Vilaseca, until I made the acquaintance of the only foreign presence here, the French physician Dr. Léfèvre, who hospitably offered me half of his house, which I accepted ever so willingly, for I could gather that his loneliness greatly oppressed him.

Soon we had modestly arranged our joint household. An Indian woman prepared our simple meals: we made our own coffee, and since I found a friendly and learned host in Dr. Léfèvre, who had already lived eighteen years in different parts of the Americas, we lived together many months in brisk activity, peaceful and happy. In general there is perhaps no easier a people who are so at home in foreign lands than the French. Every man is welcome with them, and is ever so dear when he speaks their language. They know no difference among nations.

The months of November and December as well were so rainy that until the fifteenth of this latter month I had made few trips, although Dr. Léfèvre diligently accompanied me in them. I discovered many beautiful plants, killed many unusual animals in the hunt, and decorated the patio of our house with palms and orchids. The banks and mountain ranges of the Puyacatengo River were especially rich.

This limestone range forms a group of steep, conical mountains consisting of singularly composed rock formations that are covered with virgin forest, and which offer many highly striking excursions. Knots of small palms cover the rocks, at times forming grottoes, at times narrow passes and natural bridges, and would have been worthy of the paintbrush of Claudio.[6] Every ramble therein was more or less rewarding, and each day increased my store of treasures, while we pleasantly chattered away the rainy hours in intimate and entertaining conversation. Life with Dr. Léfèvre was especially beneficial to my study of medicine; and since my friend was nothing less than an egotist, he introduced me among his patients as a likewise highly practiced physician. In the entire region I became known simply as "el naturalista," or also, since I was smaller than Dr. Léfèvre, "el doctorcito." I frequently had the opportunity to apply my knowledge of tropical fevers, and my housemate, who had lived in the fever region still longer, held a high opinion of me in this regard. In reality he was something more of a surgeon than a doctor, and whatever did not allow itself to be cured externally he liked to attribute to my underdeveloped knowledge of pathologies. Many patients visited us jointly. As the reader may perhaps surmise, the sick came to us because we conscientiously took the trouble to help when possible, although we refused to have our services respectably remunerated, something I found particularly gratifying when dealing with poor travelers.

As life passed in this way, Christmas arrived, and with it returned all the sweet memories of a day so special in my homeland. In the evenings I imagined myself with the friends of my youth, the lighted Christmas tree, games and celebrations in the domestic circle. In short, everything was so vivid that it seemed to me inconceivable to find myself in a Catholic land with no customs whatsoever to commemorate a night so holy as this. I have regularly observed that the more fanatical a people are, the less religious poetry prevails in their church celebrations. Of course, pompous ceremonies are by no means lacking; but this seemed to be always like a comedy that profaned the true religion, and to me was never more ridiculous as when a church orchestra consisting of three musicians suddenly began to play the melody "Lieben Augustins." In all likelihood they had unearthed this aria in an old violin lesson, and because of its simplicity had learned to play it by heart and with the utmost gusto. I could not reasonably fancy that they had wanted to honor me by performing this famous German composition, since in Mexican churches I had often heard fragments of Strauss waltzes; the reader will gather that one cannot assume all that much based on the selection of musical numbers. It falls to me to pass no judgment over Mexico's religious character, although I can affirm that I never found the observation of celebrations and the mass itself so little uplifting as here and later in Chiapas. The utter spiritual neglect of these people is principally to blame. In fact, the matter had gone so far that the priest of Teapa was not even embarrassed to stroll with his guitar in the evenings under the window of a doña and to bring her a serenade filled with sighs of love. But here the people are accustomed to such performances . . . so much so, in fact, that no one pauses over the matter, and they even discuss approvingly the highly affable behavior of the spirited gentleman. Bucolic morality, I thought to myself, and prudently held my tongue.

In the last days of December I made still one more excursion, to the hacienda El Rosario, which lay in the middle of the northwest mountains. The narrow and almost impenetrable trail led through exuberant and virgin forest, winding around the foot of the mountains, until the explorer comes to a small, fertile plain where more small houses, resembling our Alpine cottages, lie scattered among lovely trees. This village is called Coconá and is quite notorious because of the jaguars that here lie in wait for cattle, goats, and sheep.

A half hour further on and almost as hidden as Coconá lies Rosario, surrounded by cacao plantations and thick forests. During my several days' residence I had sufficient opportunity to wonder over the indescribable luxuriance of these eternally thriving forests which spread all the beauty of tropical vegetation before us. Every step brought something new. One beautiful scene followed another, buried deep in the shade of the forest, and wherever the sun found a small opening in order to penetrate through, there it illuminated in many beautiful refractions the ancient tree trunks and dark green, richly dewed leaves of the heliconia, palms, and ferns. Here, too, the cacao plantations again were pure delight. The short tree with its strong, handsome leaf and its stately fruit, now yellow, now red or green, delights the eye, while the membrane enveloping the grains in the pod has a pleasant sour-wine taste that greatly refreshes.

I made outstanding progress in Rosario and Coconá and returned once more to Teapa, entirely satisfied, at the end of December.

Chapter 22

The new year of 1848 began, and a new link added itself to the endless chain of time! It was the third new year that I had celebrated in America, and once again I looked hopefully to a future that could harbor sorrow and joy, life and death! On such days I indulged in far-ranging reflections and found that until now I had grown richer only in the matter of bitter experience. It seems to me that we usually judge the life of a traveler entirely too much by its physical side, and that it is too easy to forget that the wanderer is more than his mere physical existence. We speak only of how he explored this luxurious continent, or show some interest in his adventures; but regarding his emotional life we concern ourselves but slightly.

Only individuals who know the lessons of experience can appreciate this side of things, and not without reason did I select an appropriate motto for this work from Alexander von Humboldt's massive writings. Everything constantly touches man's emotional life, but this latter also plays a great role, still more for the lonely traveler who is left to his own resources. The process of meeting every danger; the complete resignation of oneself to the whims of life, in which one poisoned breath can destroy overnight; the struggle to maintain equanimity in the most different places; in sum, the striving to find a satisfying meaning in everything: it is these features that a journey in the splendid wilderness of our globe presses with the stamp of a great undertaking! Against this, how terribly small are the dangers on the sea, the physical burdens on land! The common sailor easily endures the former, while a good nature counteracts the latter. But the storms of the soul and the senses demand another helmsman: the dawning awareness of that mysterious and inexplicable power that awakens men only in the greatest moments! One therefore finds that certain moments in our lives, such as New Year's Day, provide a point for reflecting on past and future. This is not, as many might have it, a hollow propensity to revelry, a vague striving for poetry. No, it is the intimate and mysterious connection with the soul and its life.[1]

I was pulled out of my reverie by Dr. Léfèvre, who brought me an invitation of Mr. Paillet to celebrate that same day in his company. I gladly accepted this friendly request, and soon we sat, sunk deep in animated conversation at a well-set table, an authentically rare phenomenon in my current life. It was late by the time we separated from one another amid well-wishes, in order to reunite happily on the following days after our work.

I set out on my rambles in all directions with the greatest enthusiasm and brought my spoils back to the house—sometimes with difficulty, sometimes not. Thus one day I followed along a small brook, the Juiba, in its course. It lies forty-five minutes from Teapa and is so famous for its gentle waters that women and girls go to it in order to purify their laundry by washing it there. In fact, I almost came upon a division of this industrious army, but as luck would have it, on a tree over their leaders hung an extremely rare orchid[2] that I had never found and had to possess at any price, since its luxurious flower and its novelty captured my attention.

In spite of the unpleasant disturbance I might cause among the enchanting water nymphs, I could not control my desire to claim this treasure, and in a few moments, swinging upward on a vine, I was busy separating the plant from the tree trunk. Unfortunately, the roots were full of millions of stinging black ants which fell down not only on me but also on the women, who were dressed in their slips, and set off a virtual war among them. However, the disaster still was not over; for when I was no longer able to endure it from the bites, I quickly lifted up the branch and it tumbled into the brook, covering all the laundry with dust and earth. To be certain, I now had my treasure, but had also earned so profound an enmity of the women that in their indignation they wanted to pelt me with rocks. I would have received a few blows on the head as proof if one of my acquaintances had not appeared with his Indians to help me in my petty predicament. His authority brought order to the situation, and amid countless elegant apologies I abandoned the fateful brook, taking my precious orchid with me.

On January 16 I made a trip to the Cueva del Tigre ("Tiger's Cave") in the mountains, which I mentioned under the name Puyacatengo in the previous chapter. A magnificent entry over thirty feet high and resembling a Gothic cathedral door led to its interior. The cavern itself is neither particularly wide nor does it appear to be especially deep; but in spite of that, it is well worth a visit for its unique stalactites. One can comfortably walk a hundred paces forward; at that point, however, one finds the way closed by a collapsed mass of rock that towers, impregnable, to the roof of the cave. Every attempt to penetrate this mass was in vain, and I had to satisfy myself with having seen the beautiful entry and the first chamber, without being able to fully sate my curiosity. Still, the formation of the entire mountains, like one belonging to the limestone passage, offers things interesting enough for the visitor. It is one of those mountain forms that furnishes perpetual variety in its exterior as well as its interior—now through bare rock walls, now through deep, profusely overgrown ravines—and offers to the eyes one region after another in all their wild beauty, until the traveler abandons its labyrinth and turns to the agreeable valleys that stretch along the foot of the mountains to the banks of the Puyacatengo River. These limestone mountains offer many unique indigenous plants, most noticeably the begonia, which there occupies the place of our saxifrage.

On January 21 I made a small journey to the region of Chiapas and in particular to the hacienda La Esperanza. A friendly resident of the same accompanied me as guide. We traveled the path over the Juiba and followed it straight to the border, which is marked by a simple wooden cross and is tolerably passable for mules. From this point, however, many places of the road became more difficult than any I had ever seen. We had to inch forward slowly, into the heart of fathomless woods, over steep hills, and through woodland streams, while in the deep shade of the forest a suffocatingly muggy temperature forced sweat from our every pore.

An hour after we had stepped over the border we finally reached an open spot in the heart of the magnificent mountains, at the bank of the Teapa River, which rushed and tumbled over the rocks. Here the sitio La Esperanza lies on a small elevation facing the three-thousand-foot-high Ixtapangajoya, and from which it is separated only by the river. The sitio rises a good three to four hundred feet higher above sea level than does Teapa. Instead of cacao, the inhabitants cultivate sugarcane, tobacco, rice, corn, and beans with great success here, together with a lucrative cattle ranching which prospers as a result of the rich pasturage. In general, the landed estates show a seemingly inexhaustible fertility; they enjoy a climate that could not be more pleasant, are rich in surprising natural beauty, and yet are as good as uninhabited, even though in reality they have lain open to European culture for more than three hundred years.

I found myself at one of the stateliest scenes of Chiapas, surrounded by the most virgin forest intersected by countless streams . . . and with that fine and exuberant vegetation whose beauty I have so often tried to describe. It offers the selfsame trees and bushes as Teapa, except that melastoma predominate here. A few ferns actually rise as high as trees, and stately large and medium-size parasitic plants cover the ancient trunks in utter profusion. Not only the plant kingdom but also the animal and mineral kingdoms offer an immense treasure of natural wonder. There were fish, crustaceans, and worms of the most remarkable forms, and my collections increased daily with new and in-

"We had to inch forward slowly, into the heart of fathomless woods, over steep hills, and through woodland streams, while in the deep shade of the forest a suffocatingly muggy temperature forced sweat from our every pore." Travel conditions in the remoter parts of Chiapas had not improved a half-century later. (Photo courtesy of the Latin American Library, University of Texas at Austin)

teresting opportunities. Meanwhile, the area's geological formation harbored warm sulphur baths and salt springs in quantity among the concealed rock formations, and offered fine material for observation.

The sulphur baths issue in great number at the foot of a pure limestone mountain range and belong to the alkaline-saline sulphur springs. Their temperatures vary greatly; a few have only 73 degrees, while others have 86 degrees. Until now these thermal baths have been little visited, and outside of the area are completely unknown, since they were first discovered only four years before the founding of Esperanza; I was the first to observe them with any degree of care. Since they themselves may have salutary properties like those of Warmbrunn in Prussia,[3] I therefore endeavored to call them to the attention of the more intelligent inhabitants and recommended these baths to their further consideration.

The full-fledged riverbeds in the vicinity of these springs, located exactly at the foot of the Ixtapangajoya on the banks of the Teapa and Blanquillo rivers, reveal immense deposits of shale marl, which appear to extend over a large part of northern Chiapas.

A half hour's distance from these springs, in the middle of a luxurious forest, one finds the springs of kitchen salt. The water rises almost imperceptibly, is clear, and upon evaporation yields handsome crystals of pure cooking salt. In fact, these springs appear to have been known to the original inhabitants, for sunken in one of the same is found a hollowed-out tree trunk more than a foot in diameter, placed there in order to prevent it from mixing with fresh water—a trunk that might well have stood in that place since time beyond memory. In all likelihood the Indians of ancient times consumed this water as do those of the present day in their homes, without evaporating away the salt. How profitably these riches, so freely offered by nature, could be exploited, had the inhabitants more sense for industry and commerce!

From all this it is easy to see that I, although sleeping in a simple cane hut and suffering from evening chills, found myself quite contented in such an interesting place, and tried to put it to as full a use as possible, with the help of its property owners and its Indians. I spent half and full days in the woods, which more than anywhere were populated with predatory animals and poisonous serpents, in order to collect animals and plants. Often I followed the small streams barefoot, often I came back soaked or sunburned, sometimes wounded in every part of my body, ragged from my daily excursions, and for all that I could never become tired of my stay in Esperanza. In the course of the same I eventually had the opportunity to observe the relationship of the Indians to their masters and sadly discovered that the free inhabitants, even with all lenient treatment, enjoy no more freedom than the slaves of Louisiana or the Antilles. Once he has entered into the service of a hacienda, the master immediately advances him a trifling sum of money, which the servant is never again in a position to work off. For this reason a proprietor is even happy to loan to him, in order to enslave him forever. He can only leave his master under the condition that he find another who pays him for the debt, so that the Indian acquires a certain monetary value that one estate owner hands to another. The whole business thus amounts to a veritable commerce in human beings under the shelter of the law. This commerce differs from the slave trade only in that masters cannot buy the Indian in a market, even though they can easily do so on the hacienda. One also frequently hears it said that a man is of 200, 300, or 400 pesos . . . that is, an expensive worker. The hacendados also punish on their own authority the flight of an indebted worker, or any departure without their permission, with ten to fifty strap lashes, and sadly I have had to witness this procedure only too often, here as in Yucatán, without being able to convince anyone of the injustice of this cruel behavior, which threatens the entire Indian race.

From the moment that the so-called *caporal*[4] rings the bell at approximately 5:30 A.M., the Indian is at work with his woman and children, who are scarcely capable of the task, and carrying his pozole with him he does not return until the sun has set and the evening bell has sounded. Even on Sunday the caporal has them working until noon! In exchange for that the Indian receives his tiny pay, including corn, meat, and liquor, all tallied for him according to a ledger and delivered by the property owner daily or weekly. These earnings seldom more than 2 reals per day, so that he receives only a pittance in cash, and with purchases of clothing the Indian is forced to accept the generosity of his master in the form of an advance. And so it happens that as a rule the richer the hacendados are, the poorer the Indians become!

If one inquires into the reason for this moral prostration of the inhabitants, the answer is ever and always liquor, which results in complete neglect of all human development, and little by little reduces them to a tiny and deplorable heap. The Indian's freedom is provided by national laws in the greater part of Mesoamerica, and yet one can still ask with consideration of the future, why should this land be so wretched?

Still more pitiable than the Indians of the sitios, however, are those of most Chiapan villages. In their half-naked condition, these people lead a life so degenerate in regard to drinking that one cannot easily describe it. The Zoque peoples in particular play a tragic role. They distinguish themselves through their singular hairstyle, whereby only a narrow lock remains diagonally over their head. The Zoque serve as freight carriers, and with an unbelievable perseverance they haul the most difficult wares from the coast of the Pacific Ocean to Tabasco. They reach the largest villages like Teapa, for example, and there one sees them immediately drunk, tussling and rolling about; for they never spend their pay on anything other than liquor. It is remarkable that the next morning these people, often reduced to a beaten and bloody mess, set out again loaded up on their journey, as though they had lacked for nothing, and they are reduced to such a senseless condition on a journey certain to last for more than ten times longer!

In this regard one cannot reprove too much the negligence of the government. Still more, however, the guilt falls to a greater part on the priesthood of the states of Tabasco and Chiapas, which, I confess with shame, provides no good example. I have frequently seen how the padres, instead of sacrificing to the Creator with devotion, swing to and fro drunkenly at the altar, and profane all that is holy and by moral sense necessary. The burdens of the soul and the schools, together with the fostering of the spirit and the soul, lie per-

"The Zoque serve as freight carriers, and with an unbelievable perseverance they haul the most difficult wares from the coast of the Pacific Ocean to Tabasco." In fact, portage on human backs remained common into the twentieth century. (Photo courtesy of the Latin American Library, University of Texas at Austin)

fectly uncultivated. Sadly, the worthy priest Las Casas[5] has found no imitation here, where precisely such an example is needed.

A journey I made to Ixtapangajoya, a small village of 158 inhabitants, recently confirmed what I have just said. Here the inhabitants celebrated the consecration of the church. They spent the night before in gluttony, and on the following day the priest read a mass so profaned in the aforementioned manner that I turned away from it in disgust. For the scandalous church consecration the poor Indians had to pay 40 Spanish pesos,[6] so that I was doubly incensed, while to my companion I openly expressed my indignation over this boundless depravity which I had witnessed all too often. Only the stately environs of this place, the countless natural beauties, and the worthiness of my host gradually dispelled the unpleasantness of these observations.

I soon readied myself for departure, and reached Teapa once more on January 29. Upon returning I put my collection in order, planted the orchids (which to my immense satisfaction had been won with blood) in a tree on our patio, and kept up my small excursions, until fortune presented me with an opportunity to make a journey to Tacotalpa. The hacendado of Rosario had the kindness to lend Dr. Léfèvre and myself two good mules and a mounted servant so that we were able to proceed, cheaply and well furnished, on our journey.

The splendid weather we enjoyed over the last few days had dried out the road to such an extent that we rode swiftly through the forest covering the hillsides, and effortlessly descended from the heights of Teapa into the unbounded plain of Tabasco, which spread uninterrupted from the mountains to the sea coast. Lush stretches of forest alternated with panoramic vistas of the Chiapas mountains and the forest-lined rivers of Tabasco. Solitary ranchos lay concealed among dense groves of coconuts, seemingly cut off from other inhabited places. The eye strained fruitlessly to discover the path that wound its way through these forests. Here the entire country seemed virginal, as if previously untrodden, and the traveler felt himself as free and cheerful as someone who had escaped from prison. It is nothing other than what Schiller expressed so aptly with the following words: "Tranquil plant world, in your ornate quiet I perceive the movements of divinity."[7] It is that which so unintentionally elevates and inspires the wanderer and fills him with exultation in the wilderness!

It was a very hot day, and thirst had already begun to exert its frightful power as we neared the village at midday after a brisk morning's ride. We rode down to the hacienda San Lorenzo, bordering on the houses of the village, and were received in the warmest of fashions and entertained by its owner. He was a well-informed young man, highly inquisitive and a lover of the natural sciences, and although he had never left Tabasco he possessed more knowledge than I could have expected in this wilderness. Astonished, I saw on the table books about botany, the science of horticulture, history, and so forth, while I was thoroughly astounded by the garden of abundant flowers and fruit trees that he had assiduously labored to collect from all parts.

Roses, morning glory, jasmine, salvia, assorted sunflowers, hybiscus (the first of which I have seen in the tierra caliente), cabbage, lettuce, asparagus, and other kitchen greens thrive in unbelievable abundance under the shade of trees such as orange, annona, mango, guayava, star apple,[8] and zapote. In fact, the young proprietor had begun to experiment with nut trees, apricots, and peaches, but they barely survived here on account of the tremendous heat.

Tacotalpa itself, lying five leagues northeast of Teapa, was in former times the capital of Tabasco on the Tacotalpa River, a main branch of the Grijalva. These days it is a village of two thousand inhabitants with a number of good masonry houses and many cane huts. And yet even though it lies on a navigable river, it has no commercial importance outside of a negligible trade in cacao.

A mile from Tacotalpa looms the Madregal mountain with the lovely waterfall and stalactite cave of Tapijulapa, which is by all means worth a visit, even though by itself there is nothing to distinguish it from other caves of this sort. In size, however, it surpasses by far the stalactite caves of the Puyacatengo, just as it offers a generally more charming environs than do those latter.

On the return journey to Teapa we hit on another road over the haciendas Trinidad and Rosario; but we had ample reason to regret this decision. The road through the so-called *bejucal*[9] was so unfathomable that we remained on more occasion literally stuck in the mud and required a whole hour more merely to reach Rosario. Here we remained occupied until February 16 with collecting plants and animals, and returned to Teapa thereafter.[10]

Chapter 23

For most of the two months that followed I found myself in Chiapas, and in February, in fact, I knocked around the border so much that I stayed now in one state, now in another, without having to make a long journey. On February 21 I proceeded in a southwesterly direction across the border, which I reached, via an extremely mountainous road, after a few hours' journey. As soon as the traveler crosses into Chiapas he finds himself at the foothills, on which stands a huge and handsome structure, one surrounded by small cane huts of the Indians who furnish the labor of this sitio. It is one of the many properties of the wealthy Salvador Calcaño, and bears the name Azufre from the sulphur springs located in the vicinity.

To the left of the building rises a rocky, picturesque mountain, while to the right spreads an extremely fertile plain, which the waters of the Blanquillo intersect and refresh. The traveler finds himself between the hot and unhealthy lowlands of Tabasco and the mountainous and invigorating estates of Chiapas in a single point that offers all the advantages and disadvantages of the tropics. I tarried there three days, partly to augment my collection, partly to observe at closer hand the sulphur springs. These issue from the foot of the mountains, surrounded by a forest of melastoma and *limoncillos,*[1] and in terms of water volume surpass by far the springs of Esperanza. In quality, however, they are identical. Strangely enough, and just as in Esperanza, two entirely separate sulphur springs, though located in almost the selfsame place, converge here and form a rather large, milk-white stream.

The first issues from a muddy point whose water, almost clear at its point of origin, quickly assumes a yellow-white color. The water bears a sulphurous taste, repugnant, and without trace of salt; the odor betrays a great deal of unrestrained sour gas. The second major spring bubbles violently from a volcanic stone basin. It consists mainly of water carbonated with sulphur gas; this water tastes saline and is almost caustic to the tongue, and the bubbles, ascending in huge masses, give off a significant quantity of carbonated gas. The smell is a bit sulphurous, and the sediment on the rocks creates tiny polygons of salt crystals. The temperature reaches an average of more than 77 degrees. Thus, like the mineral springs I have previously described, these too lie in tranquil seclusion and are little used—in Europe, without doubt, they would provide for the health of thousands of people!

From the hacienda Azufre I set out for the largest cacao plantation, that of Santa Rosalie, which in any event belongs to Don Salvador Calcaño, and which with the ranchos counts 500,000 trees and yields an annual profit of 32,000–64,000 florins. Santa Rosalie lies two leagues northwest of Azufre in the state of Chiapas, on the banks of the Blanquillo, which is navigable from the department of Pichucalco and which together with the Chiapas River empties into the Gulf of Mexico. My earlier sketch of the course of the main river will suffice to give some idea of the location of the place here described.

In Santa Rosalie the owner met me in ever so friendly a manner. He had resided there for a long time, and had already made my acquaintance in Teapa; by chance he had mentioned more cases of fevers and illnesses and a severely injured *mayordomo* (overseer of workers) in need of medical attention. He lay sick, and the proprietor urged me to help and assist him as much as was in my power. Busy with my collection, I had to remain there a few days more in order to be able to address both objectives with favorable results. It so happened for me that things here turned out well, so that once again I did not labor without compensation.

For a brief time immediately afterward I roamed through the plantation on the Blanquillo, bordered by the haciendas La Lluvia and Rosario. Medical matters kept me extremely busy, and I finally returned to Teapa through a splendid forest country on the so-called road of Leche María without any particular incident.

It was now March 5, 1848. A few days earlier I had already resolved to make a journey to the department of Pichucalco in the state of Chiapas, but until this morning rainy weather made me doubt whether I should risk personal danger by setting out on this dreadful road. However, since I already had everything ready for departure, and believed it impossible to postpone it again, I steeled myself to it more easily; and since by happenstance other acquaintances from Teapa were making the trip, I could at least travel there in pleasant company.

We struck out on the mountain road over Azufre, which we reached without particular difficulty. From there, however, we repeatedly hit upon places where our animals at times had to wade up to their bellies in the mire. At times they, together with their riders, slipped down dreadfully steep inclines for several fathoms, and even now I cannot conceive how we were able to travel without injury on this forest path in the rainy season. The smallest streams had swollen into surging rivers and threatened to take everything with them. In short, the brief excursion offered a thousand adversities known only to those who have traveled similar roads in the Americas. Given such circumstances, the reader can easily imagine how little inclined I was to consider more closely the surrounding areas. And yet at moments we encountered such a picturesque spot, a vegetation so exuberant, that we involuntarily halted our mounts and abandoned ourselves for a few minutes to quiet contemplation of this splendid scene.

We had already ridden for six hours when we approached the banks of the Blanquillo, which we had previously glimpsed from the heights of our convoluted trail. The road passed along sitios of cacao that adorned its banks. At last we arrived at the hacienda Cosoyapita, where we had to cross the river; we ventured upon a dog swimming alongside our horses, and entered Cosauyapa on the left bank, from which point Pichucalco still lies a league distant. In short, we had reached the object of our journey. A luxurious avenue of coconut palms decorates the entry to the village, which extended to the foot of more small hills that send down the various rivulets of the Blanquillo and supply the inhabitants with drinking water.

Although the main town of the department, Pichucalco has scarcely more than six hundred inhabitants, almost all of whom live in cane huts. The few owners of cacao plantations excepted, this village has only poor inhabitants; the greater part of them are Zoque Indians who busy themselves with corn farming, stock ranching, or the transport of commercial articles or of people themselves. The Indian form of conveyance here is nothing unique, and I have already mentioned this travel method earlier. Still, in this place it distinguishes itself from that of Yucatán, insofar as in Chiapas one furnishes a form of sedan chair with a roof, and is conveyed many leagues, from village to village, on the backs of a few Indians. The rocks of the mountains, unpassable for horses, make a sedan chair almost indispensable and altogether universal. The Zoque Indians distinguish themselves in this business through their strength, perseverance, and safety. With a certain natural swiftness they hasten with two to four hundredweights[2] on their backs uphill and downhill, without so much as a single unfortunate spill.

Pichucalco, although in fact an important town in the region, presents a clear picture of the poverty of Chiapas. For a few years now it has consisted of two or three houses built of stone, and today the church itself is nothing more than a huge cane hut with an altar! One encounters the few comforts only in the haciendas of the richer cacao planters.

I dismounted at the simple cane house of a French doctor, Dr. Louis Bouchot, who over time had drifted here from the Belgian colony St. Thomas. I do not need to mention beforehand that he received me in the kindliest fashion, for living in a wilderness such as Pichucalco, lacking all connection with Europeans, my arrival at his house was a day of joy for the both of us. Dr. Bouchot was a young man of charming character who, since he reached America in the year 1845, had sought in vain those golden mountains of America that one imagines beforehand in Europe, and for that reason had given himself over to a certain resigned melancholy. The coming of a European had to be all the more pleasing to him; he was always interested in what was happening in his own country. He hospitably offered me half his house, and since I was thinking of passing a bit of time in that region I happily accepted this offer, all the more since otherwise I would really have been without accommodations.

All in all, the vegetation of this region differs little from that of Teapa. Orchids and parasites are as frequently encountered here as on the banks of the Teapa River. In truth, on account of the fact that woods in the vicinity of the village were often cut down, at first glance I would prefer to call the area less majestic than that of the land's eastern mountain slope. I made numerous excursions during the time of my residence there and can only describe the banks of the Blanquillo in the vicinity of Istacomitans as rich and fascinating. So too is the road behind the San Vicente River, and that point in the mountains of Chiapas where one finds a vegetation resembling that of Mirador and Huatusco in the state of Veracruz. The oak and fir of the higher mountains are like those I had found on the road to Mexico. Like all regions of Mesoamerica, Chiapas is rich in animals of all forms; this is especially true for the inaccessible regions of Soconusco, while toward Verapaz an extraordinary variety presents itself as well.

Luck would have it that I spent the last days of carnival in this small village, which this year was to be celebrated in an especially ceremonious fashion. Don Romualdo, a public land surveyor of Chiapas and a refined man (something uncommon here) who had emigrated from Guatemala, was going to offer a never-before-seen spectacle to the public, in association with Dr. Bouchot. It was a drama scheduled for presentation during the last days of the festival, and to which we looked forward with all anticipation and curiosity. Everything was in a stir of activity. Against their will, the educated people of the district had to become actors, and day after day the inhabitants spoke of nothing other than the rehearsals and the performance. In the plaza they had erected a temporary stage from poles and thatch, a stage embellished as well as possible by cotton decorations that the schoolmaster had painted. A form of theater box was set up from stout cane under the open sky; in short, they tried as much as possible to furnish all necessities of a theater.

The fervidly yearned-for evening drew near, and a significant body of people had gathered here from far and wide. Most of the spectators had brought along their chairs, and since the theater was barely illuminated, one saw the people bringing a lantern along with their chairs in order to be able to distinguish their immediate surroundings! The traveler becomes a solitary stranger amid this mass of humanity, which impatiently awaited the beginning of such an extraordinary performance with lantern in hand. The reader can easily imagine the temptation to compare this place with the theaters of Europe, the awareness of finding himself in a small town of Chiapas and yet attending a dramatic presentation of the first order! I cannot deny that this forum, constructed in authentic tropical style from poles and thatch, and lit by the lanterns of the spectators, had something all its own, something quite unique. Let the reader consider the dress of the people, rich and luxurious for the well-to-do, interspersed among them the half-naked Indians. He will thus understand that I could never have been happier than on this evening, even if I were visiting the Old World's finest theater.

Concerning the performance of the drama, I must hold my tongue. But I cannot leave unmentioned that the poet García Gutiérrez's fine tragedy *El trovador* at times provoked resounding laughter from the public.[3] The children's show, directed by Dr. Bouchot, found much approval; it was encouraging to see that everyone was won over, and it would have been gratifying to be able to deliver something of higher quality. The discussion over this highly entertaining evening had no end, at least for as long as I was in the village. It was an epoch-making event for the population there. Certainly the disinterested labors of two men merit praise, men who had taken the pains to instill a sense of the more beautiful things in a people who until now had known no greater amusement than games of chance. Perhaps through theater some restraint might be placed over this destructive and deeply rooted passion, which convulses the moral foundation of Mexico in the most powerful fashion! I have to believe that even in this unknown corner of the world, the people might prosper just the same without the game of monte! Old and young, spiritual as well as secular authorities, often sat here day and night at the gaming table, and would lose everything to which a gambler might take an eye. Here I saw gambling in its most destructive consequences, and satisfied myself that the well-being of the community often depended on whether or not prominent men sat at the gaming table!

After the festival most of the hacendados returned to their estates, and

Pichucalco seemed abandoned. After a few weeks, when they mustered the National Guard in order to send them to support the government in the Ciudad Real,[4] life returned once more to the village, all the more since two divisions refused to march, and were forced by a third to hand over their arms. Although the bullets whistled all around for a while, they wounded only a few; but the uproar was tremendous and everything flew into vivid motion. After a few hours peace was once more perfectly restored, and I had before me a scene of the sort that I had so often witnessed in Mexico, and whose origins are to be sought only in the ambitions of a few.

I spent more time in the land of Chiapas and returned to Teapa on April 19 in the company of Dr. Bouchot and a few other gentlemen. There we intended to spend Easter. Upon my arrival I found still nothing from Europe, but from Yucatán came the most frightful news about the Caste War itself. The Indians had already seized almost the entire country except for Mérida and Campeche, killed countless whites, destroyed villages and haciendas, and almost without opposition pursued their plan of insurrection.[5] Many families had immigrated to Tabasco and the West Indies, poor and forsaken, looking for a new homeland. In hope the Yucatecans trained their eyes on the island of Cuba, from where they vainly expected help. Recently the Yucatecan government had sent a commission there and had discussed placing themselves once more under the Spanish scepter, if Spain would send protection against the aborigines—but this help never materialized. The informed might suspect that English politics were in play here, something that succeeding events proved quite well.

Easter passed, and I resided in Teapa until April 16,[6] just as before. On this day, however, correspondence from Europe finally arrived, instructing me to prepare and irrevocably set out on my return journey to Europe.

Chapter 24

According to my plan, the return journey was irrevocably set to begin: sparing no expense of labor and effort, I thus started to pack and to put my collection in order. It was overwhelming, as here I had laid a bundle of palms, there another plant or an animal in preservation, until the hour of departure would be arranged with certainty. At the same time, I began to sell off whatever instruments would no longer be useful to me. In this way May 13 almost arrived unnoticed. It was a day all the more remarkable, since on the same day we received, through English newspapers, news of the March events in Vienna.[1] At that moment even Dr. Bouchot had arrived in order to see me one more time before my departure. There we were, the only three Europeans, by chance gathered together on the day that announced so many and in those days still unbearable events even in the secluded valleys of Chiapas. Charmed by the highly promising changes, together in the quiet solitude of our flower-decorated hut, we drank up the last two bottles of French wine still in our possession, toasting the well-being of Europe.

Loaded with the warmest wishes for a fortunate journey home by all acquaintances, on the morning of May 15, 1848, I mounted my horse to make the first stage of the return. Dr. Léfèvre, Dr. Bouchot, and Don Pedro Pedrero accompanied me as far as Eremita, where I loaded my crates and luggage onto a canoe in order to send them down the river. I set out on horseback on the road to San José, a beautiful hacienda five leagues downriver. On that day the sun shone with such force that it threatened to smother us, and after a ride of exactly three hours we arrived not a little exhausted at San José, to which point Don Pedro, ever hospitable, had accompanied me.

San José is a neatly laid out cacao plantation on the banks of the Teapa. Order, rustic comforts, and an impressive cleanliness characterize this property. They received me with all hospitality, and before long a hearty breakfast was served up to our refreshment by a few lads and maidens, who, per national custom, remained standing with crossed arms beside our chairs for further service. This practice, native to Tabasco and Chiapas, has a distinctly oriental quality, and doubtless owes to the time when all Indians were bondsmen to the whites.

While I had already reached San José by 11:00, the canoe with my things progressed so slowly down the countless bends of the river that it only arrived at 8:00 that evening, enabling us to depart with it the next morning. Still, the evening passed not unpleasantly in conversation with Don Pedro, and at last we slept on bedding consisting of cane with an animal skin pulled over it. But whatever the limitation, it was still more pleasant than sleeping on the canoe.

At daybreak I boarded the small canoe in order to travel in leisurely fashion down that same river which, because of its stiff currents, had earlier cost us so much time and effort to ascend. Now in the dry season its water seemed scarcely to flow. Immense masses of tree trunks, invisible on that previous journey, partially obstructed our passage, and we were able to get through only with much toil and caution. Not until the vicinity of the Puyacatengo's outflow did the river become navigable and the journey quicker and more pleasant. Still, the May sun on the shadeless water tormented us in a most frightful manner. Fortunately, my Indians gallantly rowed upon it faster and faster the further downstream we went. We hastened past the river's upper branch and the cacao plantations that I have so often described above.

The last beams of light had already begun to disappear when we glimpsed San Juan Bautista in the distance. It seemed to lie on an island in the river; the white houses peeped out cheerfully from among the charming clusters of trees, and the evening bells chimed peacefully to us over the waters. The city presented such a picturesque tableau, and with so many poetic touches, and yet I could not resist an eerie feeling. For all its charm, Tabasco is and remains nothing more than a cemetery for Europeans, and the fragrant groves around it exhale only deadly poisons into the foreigner's veins.

My esteemed friend Lobach had already abandoned Tabasco forever; I therefore accepted the invitation of Herr Vilaseco, whom I had met in Teapa, to stay over with him. Of course, I was thinking of traveling again soon, but destiny willed that I should fall sick there, and not until May 22, that is, six days later, was it possible for me to venture onto the river again. I cannot thank warmly enough the hospitality shown me by Herr Vilaseca, Mr. James Cabot, and Mr. Paillet, and if I mention the names of these gentlemen, it is only in order to give with these words a small token of my appreciation.

During the brief time of my current stay, Dr. Humboldt and his wife arrived here as well. A nephew of the famous Alexander von Humboldt, he was the first Austrian whom I had come upon until now. He had lived for a long time in the interior of Mexico and there had married, but now, through the vicissitudes of his father-in-law, General Urrea, was forced to withdraw to Tabasco.[2] Sadly, our time together was limited to only a few hours, for on the last days there I had to provide myself with letters of recommendation to Guadalupe de la Frontera, which was now in the hands of Americans, and to make my visits of farewell, among which included one to the governor of Tabasco.[3]

Here also, agreeably accompanied by all my acquaintances, I once more boarded a small canoe in order to journey slowly down the Grijalva or Tabasco River. I had scarcely traveled more uncomfortably than on this canoe, since when it is fully loaded the passenger can hardly stretch out his legs; thus huddled up, he must also suffer a heat that is truly indescribable, and which the natives themselves are scarcely capable of enduring.

Just as night fell the journey became tolerable; we set out by clear starlight without stopping, and were even able to pick up the pace in the cool of the evening. We greeted the morning at Chilapa, twelve leagues from San Juan Bautista, where the Macuspana River empties into the Grijalva, which here had an extraordinary width and exhibits traces of flooding, especially on its right bank. On the left bank stands a small, picturesque rancho surrounded by mango trees, which were so full of inviting ripe fruit that we decided to enjoy our breakfast here. After we had prepared our chocolate, helped ourselves to mangoes, and stretched our limbs, we set out again on our scorching journey. The previous day the sun had seemed to burn, and today it proved unbearable, assuming such a fury at midday that we saw ourselves forced to seek an hour of shelter on the shady bank of the river. Moreover, our thirst became an unbearable agony, for our drinking supply was at an end, and the sea filtering up to this point made the river water brackish and unusable. A few miles away from here on the banks of the Río Seco lies a small rancho; no other plantations are to be found, and even the rancheros further on have no other roads than the river, which with its tributaries is the only point of connection in the country. Animals and birds are the exclusive lords of this broad expanse of land from the Idolos River[4] to the sea coast. So, too, the sole masters of the river are the alligators, who swim along slowly on the water like long tree trunks. On the whole the banks, although continually level, could be called enchanting, and always gave a faithful picture of the superabundant vegetation of Tabasco that I have so often described. Toward 5:00 we reached the so-called *manglares* (mangrove forests), an hour before the river's mouth. Soon we glimpsed the wooden houses of Frontera and in a short time found ourselves before the customhouse, then controlled by the Americans, where I was treated with all indulgence and received permission to carry my collection out of the country.

Guadalupe de la Frontera, the seaport of Tabasco, lies three nautical miles from the mouth of the river, on its right bank opposite the island “del Buey.”[5] A small cluster of houses constructed from wood and cane lie scattered on the scorchingly hot sandbanks, which only the splendid ocean breezes cool the place somewhat. Now in the hands of the Americans, the town swarmed everywhere with officers, soldiers, and sailors who belonged to the battle steamer and to a gunboat whose captain was simultaneously the governor of Frontera.

I went down to the house of Herren Watson, Chabot & Co., who have a branch office here, and by whose agent—an old acquaintance, as it turned out—I was received. The simple but functional wooden building with warehouses stands scenically beneath the shade of stately palms on the banks of the Tabasco River. An unobstructed view of the river's mouth, the sea, and the island lying opposite made this place in its own way a pleasant location, all the more so in the rainy season, when the floods that occur so frequently elsewhere are not to be feared. As I said, I set up my quarters here, not knowing when and to where I would travel next, surrendering myself to a bit of peace after such a tiresome journey, something that was indispensable for my terribly shattered health.

The next morning I presented myself to Herr Wilhelm Lobach, the brother of my staunch friend. Herr Lobach was also on the point of departing, and I had the considerable pleasure to find him one of the friendliest and kindest of men. Since no ship was ready to sail for Havana and I was committed to reaching that port, Herr Lobach therefore advised me to travel with him on the schooner *Portia* to Veracruz, and from there with the English steamship, something for which I found myself forced to accept, since I had no other way out. In this way I hoped to reach Havana by sail in eight to ten days.

The time passed pleasantly enough with the immense number of foreigners who were gathered here at that moment, and we shared in common company the maritime religious service on May 28, on the warship *Aetna.* The brigantine *Aetna* was a ship of more than two hundred tons and carried only a few Paixham cannons in the middle of the deck; they weighed 17,500 pounds, and easily fired 126 pounds some eight hundred fathoms. I had never seen such marvelous pieces of work as these cannons and the turret mountings on which they were set. The *Aetna* could easily fire deadly shots with them in all directions. The deck glistened cheerfully beside them, as did all the cabins of the ship, and showed such order that I was filled with respect for the North American navy. No less trim was the war steamer *Scourge,* which diligently patrolled the coast every two or three days, and sometimes brought back one or another sea pongo.

As favorable as the Americans' position was, however, they as much as the Mexicans most eagerly awaited the official news of a peace treaty. After this long-lasting war, the Americans yearned for their homeland. The Mexicans wished to remove from their necks these "malditos Yankis" who dictated their laws and decrees, foreigners to whom they were never accustomed, and whom they condemned *a todos los demonios.*[6] I myself yearned to depart, for the temperature here never sank below 95 degrees, so I could not think of repairing my health until I was once more on the open sea. The departure date was in fact set when an American schooner arrived unexpectedly, one that was to load itself up with dyewood for transport directly to Havana, and which was to set sail for there again at once. Somewhat unwillingly I changed my already determined travel plans; so great were the advantages that this vessel offered me that I immediately relinquished the agreeable journey and companionship on the *Portia* in order to save time and money (100 pesos). The *Portia* sailed on June 5, and we were to set out the next day. This was extremely appealing, since now all life had suddenly abandoned Frontera.

On Tuesday, June 6, I boarded the schooner *Arietes.* It was a small but seemingly quite sound and rapid-sailing vessel of 120 tons from Baltimore. Captain John H. Jürgens, toward whom I nursed a certain suspicion whose grounds were not clear to me at the time, now boarded in order to reach Havana. It was loaded up to the upper deck's parapet, and so overfilled with dyewood that a passenger could not take three steps; unpleasant enough for a monotonous sea voyage, but soon it was to become more annoying still, and my angry misgivings were quickly fulfilled.

A gentle wind blew on the first day. We forced our way down from there to the bar, and at that point took on board the pilot, who to our considerable annoyance announced to us that today, with nine feet of water and with our schooner requiring more depth, we could in no way pass the sandbar. With the open sea before our eyes, we had to lay anchor in peace straight out at the mouth of the river, for today and for the entire following night, in order to be able to set forth in the morning, luck willing. Only at 9 A.M. the next day could we hoist anchor and risk crossing the bar. But it also happened that our keel struck the sandbar a few times with considerable force; the schooner escaped through the last space, we at last had reached the open sea, and a rather favorable wind drove us swiftly down the coast and toward the northwest.

Little by little now the small scenes grew smaller, the trees balled themselves into dark green bunches, and the land, with its ribbon-like sandy coast, bounded the waters to the south. Once more, and not without sadness, I glimpsed the mainland of Mesoamerica, looking back at that stretch of land which I had traversed for almost three long years, with all the joy and sorrow of a lonely wanderer! I now said farewell forever to a land in which all my young wishes and fantasies had been realized, in order to set course for Europe, my fatherland, which in the meantime was half forgotten and had quite possibly lost all its charm and attraction. For as long as a point of land was still in sight, I stared off toward the region through which I had so often wandered, mute in astonishment at the splendid nature scenes; over toward the regions that were a demanding school of experience but also a wellspring of memories, inextinguishable, ever fresh and gratifying. The land now vanished, and I openly acknowledge that my eyes were moist and now wandered over the endless waves of the ocean, not without sadness. I had to tell myself that up to now a wonderful luck had accompanied me throughout my travels and had protected me in a most striking way in this life!

We sailed quite rapidly toward the Gulf Stream with good winds, although the sea was high and stormy. The waves had picked up considerably when an evil smell suddenly descended upon the ship, a smell that those in the cabin were not able to endure, and an almost epidemic nausea overtook all. It soon became clear that the water in the ship's hold had spoiled, and now stirred up by the motion of the waves, exhaled its poisonous vapors throughout all the cabins. This odor, which could be so fatal for us,[7] had only now begun to emerge, and was a reprehensible consequence of the captain's negligence. For this reason alone I could have initiated a complaint against him with the first port authority, if I were not the only passenger on board, and for that reason without witnesses.[8] As if this were not enough, he also insisted, in spite of the fact that I had paid the 40-peso passage, to serve me with costs so entirely and wretchedly in breach of our agreement that for the duration of the entire journey I could not once eat a satisfying meal. We had not a piece of fresh meat on board, no wine, not even an egg, and day after day I had to subsist on repulsive salted meat and coffee that was even worse. Even the sailors grumbled, since it sickened them one after the other, so that at last, excluding the captain, there were scarcely four able-bodied men on board! In the end we might have endured all this with the help of heaven, but as if God's punishing rod hung over this ship, day after day we suffered powerful storms, the so-called *turbonados*. Already on the first afternoon there commenced a dreadful thunderstorm with powerful gale winds, so that the ocean seemed to churn to its very bottom. The evening came and now offered only lightning bolts by the hundreds, accompanied by terrifying thunder, a truly horrific display. Even the captain's courage had sunk, since in the Gulf of Mexico many ships are set afire by lightning in the summertime. Moreover, St. Elmo's fire terrorized him; it danced magically around the mastheads like a will-o'-the-wisp. And in reality I was so greatly fascinated by the singular display of nature—

an authentic scene of raging elements in whose center a small ship, like a soap bubble plays on the waves—that I could not help but recall the stories of *luces de santalmo* (this electrical fire), and could perfectly understand how these legends came about![9] Fortunately, the thunderstorm passed over, but the sea raged on still longer, while we tacked the entire night with the worst wind.

Our journey began with all sorts of horrors with which I would prefer not to tire my readers. But I do wish to give them a description of this most unpleasant and dangerous of all my ocean voyages, and so I provide a copy of the private ship's log in abbreviated form.

June 8. We reached the Campeche bank with a not very favorable wind. At 4:00 an unquiet sea with calm wind, for a few seconds powerful smell of sulphur. A volcanic movement at the bottom of the sea appears to be the source of both occurrences. In the evening the storm and the tempest of yesterday return. The helmsman and two sailors fell ill because of the putrid waters in the ship's hold. My indisposition and that of the rest persists.

June 9. Rather lovely weather in the morning. A sailor lies gravely prostrate with typhoid fever. In the evening a thunderstorm, with high seas and full gusts of wind. The schooner rolls horribly, in consequence of which the yards must be shortened. We pass the night without sleeping.

June 10. We have fortunately passed the sandbar and reefs of Campeche. At 2:30 in the afternoon Cape No Te Perderás in sight on the western point of Yucatán, at 5:00 the port of Sisal. We alter our course in order to pass the Alacranes with a light northeast wind. Through constant tacking we manage it, in spite of repeated stormy weather.

June 11. Wind gusts toward noon, then clear weather with unfavorable winds. The physical health of the ship's crew does not improve.

June 12. We continue to tack. Toward evening, breezes blowing strongly against the current; very high seas.

June 13. Horizon altogether cloudy, stormy weather with rain. In the evening a northeast wind, with frightfully high seas.

June 14. Lovely weather in the morning. In the evening ghastly storms. The storm sails were set. Tremendous despondency on the ship during the sleepless night that follows. The captain reads from the Bible.

June 15. The gale wind persisted, the sails remained shortened, our continued tacking brought us to the Florida banks. More birds and fish in the vicinity of the bank.

June 16. Wind and monstrous, contrary weather. In the evening a magnificent American steamer roared alongside us. The general indisposition on board our ship continued.

June 18. Lovely weather, dreadfully high seas running against us at first, but later a favorable wind. To our advantage, the Florida current drags us to the east at three miles per hour.

June 19. Land in sight this morning. The coast of the island of Cuba becomes clearly visible at 9:00.

Thus at last we neared our fervidly desired goals, and a joy took hold of everyone, as if a journey around the globe had come to an end! But who would not have rejoiced after such a horrifying and torment-filled ocean voyage that, instead of four days, had lasted fourteen? I had spent two weeks sick and almost without food through everlasting stormy weather on a dangerous sea among banks and reefs. Everything around me on board was sickness and suffering, the ship's typhus meanwhile scourged me, captain and sailors were already in despair—and I should not have rejoiced to be delivered suddenly from all these evils?

I knew Cuba, but it never seemed so beautiful to me as today, and as we dropped anchor at noon I could scarcely wait for the visit of the military- and customs-boat, in order to be able to rush to the land and there satisfy my ravenous appetite. A fonda or eatery that earlier I would not have visited for money seemed to me today the most superb *trattorio* in the world, and I do not remember the time when an authentic Spanish meal, with stew, onions, and garlic, had tasted better than at that moment.

Chapter 25

Only after my strength had returned somewhat did I begin to deliver my letters of recommendation, with which I was amply provided on this occasion. I gratefully remember the friendly reception shown to me everywhere by all, but above all that of my trustworthy countryman Herr H. Heinen, in the house of Herr B. May & Company, whom I had known from my first visit and who honored me continually with his admirable friendship.

For my residence on this occasion I selected the Washington, where for 2 Spanish pesos I had room and board. I had just settled down to read my correspondence from Vienna, letters that ended the prospect of longer residence in Havana, when the harmonious tones of a military band rang out to me, and I could not resist taking in a pleasure that had been so long denied. I hastened to the Plaza de Armas, which, in its antique splendor, with its stately palms, evergreens, bright gas lights, and good music, drew a crowd of people in the evening, and I soon found myself among a large number of Germans whom I had either met in the year 1845 or who had arrived here since then. Among the latter was to be found Herr F. Schacherl from Vienna, who had stopped here on business. The opportunity surprised me ever so agreeably, as he was every bit my countryman, and was likewise planning a journey home. We understood one another quickly and from that moment on became inseparable friends.

Straightaway we passed the evening in cheerful conversation. It put me ever so much in mind of Vienna, which I had not seen in three years. Later we hastened away to our quarters, but all the same, I could not close an eye. In a few hours I had lived through too many pleasant memories, as though my spirit had been seized by some nameless excitement. The following day I wanted to begin my rambles in and around Havana; sadly, however, I awoke sicker and could only leave the room to act upon this wish after four days.

While describing my first visit to Havana (chapter 2) I have mentioned the beautiful harbor, the streets narrow although adorned with opulent stores, the sumptuous *cafés conditorios*, a few lovely buildings, walkways, and plazas, and the immense luxury in general. For that reason I will now restrict myself to those things which I saw on that occasion and did not have the opportunity to describe earlier.

The most important of these is the Tacón Theater. Through the densely populated streets of Calle de Obispo and O'Reilly, one comes to both the city gates, which lead to the Paseo de Isabel II, and on which countless volantes drive to and fro with the well-to-do of the fair sex. Showing off their gracious forms in white clothing, they use their fans to cheerfully greet those who are traveling or merely out for a ride, while the pedestrian is condemned as everywhere to let himself be thoroughly dusted over from top to bottom. It was 7:30, and the carriages made for the city or the theater, an imposing figure that stands opposite the city gate on the side of the Paseo. A lobby luxuriantly illuminated by gas, with quarters for refreshment on both sides, with an elegant fountain in the center, forms the entry into the interior. Its size and luxury, airy box seats resting on slender columns, and marble-covered lobby could only be equaled by a few theaters in the world, and can only be placed beside the great theater of Mexico City. Equally luxurious are the costumes and scenery. The productions are first-rate, since Madrid trains the artists; only the orchestra leaves something to be desired.

Equally worth seeing as an institution of the arts is the so-called Liceo de Havana. A magnificent building serves for this academy, which provides instruction in all the fine arts nine months each year. In the summer, however, the students and music lovers suspend their music practice every Saturday and give an opera performance to which only the members and their invited guests are admitted. Since I belonged to the latter group, I showed up on the evening of July 1, around 8:00, in order to attend one such engagement. In a small auditorium, splendidly lit with gas, Havana's *haute volée* had gathered with quality orchestra. Today they performed Bellini's *Sonnambula;*[1] soon the actors appeared in fine costume with the choir and presented this opera with truly astonishing verve and virtuosity to the credit of the musicians and themselves. Only at 11:30 did we depart from this praiseworthy institute, not a little surprised by the achievements of its students. In addition to these institutions, there is, above all, the Promenade, which serves the public as a sort of entertainment. In addition to the Plaza de Armas, the Paseo de Isabel II, and the Tacón, there is also the Alameda de Paula, newly erected by the recent Governor Villanueva. It is found above the shipyard, alongside the harbor, and offers an ever so pleasant stroll in which the solitary traveler enjoys the scenery and fresh air of the sea and those of Regla, to which point a steam ferry crosses from here every five minutes.

Regla is a small city on the other side of the bank of the harbor, with an iron-casting works and a horse train to Guanabacoa. On a small knoll stands a charming church from which one has the most beautiful view overlooking Havana, the harbor, and the sea. Further on to the right of Regla lie more private hospitals, and at isolated points on the left, powder magazines. All in all it makes an extremely cheerful and charming scene, and many individuals come here in the summer. More popular as a country residence is Marianao, lying three leagues from Havana, and to which the omnibus travels several times daily.

The road to that place leads over El Cerro, where is found the previously mentioned Bishop's Garden, and from there on a good street over Puentes Grandes and Quemado, both large, highly popular villages, toward Marianao. Throughout this brief journey the traveler enjoys a beautiful view of hills and valleys lush with coconut palms. Havana shines especially beautiful in the distance with its evening lights, for it seems to stand in the middle of the ocean waves.

A large hotel called the Bilbao receives and entertains the *habaneros* who frequently wander there. In the vicinity stands a magnificent sixty-foot-high bridge built from square-cut stones, three hundred paces long, which leads over a small stream trickling along a very deep bed, to the interior of the island. It is a monument to the Spanish riches of olden days.

In Havana itself it is worthwhile to visit one or the other cigar factories, whose number, by the way, is very large, and which employ some two hundred to three hundred workers, both white and colored. One such factory often produces forty thousand to eighty thousand cigars in a day, and at the end of this book I will show how much tobacco Havana produces in general.[2]

In closing, I cannot let pass unmentioned an association that redounds to the greatest credit of our countrymen: it is the German Support Society, whose task it is either to help poor Germans through resources in Havana itself or to secure for them means to continue their journey. If the reader considers the trifling number of settled Germans, approximately 120, and sees the powerful assistance they offer their countrymen, then he will be filled with great admiration for this noble effort. The society, which has existed since 1819 but reconstituted itself again in 1846 under new statutes, has since its first year collected 31,000 Spanish pesos through contributions, of which 28,000 were handed over as assistance. For that reason, it is truly an immense pleasure for me to report this honorable service to our fatherland and to declare the deep respect with which I was filled for my fellow countrymen in Havana!

Just as on one hand this city had so many institutions worth imitating, so too on the other hand it is to be deplored that the sole museum of natural history stands on the point of collapse. To be certain, I made the invaluable acquaintance of Don Felipe Poey, professor of natural history, who owns a rather splendid private collection; in spite of that, however, my expectations regarding the riches of the island remained but little satisfied. The scientific life has taken no firm hold in Havana, something that is to be regretted with so much talent on hand.

I had passed more weeks in Havana in this way once again, and already Herr F. Schacherl had set the day of his departure, while I still waited in vain for the arrival of my travel money. Doubtless I would have waited much longer still, for the source of money from which my stipends originated in Vienna was exhausted. Thanks to the friendship of my honorable comrade Heinen I could finally set out on the return journey at the same time, and on July 6, accompanied by all our friends, we boarded the *Lyra,* a 215-ton North American packet sailer.[3]

Thirteen days later we were in Philadelphia. Once arrived in the United States, I toured in a short time the states of Delaware, Maryland, Pennsylvania, New Jersey, Connecticut, and New York, saw the principal cities of the republic with all their places of interest, and on August 5, 1848, stepped aboard the steamer *United States,* to say good-bye to America.

We made the journey over the great ocean to Le Havre-de-Grâce in twelve and a half days, so that two weeks after my departure from New York I found myself in Paris, and after a long stay in the greatest cities of the French and Belgians I arrived safe and sound in Vienna on September 4, 1848. Thus my journey was at an end. It had lasted more than three years and had covered nearly 47,500 miles!

Notes

Introduction

1. Howard F. Cline, "Regionalism and Society in Yucatan, 1825–1847: A Study of 'Progressivism' and the Origins of the Caste War" (Ph.D. diss., Harvard, 1947).

2. The most complete biographical information on Heller appears in J. Rumpf's lengthy memorial speech, subsequently published as "Professor Karl B. Heller: Nekrolog" in *Jahres-Bericht über das Gymnasium der K. K. Therianischen Akademie in Wien, 1880–81* (n.p., n.d.).

3. On the emergence of botany and its links with global imperialism, I am indebted to Lucile H. Brockway, *Science and Colonial Expansion: The Role of the British Royal Botanic Gardens* (New York: Academic Press, 1979); Richard H. Grove, *Green Imperialism: Colonial Expansion, Tropical Island Edens and the Origins of Environmentalism, 1600–1860* (Cambridge: Cambridge University Press, 1995); Patricia Fara, *Sex, Botany, and Empire* (New York: Columbia University Press, 2003); and Evan Widders, "Science, Medicine, and *Criollo* Culture in Late-Colonial New Spain" (Ph.D. diss., University of California, Santa Barbara, 2005).

4. Regarding the origins and nature of Theresianum, I am indebted to Gary B. Cohen, *Education and Middle-Class Society in Imperial Austria, 1848–1919* (West Lafayette, Ind.: Purdue University Press, 1996), 13–14.

5. Respectively, *Das diotropische Mikroskop* (1856) and the charmingly if anonymously illustrated *Leitfaden der Naturgeschichte* (1871).

6. These biographical tidbits come from Leo Santifaller, ed., *Österreichisches Biographisches Lexikon, 1815–1950*, vol. 2 (Graz-Köln: Verlag Hermann Böhlaus Nache, 1959), 260–261.

7. *Darwin und der Darwinismus* (Vienna: self-published, 1869), 7.

8. This account of the Austro-Hungarian Empire borrows principally from Steven Beller's synthetic *Francis Joseph* (London: Longman, 1996) and Paul Hofmann's *The Viennese: Splendor, Twilight, and Exile* (New York: Anchor Press, 1988).

9. Mark Twain, "The Awful German Language," in *A Tramp Abroad*, vol. 2 (New York: Harper and Brothers, 1879), 276.

10. Two works in particular have been instrumental in calling attention to the myths and preconceptions to be found in memoirs of foreign travel: Edward W. Said's *Orientalism* (New York: Pantheon Books, 1978) and Mary Louise Pratt's *Imperial Eyes: Travel Writing and Transculturation* (London: Routledge, 1992).

Chapter 1

1. In the early stages of his explorations Heller traveled with Theodor Hartweg (1812–71), a German botanist who carried out numerous collection projects for the British Horticultural Society. His missions took him to many parts of the Americas, including California, Mexico, and Colombia.

2. Heller adds a parenthetical note placing the value of a ton at 2,200 pounds.

3. This rather poetic passage found its way almost verbatim into Heller's 1880 necrology.

4. The Ilhas Desertas, or Desiertos, consist of three small islands southeast of the Madeiran port of Funchal. They are Deserta Grande, Bugia, and Chão. The Desertas take their name from their absence of water and the consequently barren soil; they are home mainly to seabirds, monk seals, and tarantulas.

5. This is Heller's roundabout way of saying that they accidentally fell into the sea.

6. Heller gives all temperatures in Réaumur (a precursor of metric temperatures), which uses 0 and 80 as water's freezing and boiling points, respectively. I have converted all temperature readings in the text to Fahrenheit.

7. A reference to Madeira's sweet-tasting malmsey wine, which victims of tuberculosis often believed to have medicinal properties.

8. Heller possibly refers to Uduard Friedrich Poepping, a Leipzig professor who underwrote collecting expeditions in order to create a natural history museum in Leipzig in the 1830s.

9. By "mollusks" Heller presumably refers to jellyfish.

10. That is, a kneeling chair.

Chapter 2

1. A *Joch* is an east European land unit, another of Heller's grab-bag collection of weights and measures. It is the equivalent of 1.06 acres or 4,316 square meters.

2. Heller uses the English term here.

3. The Windward Islands principally consist of Martinique, Dominica, Grenada, Saint Lucia, Saint Vincent, and the Grenadines.

4. See chapter 16.

5. Heller's observations are hardly surprising, since the Haitian peasantry was concentrated in the nation's mountainous interior and would not have been visible from a ship cruising the coastline.

6. Heller's note: "A Haitian thaler is the same as 50 xr. Cms." When Heller touched down in Haiti in October 1845 the president was Jean-Louis Pierrot, an eighty-four-year-old black landowner whom the nation's mulatto elite had installed as a figurehead. Pierrot spent most of his term on his own plantation and was overthrown the following year.

7. The *Imaum* was a seventy-four-gun Bombay-built vessel that Sultan Sayyid Said of Oman gave as a present to William IV in 1836. Rechristened the *Liverpool,* it

became a part of the British fleet and was stationed in Jamaica during the 1840s. The navy finally scrapped this legendary vessel in 1863.

8. The Spanish first came to Jamaica in 1510, but their settlements remained poor and undeveloped. In 1564 the British seized the island as part of a short-lived expansion campaign of Oliver Cromwell.

9. That is, when approaching Havana from the sea.

10. Ferdinand VII was born in 1748. He claimed the Spanish throne in 1808 when Napoleon took Ferdinand's father, Carlos IV, into custody, but he did not definitively establish his claim until Napoleon's defeat in 1814. Conspiratorial and authoritarian, Ferdinand ruled until his own death in 1833, during which time he presided over a period of ferocious repression, absolutist pretensions, and the loss of virtually all of Spain's American colonies. Cuba remained connected to the empire and thus became the home of the unpopular monarch's statue.

11. Isabel II (1830–1904), daughter of Ferdinand VII, ruled Spain from 1833 until her overthrow by Liberal generals in 1868; during most of that time her mother exercised power as regent. During that time, repeated rebellions on the part of Ferdinand's brother Carlos—the so-called Carlist Wars—plagued Spain. In 1868 Heller would become the science tutor of the exiled Isabel's son, the future Alfonso XII, who studied at the Theresianum Academy for two years.

12. "Christopher Columbus gave a new world to Castille and León."

13. By "trade in white workers," Heller presumably refers to the practice of bringing indentured servants from England. They were notoriously susceptible to tropical disease, and hence the practice gave way to African slavery.

14. Britain ended its participation in the slave trade in 1817, abolished slavery itself in 1834, and in 1838 did away with the apprenticeship system, which held former bondsmen to their estates as indentured servants. One common interpretation holds that Britain ended the trade and manumitted its own slaves in order to prevent resold African laborers from passing into the hands of its Caribbean rivals. As so many historians have pointed out, however, Britain ended slavery and mercantile protection at a moment when dynamic internal markets allowed it to open itself to free trade, a fact that spelled the end of the great boom on islands such as Barbados and Jamaica. Heller saw the region at a moment when the British and French sectors were in patent decline and when the Spanish sector was undergoing a rebirth in the form of Cuban and Puerto Rican sugar.

Chapter 3

1. "Scorpion Islands."

2. A slip on Heller's part, since he had departed on November 9.

3. That is, when seen from the sea.

4. Heller refers to the so-called Pastry War of March–November 1838, in which the French government demanded the inflated sum of 600,000 pesos indemnification for damages done to French citizens in Veracruz, including a French-owned bakery. During this war French marines occupied the fortress of San Juan de Ulúa.

5. The fortress of San Juan de Ulúa stands on a small island in the bay opposite the city of Veracruz itself. The name "Ulúa" comes from *culúa* or *gulhúa,* a word that the indigenous inhabitants of this island repeated again and again when Captain Juan de Grijalva arrived here in 1518 and discovered scenes of human sacrifice. By this term they possibly referred to the Aztecs of central Mexico.

6. "The Sheep's Pass."

7. Here Heller adds a somewhat awkward parenthetical note explaining that a league is the equivalent of a Spanish mile, a distance one traverses at the rate of five every four hours.

8. "Spanish beards."

9. "Mountain ridge."

10. Heller's note: "*Hacienda:* an estate, property, or place of tenant farmers."

11. Sartorius's own recollections of the time and place appear in *Mexico about 1850* (Stuttgart: Brockhouse, 1961).

Chapter 4

1. Heller's note: "The Mexican thaler or peso equals 2 florins, 8 kreuzers."

2. The three regions translate as, respectively, "hot land," "temperate land," and "cold land."

3. That is, "down in the dumps."

4. Heller reports accurately here; I myself have had the opportunity to see parrots feasting on sour oranges.

5. Heller's note: "*Tasajo* in Mexico is beef cut into strips, salted, and dried."

6. Heller appears to describe an early version of a Veracruzan music now known as *son,* a type of ballad sung to the accompaniment of guitar. The genre is common through the Spanish-speaking circum-Caribbean.

7. Heller's note: "In Mexico the term *machete* refers to three-foot knives with which everyone is to be seen, and with which they carry out all conceivable work."

8. Heller's note: "It was the so-called Dance of Montezuma."

9. A village headman. The term was of Taino origins, but the Spanish carried it with them everywhere in the Americas.

10. Heller's note indicates this particular species as *quercus insignis,* which goes by the common name of aleppo oak.

Chapter 5

1. It is entirely in character that Heller would interrupt his sorrowful and deeply personal narrative here to insert the following botanical note: "*Anone murcata Linné,*" or soursop.

2. "Two Bridges."

3. Heller inserts a note identifying these as sweetgum, tejocote or Mexican hawthorne, and benthamia, respectively.

4. *Arum escultentum,* a type of root crop similar to yucca.

5. That is, Nahuatl.

6. Heller's note: "The term *lasso* applies to rope furnished with a noose, with which one principally captures horses and horned cattle."

7. In his ever-changing units of measure, Heller uses the term *Klafter,* or fathoms, for which I have substituted "body lengths."

8. Heller's note: "I'm not going."

9. The word *tienda* simply means "store," although in the context of rural Mexico, *tiendas* or *tendejones* often retail liquor along with their collection of hardware and foodstuffs.

10. Of course, Heller had no way of knowing what this old woman was really trying to communicate. As with a number of his other observations concerning indigenous culture, what he advances is largely conjecture.

11. A slip on Heller's part: Mexico gained its independence in 1821.

12. The revolt in question began when the Mexican president, General Joaquín Herrera, seemed disposed to consider U.S. special commissioner John Slidell's offer to purchase California. Although probably nothing more than a delaying tactic on Herrera's part, it opened the door to his enemies, chiefly General Mariano Paredes, who was linked to interests plotting to crown a Spanish prince as emperor of Mexico. The U.S. invasion soon put an end to this scheme. Paredes himself fell in August 1846, at which point a junta consisting of Valentín Gómez Farías and General José Mariana Salas recalled General Antonio López de Santa Anna to lead the Mexican resistance.

13. A *medio* or *medio real* was a coin common in early national Mexico; it was only retired when the French imperialists introduced the system of *centavos* (pennies) in the 1860s.

14. It is curious that Heller should find it necessary to explain this point, since the stocks were a common practice in Europe in older times.

15. "Cockfighting with knives."

16. "Cockfighting with beaks."

17. Obsidian is a glassy, black volcanic stone that can be chipped to an extremely fine point. It provided the basis for pre-Columbian weaponry throughout Mesoamerica.

18. *Teocalli* is a Nahuatl term that in reality means "house of the god." A teocalli is a four-sided, truncated pyramid, usually constructed on top of a terrace. Its platform was apparently used for ceremonial purposes.

19. This temperature reading is dubiously high. However, it seems plausible that Heller may have suffered a heat stroke.

20. Heller's note: "*Xiphophorus Helleri bimaculatus* and *gracilis Heckel.*" These were the fish he discovered.

21. In the original text, Heller's rendering of the "hieroglyphics" appeared directly after the words "... an inkling of their meaning:".

Chapter 6

1. Heller states that this is a Plösslsches telescope, possibly a reference to a particular brand.

2. Literally, "honey water."
3. The name Los Derrumbados literally means "the tumbled-down rocks."
4. That is, lima beans.
5. A type of squash.
6. "The summit."
7. The jalap root, or *Ipomaea purga,* has long been used as a purgative.

Chapter 7

1. Heller's note: "In Mexico they are called soldier ants."

2. Heller's note: "In that place I found only Swiss orchids and *Trichopylia tortilis.*"

3. In modern Spanish these terms have varied meanings, but all can refer to a group of animals—a herd, a pack, or a team.

4. By "resting" Heller presumably means a prolonged period of inactivity, since one hundred leagues would be much too far to travel in a single day, and would therefore require the teams to rest for several evenings over the course of the journey.

5. This and the previous two paragraphs give some idea of the varying rates of travel that one could expect in nineteenth-century Mexico. When going over level ground from Chicuhuite to Córdoba, Heller traveled at a rate of 1.54 leagues (5.4 miles) per hour. When traveling the barranca-filled terrain from Córdoba to Huatusco, he averaged a mere .8 leagues (3 miles) per hour.

Chapter 8

1. This melodramatic passage is one of the few instances in the text where Heller attempts to reproduce actual speech.

2. Heller's note: "The casa constitoriales, called casas reales under the Spanish, were handsome buildings in which travelers passing through found free lodging and partial provisioning. The new Mexican government has let them deteriorate to a considerable degree."

3. By "town of the third rank" Heller presumably refers to a nineteenth-century census practice that classified populations as *pueblos, villas,* or *ciudades,* the last being the largest.

4. Heller's account of religiously devout bandits seems a bit dubious, but given the many inconsistencies of folk piety it is not altogether impossible.

5. A gauge is a measure of the interior diameter of a shotgun barrel; an eleven-gauge barrel is approximately .746 inches in diameter.

6. "Wait, wait! They're bandits!"

Chapter 9

1. Cholula was hardly "the cradle of ancient Mexican civilization," but here as elsewhere Heller does the best he can with the limited archaeological knowledge of his day. Although the city traces back to settlements perhaps as old as 1700 B.C., its

true florescence came in the period A.D. 150–725. It reemerged after a Toltec occupation somewhere around 1168, with subsequent domination by the Aztecs. Though large and long-lived, Cholula was fated to be a client to powerful central Mexico states.

2. What Heller refers to as "mandelstone" would today be termed "amygdaloid," an igneous rock containing numerous gas cavities filled with quartz or other minerals.

3. Heller's note: "Malinche or Malintzin, a woman's name, which is now held as synonymous with María."

4. Heller possibly errs here. The great age of church construction in Yucatán was the seventeenth century, and many of the churches he would have seen in Yucatán were two hundred years old or less.

5. At this point Heller inserts a lengthy section of Hernán Cortés's letter to Charles I of Spain. The passage consists of a description of the city (then Tenochtitlán), its layout, and its inhabitants. Rather than tire readers with a literal reproduction, I refer them to *Hernán Cortés: Letters from Mexico,* trans. and ed. R. Pagden (New York: Orion Press, 1971), 102–8.

Chapter 10

1. Heller refers to this as "the new Mexico," which I have rendered throughout as "Mexico City."

2. In Mexican terms, a *colegio* would be the equivalent of high school, attendance at which was a privilege available to relatively few in those days.

3. Heller was prophetic, since Mexicans never did produce anything more than the base, or *zócalo,* from which the great plaza now takes its name. The equestrian statue of Carlos IV now stands in front of the National Art Museum.

4. More a monument to the sun god than a functional device, the so-called Aztec Calendar once stood at the top of the main temple. The Spanish buried it when they conquered the city in 1521, but it was rediscovered in 1760 under what is today the *zócalo,* or main plaza. It remained embedded in the exterior of the Cathedral's western tower until president Porfirio Díaz had it removed in 1885 and rehoused in the national history museum. The Aztec Calendar remains a cornerstone of Mexico's artistic and cultural patrimony.

5. Manuel Tolsa (1750–1810), a Valencia-born architect, worked in Mexico from 1781 until his death. He built the College of Minería and the towers of the metropolitan cathedral. Tolsa is probably best known as the creator of the previously mentioned equestrian statue of Charles IV, erected in 1803.

6. Heller's note: "This lone tree is found in the vicinity of Toluca. Herr Karwinski claims to have seen forests of it in Tehuantepec, to be certain, but Herr Hartweg, who traveled this region as well, and whose authority I consider highly competent, contradicts this assertion."

7. Heller errs. The mother of Huitzilopotchli (principal Aztec deity), and the figure represented in this famous statue, is Coatlique. Teoyaomiqui was the god of flowers.

8. Heller's note: "One such *teponaztli* is even now found in the possession of the Indians of Huatusco, who preserve it as a great sacred relic, and only use it at certain times, without anyone knowing how to explain the matter. It is unbelievable from how far one hears the sounds of this drum. With clear atmosphere one still clearly perceives the beats at the distance of an hour."

9. Heller's note: "$5,000 had already been offered to the Museum for this artwork."

10. Pedro de Alvarado, Cortés's lieutenant, later led the conquest of Guatemala and died in northern Mexico fighting an Indian war.

11. The *voladores* was a Mesoamerican acrobatic show in which several men climbed to the top of a pole; to their waists they fastened ropes that had been coiled around the pole. The men leap off, and as the ropes gradually uncoil, the centrifugal forces send the men spinning ever further outward until they reach the ground. The *volador* is still performed in some parts of the country.

12. Literally, this term means "table of the host." In restaurants it refers to the full-course meal available for the price of the entrée.

13. Chapultepec ("the hill of the grasshoppers") began as a fortress under the instructions of New Spain's reforming administrator José de Gálvez, who was active in the Americas in the years 1765–72. It was completed later in the eighteenth century under his brother Matías de Gálvez (viceroy, 1783–84) and the latter's son Bernardo de Gálvez (viceroy, 1785–86). It served as the home of Mexico's head of state until President Lázaro Cárdenas (1934–40) relocated the presidential quarters elsewhere and converted Chapultepec into a museum.

14. See chapter 19.

15. As in other points of the text, Heller's archaeological knowledge is lacking: Teotihuacán preceded the Toltec culture by a millennium.

16. Mexico abolished titles of nobility in 1826.

17. Following a relatively stable and prosperous period of 1841–44, Santa Anna was overthrown by a coalition of Federalists and Moderates in late 1844, a revolution sparked in part by his plan to wed a fifteen-year-old girl. Exiled in early 1845, he returned in August 1846 to lead the Mexican defense against the U.S. invasion.

Chapter 11

1. Heller's note: "Outstanding among the trees are the white pines, *Russelliana,* the Chihuahua pines, and the sacred fir. Among the flowers: pentstemon, turtlehead, bouvardia, cigar flowers, cinnamon, and nightshade."

2. Cerro de las Cruces lies in the province of Mexico. On October 30, 1810, it was the scene of a momentous battle in which Miguel Hidalgo defeated a Spanish force. But his own supply shortages, heavy losses, and fears of mob violence in Mexico City caused Hidalgo to retreat, thereby costing him the momentum of the war.

3. The actual distance is 58 kilometers, or 34.8 miles.

4. As previously stated, in 1824 Mexico adopted a Federalist constitution, which granted considerable autonomy to its states. Centralists overthrew this constitution in 1835 and restored greater power to the Mexico City–based national government.

5. Yet Heller spoke appreciatively of fondas when quartering his servant in one in Mexico City.

6. One of Mexico's smallest states, Colima lies on the Pacific Coast, nestled between Jalisco and Michoacán, at approximately the same latitude as Mexico City.

7. Mariano Salas (1797–1867) was a key Mexican general during the first half-century of independence. In August 1846, amid the chaos of the U.S. invasion, he led a coup that restored General Antonio López de Santa Anna to favor, and he served as provisional president himself until December of that year. Salas sided with the French during the occupation of 1861–67, and died in obscurity several months after the intervention's collapse. Whether his actions were responsible for the debacles of 1847 and 1848, as Heller suggests, is highly debatable. More likely, Mexico's problems were symptoms of an untenable situation.

8. "Long live Santa Anna and the Federation, and death to Paredes!"

9. Heller's problem was that he depended on periodic stipends sent from Vienna, stipends that the U.S. naval blockade threatened to cut off.

10. Heller's note: "it chiefly consists of agaves, cacti, nightshades, Labiaten, irideae, and gramineum. The fauna is richer. Especially well represented here were Carabiciner, Saparden, Heteromeren, and scorpions."

11. By this, Heller presumably means that they spoke Nahuatl.

12. There were no bulls in the Americas prior to European colonization.

13. Heller's note: "In this place are found many small labiateae, irideae, nightshades, wood sorrel, euphorbia, plantegineae, and in full bloom beardlip, ranunculus, buttercups, and ranchería clover." To this last item Heller fixes the scientific name *Trifolium heller* (*Zahlb.*), although modern plant taxonomies classify it as *Trifolium albopurpureum*.

14. "From below."

15. Heller's note: "The most prominent are: three forms of lupines, two Indian paintbrushes, sweet pea flowers, flowering currant, sage, horehound, monkey flowers, nightshades, apocynaceae shrubs, lady slippers, nemophila, wood sorrel, clover, sunflowers, crucifera grass, euphorbia, blue witch, Porulaceen, star chickweed, cigar flowers, St. John's Wort, honeysuckle, nightshade (growing wild) beside very handsome grasses and cyperaceae."

16. Heller's note: "Among the things found are ranunculus, some lupines, sunflowers, hellebore, and much beautiful grass."

17. It is unclear whom Heller refers to here. The most renowned Robertson to travel Mexico in the nineteenth century was William Parish Robertson, whose *A Visit to Mexico* (London, 2 vols.), which describes a journey begun in 1848, was not published until 1853.

18. The volcano of Orizaba is Mexico's highest mountain. By nine thousand feet Heller would have begun to experience significant effects of altitude sickness, including dehydration, headaches, and shortness of breath. His ability to climb beyond fourteen thousand feet doubtless reflects his youth, his overall physical condition, and his experience in the mountains of Austria.

19. In this somewhat awkward phrase, Heller means that because he sat on the side of the mountain he could not enjoy the 360-degree view available at the summit.

20. One *Metze* equals 3.44 liters.

21. "... der Glaube selig mache."

22. Heller's note: "Mock oranges, Montezuma's rose, gentian sage, echiums, figwort, and Iprodeen."

23. Heller's note: "The only orchids found here are *Laelia autumnalis* and bletilla. Quite beautiful are the Achimenes Gesnerien and Lamourouxien which are covered with flowers."

24. Heller's note: "Dogwood, cestrum, night jasmine, and *Rebus trilobus Moc. et Ses.*"

Chapter 12

1. Heller's note: "The harfita del pastor is a five-foot-long section of wild cane, upon which a few strings are stretched, and on which, high on the side, a small hole is found, from which when one blows into the cane, the air passes over the strings and makes them resound. In the moment when the traveler finds himself in motion, he lightly touches in different places with the fingers in order to be able to bring forth the necessary tones."

2. This is the so-called *patio* process used during the sixteenth-century mining boom of the Andean colony.

3. Horn silver, or cerargyrite, is a mineral rich in silver chloride.

4. Heller's note: "Popocatépetl and Itztaccíhuatl."

5. Located in what is today the western part of the Czech Republic, Karlsbad is noted for its mineral baths.

Chapter 13

1. In this regard Heller certainly appears foresightful, although it is possible that he reconstructed his letter from memory after the event, and in the process subtly altered the contents.

2. Heller's note: "These objects arrived only after I had been in Europe for a year and a half."

3. Heller says "physical instruments."

4. Heller apparently meant no irony by juxtaposing this sentence with the previous one.

5. "Dry Ravine."

6. "Badlands."

7. Heller refers to the Battle of Cerro Gordo (April 19–20, 1847), in which the U.S. forces under General Winfield Scott defeated the Mexican defenders led by General Antonio López de Santa Anna. The defeat left Mexico City open to the invaders.

8. An odd comment, since Heller would seem to have been *between* Orizaba and the rising sun.

9. Heller speaks figuratively, referring more to potential danger. The sea at this moment would have been relatively calm.

10. Heller's note: "The mosquito, a very irksome fly of genus *Simulia.* See Chapter 3 above."

Chapter 14

1. Possibly Heller refers to Champotón, which does indeed have a small stone bulwark along its coast.

2. Heller's meal constituted a relatively new luxury. The canning process only came about in the 1790s, with a series of subsequent refinements over the course of the nineteenth century.

3. In Heller's time the sea reached to the city's walls. Land-reclamation projects have since pushed it back for the distance of several city blocks. Then as now, the city was divided into two parts: the *intramuros* section, located within the walls; and the *extramuros,* or various barrios located outside the walls. In Heller's day the former was home to the more affluent Campechanos, but over the course of 150 years most residents left the inner city, which is now dominated by tourism, commerce, and government administration.

4. Heller uses the phrase "Richter der politischen Angelegenheiten" ("judge of political matters"), which I take to refer to the position of *jefe político,* an appointed official whose function was to oversee a wide variety of administrative affairs within his designated district.

5. The term Heller uses is "parish church," but presumably he means the Cathedral, given its age and prominence.

6. Possible Heller refers to the *coa,* a shorter, hook-shaped machete whose name is of Taino origin, and which still enjoys widespread use in the peninsula.

7. A rather dubious assertion on Heller's part. Either human feet have grown over the past 150 years, or else he exaggerates.

8. The word choice here is curious. Heller refers to "Landsitze," which most properly would indicate "county seat," or the Spanish *cabecera.* However, the following description refers to the affluent rural getaway houses known as *quintas.* Quite probably he meant to say that *quintas* were often found in the lesser *cabeceras,* a way for the wealthy from Mérida and Campeche to escape the big city without sacrificing all the amenities of urban life. Hence I have employed the word *quinta.*

9. The first Spanish contact with Yucatán was the 1517 expedition of Francisco Hernández de Córdoba. Serious efforts at conquest began under Francisco de Montejo in 1526 and were not concluded until 1544.

10. At the time of Heller's arrival, Yucatán had recently been the scene of Santiago Imán's Federalist revolt (1836–40), the peninsula's subsequent separation from Mexico, and Mexico's failed reconquest attempt of 1842–43.

11. A doubtful assertion. It is more likely that the Campeche "governor" was an unofficial position more akin to the city's party chair.

12. The date of the constitution was actually 1824, a point that Heller in all probability had lost in the confusion of political events. He repeats the erroneous date a few lines later.

13. The capital of Latvia.

14. That is to say, in Europe they would have been citizens of rival powers—Prussia and the Austrio-Hungarian Empire—but in the Americas they found themselves united by a reasonably common language and culture.

15. Heller refers to Laguna de Términos, a large lagoon lying to the immediate east of the modern-day border between Campeche and Tabasco. The area around the bay was then prized for logging dyewood.

16. Heller refers to the two-month Campeche-based revolt led by merchant Domingo Barret. This revolt, more than any other, legitimized political violence and gave rise to ethnically based killings.

17. A much fuller account of the Camacho brothers' museum appears in B. M. Norman's highly readable travel narrative, entitled *Rambles in Yucatán, or, Notes of Travel through the Peninsula, Including a Visit to the Remarkable Ruins of Chi-Chen, Kabah, Ayi, and Uxmal* (New York: J. & H. G. Langley, 1843), 199–208.

18. When Heller states that the American forces occupied Laguna, he presumably means that they occupied Ciudad del Carmen, which controlled access to Laguna.

19. I have here omitted Heller's section entitled "Statistical Notes."

Chapter 15

1. Paris-born Victor Jacquemont (1801–32) was one of the most famous naturalists of the early nineteenth century. The posthumous work to which Heller refers is *Letters from India, 1828: A Journey in the British Dominions of India, Tibet, Lahore, and Cashmere* (London, 1834). The example of Jacquemont's death in a faraway land apparently did not escape Heller.

2. Scholars have advanced a wide variety of explanations for the name *Champotón.* The word *chak'an* definitely means "savanna." Depending on how one wishes to trace *putún,* the name may mean "savanna region," "savanna of chiles," "savanna of the putún [i.e., Toltec] peoples," or "region to which stones are carried." For a review of the name's etymological vagaries, see Tomás Arnábar Gunam, *Apuntes para la historia de Champotón,* vol. 6 of *Enciclopedia histórica de Campeche,* ed. Román Piña Chan (México: Gobierno Constitucional del Estado de Campeche, Instituto de Cultura de Campeche, 2003), 10–11.

3. Heller errs: the principal damage to Champotón came during the failed Mexican invasion of 1842–43.

4. "The place of turkeys."

5. The Maya term *áak'alche'* refers to the seasonal wetlands found in the southern part of the Yucatán peninsula.

6. Heller's note: "Pozole is a drink that forms a staple food in Yucatán and Tabasco, and which is prepared in the following manner: the corn, soaked for a long time in water with lime, is ground into dough between fine stones, whereupon it is mixed with water and drunk cold. They add a bit of sugar to it, and it is an extremely healthy and agreeable beverage."

7. At this point such reports were probably exaggerations, since the Yucatecan army still dominated the eastern region.

Chapter 16

1. Heller refers to Arthur Morelet, whose *Travels in Central America* (New York: Leypolt, Holt, and Williams, 1871) remains an important source of information on southeastern Mesoamerica for the nineteenth century.

2. A photograph of this important icon appears in Terry Rugeley, *Of Wonders and Wise Men: Religion and Popular Cultures in Southeast Mexico, 1800–1876* (Austin: University of Texas Press, 2001), 105.

Chapter 17

1. *Tupiles* functioned as policemen and all-purpose assistants to the *repúblicas de indígenas,* Indian peasant councils that governed native affairs in the towns. Yucatán formally ended the practice of indigenous self-government in 1868.

2. Heller was traveling in April, the hottest month of the year in southeast Mexico. Yucatecan tradition holds that *semana santa,* or Holy Week, is the worst.

3. Heller presumably refers to Mérida and Campeche.

4. The individual in question was Pedro José Hurtado, one of the last Spanish-born priests active in Yucatán. Hurtado survived the Caste War, the Liberal Reform, and the French intervention (which he strongly supported), only to die shortly after 1867.

5. The murder to which Heller alludes took place on Good Wednesday of 1843. Several Mayas involved in provisioning the Yucatecan army during the Mexican invasion of that year were returning to their home in the eastern part of the peninsula when they invaded the hacienda Uxmal and assassinated Simón Peón's caretaker, one Antonio Tacú.

6. Here and in subsequent comments Heller was wrong. Uxmal is today one of the most extensively reconstructed—and visited—sites in Mexico. The greatest danger today is the excess of tourism, which has led authorities to limit access to the steps of the pyramid in question.

7. Here as elsewhere, Heller's archaeological explanations remain a curious blend of good sense and fantasy.

8. Heller refers to the writings of famous travelers that he read as part of his preparation: Federico de Waldeck, John Lloyd Stephens, and B. M. Norman. I have thus far been unable to identify Friedrichstal.

9. At this point Heller inserts a lengthy paragraph from the writings of the Franciscan chronicler Diego López Cogolludo, together with a few words of his own meditations on the same. I have omitted this passage; for the original text see Cogolludo, *Historia de Yucatán* (Campeche: Comisión de Historia, 1954, facsimile of 1842 edition), vol. 1, book 4, p. 348.

10. It is unclear whether "per man" refers to the passenger or to the porters; in the latter case, the cost increases to 2 reals per league.

11. Again, this temperature reading seems somewhat exaggerated.

12. An extraordinary comment, given the fact that the Indians had just finished carrying him twenty-four miles overland!

Chapter 18

1. In reality, the destruction to which he alludes took place in 1842.

2. A less-than-brilliant joke on Heller's part: he means to say that he was looking for a girlfriend. The ever-proper Heller was, of course, single at the time.

3. "A mountain pass."

4. The U.S. forces occupied Puente Nacional, which crosses the Río Frío, on April 9.

5. Pedro Ampudia, a Cuban-born officer and partisan of Santa Anna who served a number of important military and political capacities in the 1830s through the 1850s.

6. That is, the house of Francisco de Montejo, still to be found on the south side of the main plaza.

7. Miguel Barbachano (1807–59), son of a wealthy family of Asturian immigrants, was governor from 1842 to 1846 and again from 1848 to 1853.

8. Heller's note: "It belongs to the agave family."

9. Heller was prophetic. In 1854 a Yucatecan named Manuel C. Villamar introduced the first mechanical rasper, thereby laying the groundwork for the later henequen export industry.

10. Only four issues of this journal were ever published. They still survive and remain very much worth reading.

11. Heller's note: "Inn, quarters, or guesthouse."

12. Heller's note: "On workdays the volantes are supplied with linen covers in order to protect their gilded surfaces."

13. While not perhaps our notion of cleanliness, it was exemplary for the time. Moreover, Heller probably underestimates the frequency of baths here; Maya milpa farmers bathed daily.

14. The feast of Corpus Christi commemorates the institution of the Holy Eucharist. It is observed two Sundays after Pentecost, situating it somewhere in mid-June. In nineteenth-century Mexico this feast was an important popular event; for a description of the rowdy popular behavior associated with its celebration, see Terry Rugeley, *Of Wonders and Wise Men: Religion and Popular Cultures in Southeast Mexico, 1800–1876* (Austin: University of Texas Press, 2001), 90.

15. It is somewhat unclear what Heller means by *Muscheltieren;* I interpret this as a reference to conches, but it might include other shellfish such as oysters and crabs.

16. That is, José María Guerra, Yucatán's first native-born bishop, and a man fated to preside over the church's triple scourges: the Imán revolt, the Caste War, and the Liberal Reform.

17. John Lloyd Stephens's description of this well, together with one of Frederich Catherwood's more memorable illustrations, appears in *Incidents of Travel in Yucatán,* vol. 2 (New York: Dover Publications, 1963, facsimile of 1843 edition), 97–104.

18. Heller's sources were correct. For a recent photo of these freshwater springs see Pritt J. Vesiland (text) and Wes Skites (photos), "Watery Graves of the Mayas," *National Geographic,* October 2003, 100–101.

19. An odd comment; Heller made the return trip in two days, about the minimum time he describes earlier.

Chapter 19

1. An obvious slip on Heller's part: they were gathering pollen, not honey.

2. Heller errs, for the clash in question took place in 1842.

3. Heller's note: "In the country they are called *tintales,* from *palo tinte,* dye- or bluewood."

4. Heller's note: "One carga equals 3 quintales or 300 pounds."

5. For the first time in this chapter, Heller speaks of "us"; apparently he rode out accompanied by a guide.

6. Heller's imperfect understanding of events in the Yucatecan interior inadvertently led him to advance the myth of a tribe of Mayas known as the Huits. As I have documented in other publications, there was no such tribe. The villages of the Caste War region all had non-Maya populations for a long time before the rebellion, nor was there anything approaching tribal organization among them. Rather, all the colonial institutions of Mexico were to be found here. The term *huit* simply referred to someone with the ability to survive in the *monte,* a trait common to all Maya milpa farmers. Nevertheless, the myth of the Huit tribe has proved long-lived.

7. It is extremely doubtful that the plot to which Heller refers actually existed. In all probability the repressive actions he endorses here reflected nothing more than Hispanic hysteria.

8. Heller's note: "With this they would suggest a long series of years."

9. Heller's note: "An alcalde whom the Indians killed, roasted his flesh, and whose bones they then burned." This report of real or quasi-cannibalism is highly dubious, although acts of extreme violence did take place in the course of the Caste War, and on both sides.

10. "Chilam Balam, an Indian prophet and priest, lived in the year 1500; see Cogolludo, loc. cit., I, p. 257." [Heller's erroneous note.]

11. This unusual document, not reproduced in any other work on the Caste War, does indeed appear to reflect certain millenarian beliefs at the Caste War's onset. Its purported signatories and "ringleaders" were in fact long dead: Jacinto Canek had been executed following his uprising in 1761, and Manuel Antonio Ay, cacique of Chichimilá, in early July 1847. However, in the history of Latin America's Indian rebellions it was not uncommon to assume the names of past heroes in order to broaden one's appeal. The reference to Juan Vázquez, a Hispanic from the town of Tihosuco, does correspond to a rebel grievance documented elsewhere: retribution to Hispanics who had first mobilized Mayas for their own political reasons, then betrayed them. What, then, of the letter's origin? In all probability it came from the area of the Caste War's genesis. Its author was probably one of the original cacique leaders (possibly Jacinto Pat), who drew upon known names to justify and explain his rebellion. It almost certainly would not have originated in the Campeche area, as Heller seems to suggest.

12. Although obviously premature, this report of Mexico's death probably does reflect a sense of despair over the outcome of the war.

13. Heller's note: "The six-foot-high Crucified Christ is fashioned out of paste, varnished dark, and authentically a masterpiece of plaster art."

Chapter 20

1. That is, 1847.

2. Heller errs. The first attempt to turn back the invaders at Villahermosa succeeded; U.S. naval forces only succeeded in taking the city on their second try.

3. That is, he carried double sets of papers: one identified him as Yucatecan, the other as Mexican.

4. Heller's note: "Sail to the wind, to the windward, full to the windward, spread the sail, press the foresail!"

5. Heller's note: "'A yard and a half, a quarter, a little over a yard, a yard, not quite a yard.' A *brazo* has eight palms, or Spanish feet, a pongo goes slightly over seven palms in the water."

6. Heller uses the surname "Secura" here, clearly a mistake.

7. Heller's note: "A *cayuco* is a small canoe made from a single tree trunk. Such canoes are fully eight to ten feet long; one calls them cayuquitos or cayuquillos."

8. Heller's note: "In Tabasco, as in Yucatán, pozole is served as an all-around meal."

9. By "four square fathoms" Heller presumably means a house measuring twenty-four feet on each side.

10. Heller's note: "*Tapestle* is the name of straw-thatched roof of the house, where the corn supply is usually stored."

11. Heller's note: "*Comején* is the name for the conical nests created by termites and destroyed by men. There are people who even enjoy eating the *comején.* I could acquire no taste for this food."

12. At this point Heller is not traveling overland but rather canoeing over flooded territories beyond the normal flow of the river.

13. Heller speaks metaphorically, of course. The vegetation had roots in the soil, but both were underwater.

14. That is, if one approaches the city headed downstream, as Heller does.

15. Heller's note: "Lobach & Co., Watson, Cabot & Co., Pablo Sastre y Mazas, and Pierre Paillet."

16. I have here omitted Heller's section entitled "Statistical Notes."

Chapter 21

1. Heller refers to the African mongoose, which preys on crocodile eggs.

2. Heller's note: "Painted." *Pinta* is an infectious skin disease caused by the tropical bacterium *Treponema carateum.* It enters the skin through small cuts and abrasions, and works its greatest effects on the face and extremities. Today doctors commonly treat it with forms of penicillin.

3. Heller's note: "Of the family mimosa, mulberry, zapote, turpentine, and byttnerincea."

4. Heller's note: "Of the family malphigiaceen, serindaceae, cucurbitaceae, asclepiadeae, begoniaceae, ampelopsis, sarsparilla, morning glory, and passion flower."

5. Heller's note: "Dracotia, climbing pathos plants, bromeliads, orchids, piperaceae, moss, and lichens."

6. French-born painter Claude Gelée (c. 1600–1682) was renowned for his landscapes.

Chapter 22

1. His philosophical reveries on the relationship between the individual and the vast, ineffable forces of nature place Heller solidly within the German romantic tradition. At the same time, these musings bring out his most awkward and convoluted prose. I have taken greater liberties than usual to make the previous two paragraphs accessible to the modern English reader.

2. Heller's note: "Coryanthus macrantha Lindl."

3. Heller refers to Cispline, a hot-springs bath known since medieval times, located in the Silesian province of what is now Poland. When Poland was partitioned between 1772 and 1795, control of this region passed to Prussia.

4. That is, a mayordomo, or hacienda foreman.

5. Bartolomé de las Casas (1484–1566), the great Spanish crusader for Indian rights, served as bishop of Chiapas from 1544 to 1547. He returned to Spain after becoming frustrated with colonial resistance to his attempts at reform, but the city San Cristóbal de las Casas still bears his name in commemoration of his struggles there.

6. Heller presumably means 40 pesos paid collectively, since such an amount would have constituted an immense fortune for an individual Indian in this remote area.

7. "Ruhige Pflanzenwelt, in deinen kunstreichen Stille vernehme ich das vandeln der Gottheit." The quote comes from the romantic poet and dramatist Friedrich Schiller (1759–1805) and is found in act 7 of his *Der Versöhnte Menschenfeind* ("The Misanthrope Reconciled") (1790).

8. That is, the caimito.

9. Heller's note: "Outgrowth of vines."

10. I have here omitted Heller's section entitled "Geographical and Statistical Notes concerning Chiapas and Soconusco."

Chapter 23

1. That is, lime trees.

2. A hundredweight was the equivalent of approximately 50 kilograms. Hence the Zoque porters, working collectively, were capable of carrying 100–200 kilograms, or 200–400 pounds.

3. Spanish playwright Antonio García Gutiérrez's (1812–84) *El trovador* (1836) became the basis for Giuseppe Verdi's *Il trovatore* (1853).

4. That is, San Cristóbal.

5. As with almost all the contemporary tellings of the early Caste War, Heller's account of the Maya rebels' success is greatly exaggerated. Heller also exaggerates the degree to which the war and its outcome were the result of "English politics."

6. The original text says February 16, but this was evidently a slip on Heller's part. The date in question would have had to be April 16, since Easter had already passed, while Heller departed from Teapa on May 15, as stated in chapter 24.

Chapter 24

1. In March 1848 a series of popular uprisings swept through Europe, promising constitutional governments and the triumph of national sovereignty over old empires. But Heller's rejoicing was premature; within a month of his return to the Continent, Vienna once again fell into the hands of reactionary forces, with the rest of Europe soon to follow. Moreover, he little suspected that the upheavals of that year would have a serious impact on his chances for employment upon returning to Europe.

2. General José Urrea accompanied Santa Anna on the latter's Texas campaign of 1836.

3. The governor of Tabasco at this time was Justo Santa Anna Cabrera (1796–1883). A member of the Federalist and later Liberal parties, he advanced legislation privatizing untitled state land.

4. "The River of Idols."

5. "Island of the Ox."

6. Literally, "to all the devils." That is to say, the Mexicans were telling the Yankees to go to hell.

7. Again, the idea was that miasmas or fetid odors produced disease.

8. In other words, sailors under the captain's command would be reluctant to testify against him.

9. St. Elmo's fire is a natural phenomenon occasionally observed during stormy weather on such places as the points of ship masts or the tips of airplane wings. A brush discharge of electricity, it is red when positive, blue when negative.

Chapter 25

1. Italian composer Vincenzo Bellini's (1801–35) highly popular *La sonnambula* ("The Sleepwalker") premiered in Milan in 1831.

2. Heller includes this information in a statistical appendix that I have omitted from the text.

3. A packet sailer was a small, swift sailboat used for rapid delivery of letters and packages.

Index